D0463236

QUICK HITS

QUICK
HITS

10 Key Surgical Strike Actions to Improve Business Process Performance

Kelvin F. Cross

AMACOM
American Management Association
New York • Atlanta • Brussels • Chicago • Mexico City • San Francisco
Shanghai • Tokyo • Toronto • Washington, D.C.

Special discounts on bulk quantities of AMACOM books are available to corporations, professional associations, and other organizations. For details, contact Special Sales Department, AMACOM, a division of American Management Association, 1601 Broadway, New York, NY 10019.
Tel.: 212-903-8316. Fax: 212-903-8083.
Web site: www.amacombooks.org

This publication is designed to provide accurate and authoritative information in regard to the subject matter covered. It is sold with the understanding that the publisher is not engaged in rendering legal, accounting, or other professional service. If legal advice or other expert assistance is required, the services of a competent professional person should be sought.

Library of Congress Cataloging-in-Publication Data

Cross, Kelvin F., 1953–
    Quick hits : 10 key surgical strike actions to improve business process performance / Kelvin F. Cross.
        p.   cm.
    ISBN 0-8144-7206-0
    1. Reengineering (Management)   2. Workflow—Management.   3. Process control.   4. Industrial management.   I. Title.

HD58.87.C76   2004
658.4'063—dc21

2003011317

© 2004 Kelvin F. Cross
All rights reserved.
Printed in the United States of America.

This publication may not be reproduced, stored in a retrieval system, or transmitted in whole or in part, in any form or by any means, electronic, mechanical, photocopying, recording, or otherwise, without the prior written permission of AMACOM, a division of American Management Association, 1601 Broadway, New York, NY 10019.

Printing number

10   9   8   7   6   5   4   3   2   1

CONTENTS

ACKNOWLEDGMENTS ix

CHAPTER 1. QUICK HITS THROUGH SURGICAL STRIKES 1

What's New About Surgical Strikes for Business Performance
 Improvement? 2
The Illumination of Surgical Strikes 5
Don't Obliterate, Renovate 7
The Return of Intelligence 8
The Surgical Strikes Approach Cuts to the Chase 8
Surgical Strikes Come Naturally If Given a Chance 9
Who Gets These Great Results? 11
The Ten Surgical Strikes—The Way the Results Are Achieved 13
The Ten Surgical Strikes—The Way to Results 17

CHAPTER 2. WHERE TO STRIKE 19

So Where to Begin? 19
Define the Core 20
The Customer Defines Value 20
The Customer Segments 22
When a Strike Misses the Mark 23
A Question of Perspective 25
A Core Process Omission 28
Characteristics and Virtues of Core Process Thinking 29
Customers + Processes = Strike Zones of Opportunity 32

CHAPTER 3. HOW TO STRIKE 35

A Plumbing Problem 35
Map Out the Details 36

The Game Plan—What It Takes   40
Discovery   41
Inspire   44
Design   47
Realize   47

CHAPTER 4. STRIKE 1: UNCLOG THE WORKPLACE   **51**

Busy but Not Productive   52
So How Did We Get Here?   53
A Magnificent Navy on Land   58
That Was Then, and This Is Now   59
Routine Maintenance . . .   61
. . . Or Radical Cleanup   62
When All Clogged Up . . .   63
. . . Focus the Hit   63
Triangulate and Strike   66
Strike 1: The Tip of the Iceberg   67
Strike 1: Unclog the Workplace   67

CHAPTER 5. STRIKE 2: ELIMINATE WORK   **69**

Eliminate Bad Customers   72
Eliminate Bad Products   75
Eliminate Failures and Failure-Related Recovery   76
Eliminate Non-Value-Added Nonsense Work   80
Strike 2: Just Say No   85
Strike 2: Eliminate Work   85

CHAPTER 6. STRIKE 3: STREAMLINE THE WORKFLOW   **87**

Profile the Workload Within the Process   89
Quantify the Process Itself   92
Initial Ideas   93
Prioritize Opportunity Areas   95
Generate Ideas and Assess Impacts   98
Overall Impact   101
Cut Cycle Time   103
Cut Value-Added Time (Not Steps)   109
Strike 3: On the Straight and Narrow   111
Strike 3: Streamline the Workflow   112

CHAPTER 7. STRIKE 4: RECLAIM LOST TIME—UTILIZE
CAPACITY AND EXPAND CAPABILITY 113

Reclaim Lost Time by Eliminating the Wait for Work 115
Unavailable Time: Use it or Lose It—Time Is Money 122
Customer Chaos Is No Excuse for Poor Utilization 126
Expand Capability 130
Expand Capabilities and Reap the Rewards 137
Strike 4: Reclaim Lost Time 138

CHAPTER 8. STRIKE 5: REDISTRIBUTE THE WORK 139

Put Your Customers to Work 140
Technology-Enabled Self-Service 147
Hire Some Help 149
Fire the Intermediaries 157
Strike 5: Redistribute the Work 160

CHAPTER 9. STRIKE 6: MANAGE FLUCTUATIONS IN WORK
VOLUME 163

Clip the Peaks and Fill the Valleys 164
Twin Peaks 165
Why Exacerbate Peak Loads? 168
The Appearance of Flexibility, the Reality of Efficiency 172
Strike 6: Manage Fluctuations in Work Volume 173

CHAPTER 10. STRIKE 7: FOCUS THE FLOWS 175

Slow-Track Versus Fast-Track Work 176
Geographic Orientation 182
Segment Focus 184
Focus the Flows on Performance to the Customer 188
Strike 7: Focus the Flows 189

CHAPTER 11. STRIKE 8: LINK AND LEARN—UNCLOG THE
FLOWS OF KNOWLEDGE 191

Close the Feedback Loops from *Within* a Core Process 194
Move Information and Knowledge Among Core Processes 195
How to Link and Learn 199
Strike 8: Unclog the Flows of Knowledge 210

CHAPTER 12. STRIKE 9: SHOW THE RESULTS   211

Establish Down-to-Earth Balanced Measures of Performance   212
Scorecard in Action   213
The Right Measure and Real Value   214
Make Clear Priorities Visible   217
Dress Up the Workers   218
Dress Up the Work   219
Build Camaraderie and Teamwork   219
Strike 9: Show the Results   221

CHAPTER 13. STRIKE 10: IMPLEMENT CUSTOMERCENTRIC TEAMS   223

Group Think—How Did I Get Here?   225
Broken Silos   227
Fast Team—Fast Results   230
Multi-Teams and the Supporting Environment   231
Common Themes   236
Culture Clash?   239
Strike 10: Implement Customercentric Teams   240

CHAPTER 14. CONDUCT THE STRIKE(S)   241

Obtain the Gains, Sustain the Gains   242
Communicate, Communicate, Communicate   242
Pilot the Strike   249
Strike Again   251

APPENDIX: THE TEN SURGICAL STRIKES   253

NOTES   261

INDEX   267

ABOUT THE AUTHOR   275

ACKNOWLEDGMENTS

Quick Hits resulted from years of work with a variety of companies in a variety of industries. Each work experience, each project, and everyone with whom I worked contributed in some way to the identification of, and experience with, the ten "Surgical Strikes." That said, over the last few years I have been consciously applying the surgical strikes and speeding up our projects with clients. Therefore, I wish to acknowledge a few key executives who have given me and my firm the opportunity to develop and deliver "quick hits": executives Victor Agruso, Joe Barrett, Steve Coburn, Tom Flanagan, Stewart MacDonald, Greg Maguire, Don Moffatt, Kirk Moul, Elias Safdie, Diane Salomon, Geof Schlakman, Gay Smith, Jon Theuerkauf, Ken Tuchman, and Bill Wilde have all provided such opportunities. The work, along with feedback and discussions, has helped me hone my craft, refine my thinking, and enable me to write this book.

In particular, I thank John Feather, my business partner, friend, and cofounder of Corporate Renaissance, Inc. Collaborating with John on our business, client projects, and as a sounding board for the ideas contained in this book has been essential to this book coming together.

In addition, my colleague and friend Chuck Malovrh provided excellent support with his meticulous reading of the manuscript, and by providing very constructive and detailed critique, as well as encouragement.

Most important was the encouragement of my wife, Caren, to get the book written and get it published. Her persistent optimism and support were critical to this entire project, from writing the book and finding the right publisher to getting through the details of numerous edits and obtaining permissions. Caren helped keep me on track.

CHAPTER 1

QUICK HITS THROUGH SURGICAL STRIKES

Companies have got to eat change for breakfast.
—TOM PETERS, BUSINESS CONSULTANT,
WRITER, AND STAGE PERFORMER

"A funny thing happened on our way to results—the right results were too small and came too slow, and the wrong results were too big and came too fast," says Steve Coburn, a chief financial officer, about his experience with business improvement initiatives over the last couple of decades.

He goes on to explain his view of process improvement in the corporate world, "Years ago we first got enamored with a sole focus on the rigor and rhetoric of the quality movement—and slow deliberate incremental improvement. Later we swung wildly to the other extreme of 'radical reengineering,' . . . which evolved into our even more radical e-business initiative—where we got what we asked for—radical results—just not the right results!

"Today we focus on the Quick Hit 'Surgical Strikes'—we identify precise targets of opportunity, and then use judicious deployment of techniques, technologies and people, to get big results."

In meeting with and consulting for numerous companies both very large and very small, the trend is unmistakable—whether executives use the term "quick hits," "leverage points," "low hanging fruit," "targets of opportunity," or say "we don't want a science project,"—the emphasis is on finding and making the "quick hits"—using "surgical-strike" projects with high benefits, but with low cost and low risk.

Regardless of industry, company, or process, there are a few key actions that work repeatedly. These surgical strike actions have been gleaned from two sources—real-world experience and classroom simulation:

1. After thirty years of working on business process improvement initiatives I have seen a variety of techniques that work (and some that don't!).

2. For the last ten years I have been running a game, a workshop in which the participants redesign a broken process. After over three hundred sessions of the game, the same quick hit techniques that work in the real world come to the fore—repeatedly.

These techniques, the small actions that deliver big results in the game or real processes, can be aggregated into ten types of surgical strikes.

What's New About Surgical Strikes for Business Performance Improvement?

In some respects—not much! The approach builds upon everyone's learning to date with TQM, reengineering, Six Sigma and the like. In other respects, a lot is new. The "surgical strikes" approach of tried-and-true principles and techniques provides a consolidated solution set—solutions ready for action. What's new is in how those principles and techniques are applied: fast and furious, with a "strike force" from the workforce.

The techniques for improving businesses and their processes are constantly being rethought and updated. To some extent, a new approach emerges when the old approach has lost its luster. The move to the "next wave" largely takes place as managers move from fad to fad (e.g., from TQM, to Reengineering, to Knowledge Management, to Six Sigma, to e-everything, to enough!). To some extent a new approach emerges when new ideas, new technologies, and new business conditions provide the opportunity.

Like previous approaches to business improvement, the surgical-strikes approach represents a combination of new conditions providing an opportunity, and the previous waves having lost their luster.

If we look at the recent history of business process improvement it was the TQM movement of the 1980s, which focused everyone's attention on business processes. Typically, during this era, the emphasis was on maintaining minute tolerances of performance within specific process steps. So the emphasis was on control and on incremental improvement projects. At times, this internal process focus expanded in scope. But at best, the expanded scope was still isolated within a department or function such as circuit-board assembly or order processing.

Within the TQM movement, and to some extent with Six Sigma at some companies, both the scale of the projects and the scope of the organization to be covered by those projects tended to be small. Otherwise known as continuous improvement, or kaizen, it was the small scale and small scope that made these projects popular and safe for the organization to handle. As one insightful article stated, "Bureaucracies Love Kaizen":

> **Chances are that once the word kaizen enters the vocabulary of your business you can kiss any hope of a breakthrough in performance goodbye. . . . Bureaucracies love kaizen because the individuals in bureaucracies interpret it to be a most noble and overtly responsible process of gradual and incremental improvement. Kaizen is contemporary (at least for North American firms), and gradual (read nonthreatening and "manageable"), and incremental (small, safe, baby steps), and "correct"(we are committed to excellence . . . blah, blah, blah). The bottom line is that it is the greatest defense to tampering with anything of significance that might "rock the boat." Keep it safe. Keep it contained. Keep it under control. Manage the risk. We wouldn't want anything too dramatic to happen.**[1]

With TQM, companies typically initiated numerous isolated improvement projects within each department and function, and typically the results were disappointing. As management either became disappointed with their TQM improvement rate, or if the rate had slowed to a crawl, they searched for something new. They found it. TQM and incremental improvement—were upstaged by reengineering.

Although reengineering shares the same sound principles of process design with TQM, the approach differed in its scale and scope. Rather than incremental improvement, reengineering calls for radical redesign. Rather than functions and subprocess scope, reengineering called for tackling a whole core process and/or whole business redesign. Rather than precise targeting, reengineering called for "carpet bombing" of the existing processes.

The more adventurous companies (both smart and stupid alike) took the reengineering message to heart and attempted to redesign (from scratch) entire core business processes. Examples of such core business processes include new product introduction, or order fulfillment. In many cases, these projects were done with lots of investment (time and money), but little return. Typically these projects had more grandiose names and ambitions, as in "Project 2000," "Blue Sky," "The Journey," "Project Customer," "The Renaissance Project," "Enterprise Project," and "Millennium."

Likewise, for many companies, the e-business frenzy was similar to reengineering in ambition, scope, and scale. For many brick-and-mortar companies, the "blank slate" for e-business meant starting new ventures for procurement and customer care.

So, with reengineering and many e-business initiatives, the scope and scale were massive and sweeping, a "blank canvas" approach. In a sense this was the high-risk, high-reward approach. And in another sense it was also the high-cost, high-benefit approach. Done well, it was worth it.

When done poorly, companies were left with the high risk and the high cost, with little reward and little benefit. For instance, one leading health maintenance organization devoted two years and hundreds of millions of dollars to reengineering their entire nationwide operation only to give up when many of the recommended changes were too difficult and expensive to implement. (The consulting firm had eaten up all of the investment dollars!)

Many companies heard the reengineering horror stories, were timid, or didn't have the nerve to go for the radical redesign that reengineering gurus advocate. Rather, they compromised and attempted the wholesale redesign of functions and/or departments within the business. Only recently have they realized the limitation of this approach.

In some cases they saw the streamlining of one department clog up another. For instance, the airlines streamlined the paperwork involved in their sales process by offering electronic ticketing. Unfortunately, in the initial roll-out, the day-to-day operations at the departure gates could not effectively handle the new approach. E-ticketed passengers were pulled aside so their tickets could be reconfirmed. In other cases the bulk of a function's activities would not exist if work were performed right the first time elsewhere. For instance, to make a billing inquiry department more efficient is a misguided effort when the bill should have been correct in the first place.

The Illumination of Surgical Strikes

During the early 1990s the business-performance improvement pendulum swung from the TQM days of independently and incrementally improving each part of the process, to the radical reengineering and e-business days of redesigning everything from scratch. In other words, they attempted to move from the lower left quadrant of Figure 1.1 to the upper right. But when you think about it—what's missing? What's missing is the "High Reward-Low Risk" quadrant. What's missing is the "High Benefit-Low Cost" quadrant. This is the essence of surgical strikes.

Now the idea of surgical strikes is to retain the company-wide perspective, while incrementally improving the few targets of opportunity that will have the greatest impact on the whole. In other words, surgical strikes are about deploying small-scale projects with broad organizational scope and impact. The intent is to achieve major benefits with minimal risks and costs and move to the upper-left quadrant in Figure 1.2. In our billing inquiry example, the surgical strike is to enable the billing process to perform the work right the first time, thereby producing correct invoices, eliminating the inquiries, and—perhaps most important—getting paid faster!

As in the case of companies careening back and forth from central-

Figure 1.1. What's Missing

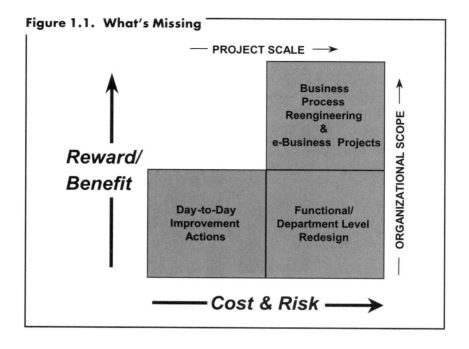

Figure 1.2. Characteristics of Four Approaches to Process Improvement

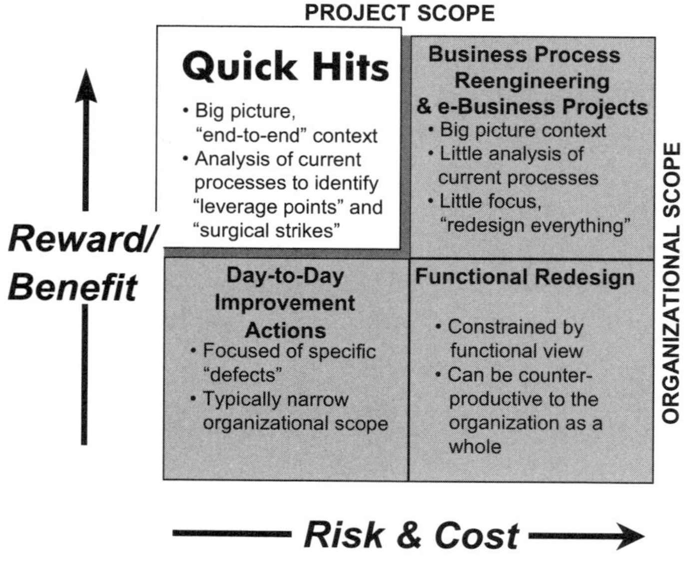

izing and decentralizing, the process improvement movement has careened over the years. Although the swings are moderating, they have ranged back and forth from a trial-and-error approach to a rigorously analytical approach. With surgical strikes, we have reached a point of relative equilibrium.

The surgical strikes approach represents the accumulation of knowledge and experience with all facets of business-process improvement. It builds upon the principles and rigor of the TQM and Six Sigma movements, as well as the radical art of reengineering, and e-business revolution. We have been to the extremes and found middle ground. But that middle ground is not a rejection of either extreme, but rather an alternative—and I believe the alternative of choice for today's business climate.

Today's business climate requires balance and moderation. Innovation and taking chances needs to be balanced by business pragmatism and fact-based management. Extreme swings in approaches have been moderating; fad-based management is rapidly being replaced by doing the right thing for the right problem—a surgical strike. As my CFO friend says, "Use rigor when appropriate, use trial and error when appropriate. Use the surgical strike that uses the best combination of tools and techniques from years of experience with all forms and means of improving business process performance."

Don't Obliterate, Renovate

So we have been to the extremes: from the safe haven of risk-free incremental improvement to the zeal of radical reengineering and e-business initiatives. However, as with many things in life, moderation is the key. The notion of surgical strikes is the notion of moderation.

Look at the homeowner as an analogy. Perhaps the renovation of a basement or a bathroom is a surgical strike. The homeowner opted not to demolish the house and start over. Nor did he or she simply settle for incremental cleaning and painting as the means to home improvement. Done for the most benefit, a one-room renovation may enhance the whole house, not just the room being remodeled. A new basement family room provides space for the kids, and frees up the living room for the adults. The additional shower enables more time in the shower for each member of the family (whether they use the old or new shower).

In any case, the family gets many of the most important benefits of a new house, without the expenditure of time and money and the hassle of getting into a new house.

Most businesses can improve their performance in much the same way as the homeowner. They can get a big bang for the buck by focusing on the little projects that deliver big results. In other words, don't obliterate, renovate.

The Return of Intelligence

The notion of a surgical strike implies intelligence. If we are not going to "carpet bomb" the old process and start from scratch, then an analysis of the current process is critical. So while the reengineering wave had many suggesting that any time spent evaluating the current process was wasted, a surgical strike depends upon it.

Look at our home improvement project. In order to renovate, the homeowner and/or the builder needs to know where the load-bearing beams reside, where the plumbing is routed, and other key facts about the existing structure. The surgical-strike renovation can then be conducted with safety and efficiency. In business, the same is true.

The time spent up front in analyzing the existing process is not only where the targets for surgical strikes will be discovered, but also where the obstacles will be found and the workarounds planned.

In many respects the Six Sigma movement marked a profound shift back to the importance of up-front analysis and understanding before making changes. The methodology is very clear in this regard with the DMAIC framework: Define, Measure, Analyze, Improve, and Control. Unfortunately, like the TQM movement before it, the Six Sigma zealots force fit the methodology on problems, and force fit problems into the methodology. In one case, a financial services organization spent more time agonizing over "What is a defect?" and "How many opportunities for defects are there?" in financial deal making rather than cutting to the chase and fixing the top few significant and obvious defects.

The Surgical Strikes Approach Cuts to the Chase

So the return of intelligence does not mean weeks and months of mind-numbing data collection and analyses. The surgical strikes approach is to quickly find and focus on the few key areas of greatest opportunity, and then select the most appropriate surgical strike action or actions.

With the right team and a little meaningful data, the right conclusions can be drawn and the right actions taken. This book is about finding the "right" actions that show up repeatedly in the real world and as corroborated in a simulated environment.

Surgical Strikes Come Naturally If Given a Chance

Over the past decade, my colleagues and I have been running a workshop/simulation exercise, a game that has the participants work in and fix a defective process. Throughout this book I will refer to the game, and the lessons learned. On each occasion that I discuss the game the text will be bounded within a box, or sidebar.

In our Quick Hits Game, all the participants go through a hands-on experience with business process redesign and implementation. The participants rapidly, and by gut instinct, obtain significant quick hits by applying the same 'surgical strike' actions that work in the real world.

The content is serious but learned in a fun, relaxed setting. In this four-hour interactive game, the participants are part of a company the processes are out of control (Figure 1.3). The flows of work and physical layout are disjointed, with tables spread out around a room, and at each table there is a specialized assembly function.

The participants are asked to assemble a "cellular phone" made from plastic Stickle Bricks. These Stickle Bricks are especially well suited to highlighting the importance of attention to detail and the impact of training and learning curve. In other words, they are nasty. They are not symmetrical. One side has two prongs and the other has one prong (for example, see the top and bottom of the "antennae" in Figure 1.4). Therefore, each piece has to be oriented properly in order for the entire assembly to come together correctly—and there is only one right orientation for each piece.

While we use this toy phone and a "factory" setting for the game (to make the work visible and tangible), the game has been run mostly in service settings (e.g., insurance, telecom, or software development) with great success.

The game begins with Round One: running a dysfunctional process for ten minutes to establish a baseline of (poor) performance. After Round One the group has about forty-five minutes to redesign the process and try again. Like reengineering, it is a "blank slate" opportunity.

Figure 1.3. The Floor Plan for Round One of the Game

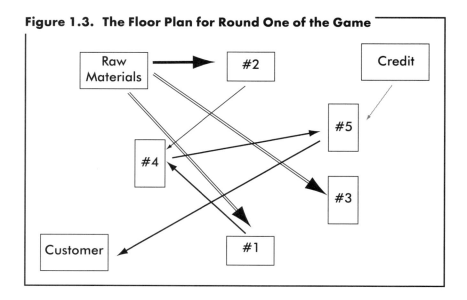

Figure 1.4. The Toy Cellular Phone

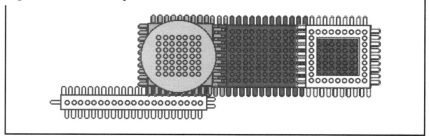

They can do anything they want, except change the product or customer demands for delivery and quality. Round Two is then run to see if the improved and redesigned process performs as expected. Usually there is a significant improvement, but it is not good enough. It takes more discussion, more changes, some additional training to get it right, not unlike the real world of change. By Round Three the process hums. Quiet and overachieving, the process delivers an outstanding level of output and performance.

In essence, the participants learn the characteristics of a good process and service design with an emphasis on measurable results. Participants see first hand the changes in teamwork and management styles at various stages of process performance, from Round One's chaos to Round Three's high performance.

Over three rounds of the game, participants experience the degree to which all dimensions of performance can be designed to improve

Figure 1.5. Average Performance Results for Over 200 Sessions of the Process Redesign Game

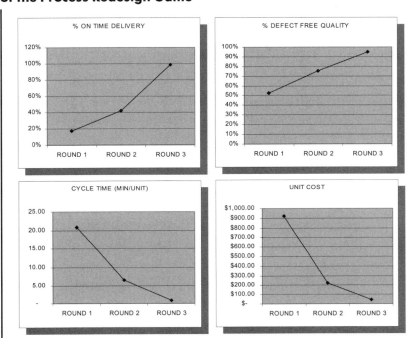

simultaneously. The team is challenged to produce breakthrough results in output, quality, delivery, cycle time, and costs. Over the last ten years, and hundreds of sessions, average performance results are shown above (in Figure 1.5).

The participants gain a hands-on experience in diagnosing process problems and applying solutions based on gut instinct and group discussion; we don't do much facilitation. Yet, time after time, we have seen the same set of actions produce these same great results.

The common theme with the game and surgical strikes in the real world are actions and results based on tried-and-true principles and fast-and-furious execution by a "strike force" from the workforce.

Who Gets These Great Results?

So why is process improvement so difficult, especially if gut feeling and instinct work repeatedly? The answer is in two parts:

1. The right people are not typically put together and empowered to redesign the business.

2. In the real world work flows among departments and buildings, and is performed by systems, by suppliers, and customers, all out of view. The game has everything in front of you—the supplies, the workstations, the customer—all within view. The real world and its improvement efforts are more complex, requiring tools and techniques (e.g., process mapping and the like) to put the process in view.

Putting the process in view requires expertise and experience in a variety of analytical tools and techniques. However, commitment to the right actions and the right results requires expertise and experience with the process itself. The best way to get around this difficulty is to have a couple of process experts teamed with a cross-functional team of people who perform the day-to-day work in a given process.

The trick is to find the surgical strike, where a small precise action will get a big result, and this requires skill. In the martial arts such as karate, a well-placed maneuver takes little effort but leads to big results. The same is true in the operating room, where a well-placed incision cures a major problem. Although less dramatic, the homeowner may achieve a major benefit from a minor renovation (e.g., removing a wall or putting in a new door). We see the same in business. If targeted well, a small precise action can get a big result.

It sounds so simple, but it isn't. It takes years of training to become a black belt in karate or a surgeon and to know how, when, and where to act. Similarly the surgical strike approach typically requires expertise to cut through the tangle of data and confusion to get a true perspective of the situation and what needs to be done. But it requires two types of expertise: (1) process analysis and design expertise found in consultants, reengineering specialists, Six Sigma black belts; and (2) expertise in the specific work and process to be improved. In other words, if the process in question involves order processing then some order processors should be involved.

This emphasis on process expertise and cross-functional involvement is not new and is well understood, but in my experience still not widely practiced—except perhaps at GE. Their experience with Work-

Out taught them about cross-functional involvement. GE then built upon that learning to go on with a very successful implementation of their Six Sigma program:

> **"The basis for Six Sigma's success has been GE's previous efforts to minimize bureaucracy, find solutions and solve problems through its Work-Out program. . . . Work-Out involves identifying people who have to deal with a particular problem, from line workers to management, and effectively locking them in a room for several days until they solve it."[2]**

The actions that come out of Work-Out and Six Sigma initiatives are typically surgical strikes.

The Ten Surgical Strikes—The Way the Results Are Achieved

Despite the difficulty, when you cut through the tools, techniques, and jargon, the same actions and principles that work so well in the game also apply to the real workplace. So what are these actions?

The way these results are achieved can be boiled down to ten surgical strikes.

Strike 1: Unclog the Workplace

Strike 2: Eliminate Work

Strike 3: Streamline the Workflow

Strike 4: Reclaim Lost Time—Utilize Capacity and Expand Capability

Strike 5: Redistribute the Work

Strike 6: Manage Fluctuations in Work Volume

Strike 7: Focus the Flows

Strike 8: Link and Learn—Unclog the Flows of Knowledge

Strike 9: Show the Results

Strike 10: Implement Customercentric Teams

These surgical strikes fall into two categories: (1) those that are direct actions to change the flows of work (Strikes 1 through 7); (2) those that provide the structure, environment, and support required to enable those close to the work to more easily make changes (Strikes 8 through 10).

In most cases these surgical strikes are intertwined. While one strike may contribute the majority of gains, there are usually a few others at play at the same time. As a matter of fact, there should always be at least more than one at play.

If a Category 1 surgical strike is conducted, it will eventually require the structure, environment, and support (e.g., organizational structure, proximity of key workers to each other, etc.) to sustain the gains.

If a Category 2 surgical strike is enacted, the intent is to enable others to conduct the Category 1 strikes.

What follows is a brief discussion of the ten surgical strikes.

Strike 1: Unclog the Workplace

Many times in the game and in the workplace too much confusion and too many people obscure the flows of work and work-related problems. You can't fix what you can't see. Just as a cloudless day is needed for reconnaissance planes and satellites, a clear view is needed to get a true perspective of work processes. Sometimes the sole act of clearing the view will clear up the process. In the game, if there are too many people involved, it bogs down, takes too long, and performance suffers. The larger the group, the more difficult it is to produce the toy phones, and the more difficult it is to bring the group to consensus on how best to change the process in the time available.

Strike 2: Eliminate Work

All too often the incoming work is taken for granted. It is processed in more or less the same manner week after week for years, because that is the way it has always been done. Sometimes the incoming work is irrelevant, or worse—destructive. Why streamline a process to handle work you shouldn't be doing at all? Why get better at handling billing inquiries when a well-designed bill could eliminate the inquiries?

Strike 3: Streamline the Workflow

The most direct route from Point A to Point B is a straight line. Yet most workflows look like Round One of the game: a convoluted criss-crossing maze of confusion. The trick is to determine points A and B and then straighten and shorten the flow of work between them. Eliminating hand-offs, approvals, and anything else that doesn't add value will shorten and streamline the workflow.

Strike 4: Reclaim Lost Time—Utilize Capacity and Expand Capability

There is always more capacity to do more work than meets the eye. Capacity is lost when specialists are idle waiting for their work, or work is bottlenecked elsewhere, or scheduling doesn't work. Uncovering and using previously hidden capacity to better serve the customer can be a significant surgical strike. Ideally, newfound capacity can be put to good use in performance of productive value-adding work, such as handling: more volume, new products, new services, new capabilities (e.g., for delivery, for customization and for experimental ventures).

Strike 5: Redistribute the Work

Who says you have to do all the work? Could the customer do some of the work? Should you outsource some of the work? Are there intermediaries in your business and its processes that could do some of the work more effectively and efficiently? Are the "right" employees doing the "right" work? If someone else or another organization can do some of the work more effectively, why not have them do it?

Strike 6: Manage Fluctuations in Work Volume

Fluctuations in work volume are many times overlooked and/or mismanaged. Rather than clip the peaks and fill the valleys with work, companies do things to exacerbate the peaks and valleys of work. Staffing levels fall out of sync and the work either doesn't get done, or the staff is idle while waiting for work. The surgical strike is to either manage staff levels to the ebbs and flows or to manage the ebbs and flows to the staff level.

Strike 7: Focus the Flows

When a process and/or a service experience is designed to be all things to all people, difficult work is mixed with easy work. The easy work is delayed by the difficult work. Or an experienced customer is processed the same way as a new and inexperienced customer. The experienced customer is annoyed by excessive handholding, while the inexperienced customer still feels neglected. The surgical strike is to set up processing tracks to provide focus (e.g., a fast track for the easy work and a slow track for the difficult work).

Strike 8: Link and Learn—Unclog the Flows of Knowledge

While we have talked about unclogging the flow of work, here we are primarily talking about unclogging the flows of knowledge. However, unlike the amorphous concepts of knowledge management this is about defining and using specific feedback regarding the business and process performance. For example, if billing inquiries result from hard-to-understand bills, then those who design the bills need feedback from those who handle the inquiries. Typically such links are lost in large organizations and nothing improves.

Strike 9: Show the Results

The four-quadrant scorecard we use for the game provides clear focus for everyone as to the criteria and expectations for process performance. The scorecard balances external measures of quality and delivery to the customer, with internal measures of cycle time and cost. As results improve, the group becomes more motivated. Visible results drive visible improvements, which drive visible results, and so forth. The role of measures cannot be overemphasized in the game or in the workplace; they must be balanced, tangible, visible, and actionable. Then they will motivate behavior that leads to continuous improvement.

Strike 10: Implement Customercentric Teams

Teams are the answer when workers and managers are given a chance to rethink and redesign the way a process operates and the way it is organized. Having facilitated process redesign initiatives in a variety of industries (from steel factories, to software developers, to financial services) and in all core processes (such as new product development, order fulfillment, service delivery) this same conclusion is reached. The small, self-managed, customercentric team structure is a common solution. And rather than taking months to design and implement such a structure (as was the case during the glory days of reengineering), such teams are now designed and implemented in a matter of weeks.

The Ten Surgical Strikes—The Way to Results

A successful surgical strike is based on speed and a blend of new economy and old economy thinking. As Gary Hamel says in his recent book *Leading the Revolution*, "Post-industrial executives will need to embrace an amalgam of the two. Every Internet company must master old-economy necessities like flawless customer service and Six Sigma quality; every Fortune 500 behemoth must internalize the virtues of heretical thinking, ready-aim-fire prototyping, and grassroots innovation."[3] Quick hits through surgical strikes provide the means to lead the revolution.

CHAPTER 2

WHERE TO STRIKE

The customer is the most important part of the production line.
—W. EDWARDS DEMING

So Where to Begin?

By definition a surgical strike implies a precise target—in this case a target of opportunity. But how do we find these targets?

There are opportunities for surgical strikes in almost any industry and any company. They can be found in almost any function or aspect of a business: products, services, pricing, public relations, human resources, process, technology, outsourcing, deal making, relationship management, and day-to-day operations. The list goes on. However, it is through a business process view that many of the most significant surgical strikes can be found.

What is counterintuitive about surgical strikes is the unexpected places they can be found, even in non-key areas which are on the critical path to the key ones. For example, the clear identification of core processes and a realistic assessment of their performances can lead to the identification of a surgical strike. In one instance, an outsourcing company had an exceptional sales team that could get in the door and an operations group that was extremely "buttoned up." They excelled in both lead generation and day-to-day operations. The surgical strike lay in helping them overcome obstacles in the client-visible transition period—implementation—from the end of the sales process to the start of steady state operation.

In another case, a CEO laments: "In our sales process we continue to make bad deals with bad customers. I thought we agreed to focus on the money-makers and abandon the losers." Here the surgical strike was to define clear customer segments, determine the profitability of each segment, and either re-price to make the nonprofitable profitable or abandon the nonprofitable segments altogether.

Define the Core

At the core of any business are (1) the core customers and (2) the core processes by which work gets done on the customers' behalf. You can never forget that ultimately processes are in place to serve customers. On second thought, I guess you can forget. I observed and learned that lesson the hard way—a few times!

For example, during the 1980s I worked at Wang Laboratories as the head of Industrial Engineering, and worked on numerous process improvement/redesign projects. I even published an article entitled: "Wang Scores 'EPIC' Success . . ."[1] EPIC stood for Experimental Process Improvement Challenge. We completely redesigned the way circuit boards were assembled, changing from functional departments to work cells. The new process did achieve "epic" success. Unfortunately we got very good at producing a product the customer didn't want. Likewise, with the redesign work in the new product development process came dramatic improvements in time-to-market—with new products no one wanted!

So the big lesson was to view every process improvement project in a larger context. How does the process in question ultimately serve the customer? What steps add value and what steps do not? To answer these questions you have to know something about your customers and their perception of value.

The Customer Defines Value

In the brick-and-mortar world, face-to-face service encounters provide a tailored experience—all based upon a judgment call by the service provider. The guy in the small-town hardware store knows you, your skills, what projects you have under way, and what tools you may own. He may suggest certain approaches and related tools based on his knowledge of you. Likewise at the small-town local bank, the loan officer knows if it is your first time buying a house or your fifth transaction this decade. Your experience with the loan process dictates the experience, such as the degree of interaction provided by the loan officer. Outside of rural America, those days are gone, but the need to deliver the appropriate service to each customer remains.

So let's follow up on the banking experience. For the sake of simplicity, let's assume there are two types of customers: inexperienced and experienced. The inexperienced desires more help and handholding throughout the process; the experienced homebuyer just wants to know the closing date and time. The savvy banking customer shuns handholding during the mortgage application process. Such handholding would not add any value and would likely be outright annoying. Conversely, the naïve first-time homebuyer will value the handholding and extra attention. The trick is to quickly identify the customers and their particular service needs, and then treat them accordingly. The perception of which encounters with the bank add value and which encounters do not will depend on which individual you ask.

Now think of the additional complexity brought about by technology and e-commerce. In the e-business world the customer experience must be designed for their technological ability, as well as their experience with the mortgage process. The technologically savvy customer desires little handholding regarding the use of computer-based applications and status reporting. Conversely, the technologically naïve customer requires extra care and attention (Figure 2.1).

Figure 2.1. Customer Desires

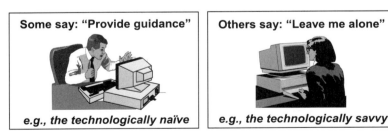

Some say: "Provide guidance"   Others say: "Leave me alone"

e.g., the technologically naïve   *e.g., the technologically savvy*

In the e-business world the customer experience depends upon process (define the customer type, provide the right experience through a defined process, and collect the right data). The first step in e-process design (or any process design) is to define and design the desired customer experiences.

The Customer Segments

The result of evaluating the customers' desires for service is a "Customer Value-Needs Profile." See Figure 2.2. Such a profile segments the customers according to their respective needs for service and a particular service experience.

Figure 2.2. Customer Segments Based on Needs

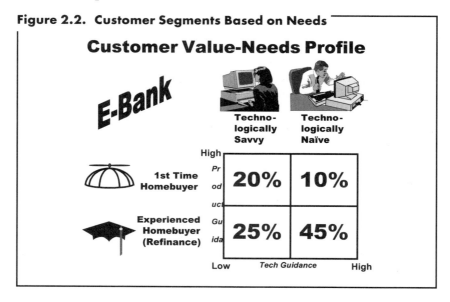

In this example, the "Product-Naïve 1st Time Homebuyer" who is also "Technologically Naïve" represents 10 percent of the customers. Such a customer will likely require a high degree of guidance with both the product and the technology by which they receive service. Conversely, the 25 percent "Technologically Savvy—Experienced Homebuyers" require little guidance.

When the "Value-Needs Profile" is translated to a view of the customer experience, a variety of paths are depicted (Figure 2.3). The savvy customer skips the "Receive Guidance" steps, while the naïve customers do not.

Only with an understanding of customer requirements and desires can an effective surgical strike be conducted.

Figure 2.3. Customer Segments—Experience Should Vary

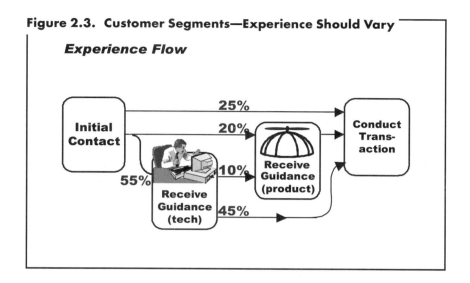

When a Strike Misses the Mark

Like me, some big companies learned the hard way. As I mentioned earlier, a recent article exclaimed: "Banking giant First Union Corp. is hiring 2,000 tellers in an admission it's misjudged how much customers want to see real people for their banking needs." What First Union didn't grasp is that, while customers were moving in great numbers to "direct banking" (phone, kiosk, or Internet), the migration was not going as fast as anticipated. An Associated Press article described the situation:

> Banking giant First Union Corp. is hiring 2,000 tellers in an admission it's misjudged how much customers want to see real people for their banking needs. . . . The news comes after about 5,800 First Union workers were laid off in March . . . in an effort to boost profits. [The intent was to establish a] . . . concept that relies heavily on technology such as personal computers, ATMs, the Internet and telephones to use fewer employees in each branch. . . . Now First Union management has found that even

> though customers don't need to come into a branch,
> they come in anyway and demand service.
>
> Lawrence Cohn, an analyst with Ryan, Beck &
> Co. said he thought the bank was just "over-
> zealous" in their cost-cutting efforts. "Did they
> manage this process properly? The answer is obvi-
> ously not. It cost them money to lay people off. It's
> going to cost them again to hire people. Did they
> waste a lot of money in here? Absolutely," Cohn
> said. "On the other hand it's an ongoing business
> and you've got to handle the business. They made
> a mistake and they recognize it."
>
> "The bottom line is we value our customer rela-
> tionships," said a company spokesperson.[2]

The bottom line is many customers valued face-to-face interaction, whether it was really necessary or not. In this case, the surgical strike of reducing face-to-face banking capacity and increasing direct banking capacity, was a strike that missed the mark.

To use a military analogy, the missile hit the wrong target. Remember the Gulf War, when a smart bomb—delivered through the right window—could take out a big chunk of Iraq's defense communications system. But, if it were delivered through the wrong window nothing much would happen. Well, First Union missed the building and hit their own people—their customers and employees. Both were damaged, as in a case of casualties due to friendly fire.

The trick is to find the surgical strike, where a small precise action can get a big result, but it has to be the right result. So the first step is to clearly understand the customers' perceptions of value; know how many customers' desires there are for each level of service; how that volume is likely to shift over time; and then be ready to react if it doesn't go as expected. To First Union's credit, they tried something; it didn't work as expected, so they learned something, rapidly adjusted, and moved on—a new economy imperative.

So once you know what customers desire, what are the few core processes that deliver value to the customer?

A Question of Perspective

I once asked a company "What are your core processes?" They said, "Well, we have sixty-five core processes." I thought to myself, "We are using entirely different definitions of 'core.'" I try to think of "core" from the customer's perspective.

A customer's experience with any business goes something like this. Customers have a recognized or unrecognized need. The first company that offers a product to fill that need is likely to get the customer's attention. So they first hear of the product or service as an output of the development process. Next they get sold on the idea of buying the product or service (the customer acquisition process). For some products and services there is an implementation phase, from signed contract until available for use. Then there is day-to-day use of the product or service, followed by distinct after-sales service encounters such as maintenance, repair, or enhancements. It is this customer perspective that define processes that are truly "core."

Figure 2.4 suggests a definition of core processes for a technology solutions provider, and a definition for each.

In many respects, a company's core processes are the cylinders that make up the engine of the company. In order to be effective, the engine must fire on all cylinders.

Having a finely tuned high-performance engine requires all of a company's cylinders to be firing by design, and not to be reliant upon intermittent blasts of individual genius or luck. In other words it is process design, and adherence to the process design, which enables scalable growth and sustainable, repeatable great performance.

Each core process plays a critical role in the company's success, from the planning process to the service delivery process.

■ *Business Planning*: Strategies and plans must be revised routinely to adapt to changing conditions with the growth in people, products/services, and changes in technologies and competitive landscape. A traditional strategic plan, done once each year, will not work. In today's environment, the planning approach has to be seen as more of a framework: adaptable and flexible enough to welcome revisions as conditions evolve and new opportunities arise. In a sense, the output of the planning process is the broad allocation of power and

Figure 2.4. Core Processes for a Technology Solutions Provider

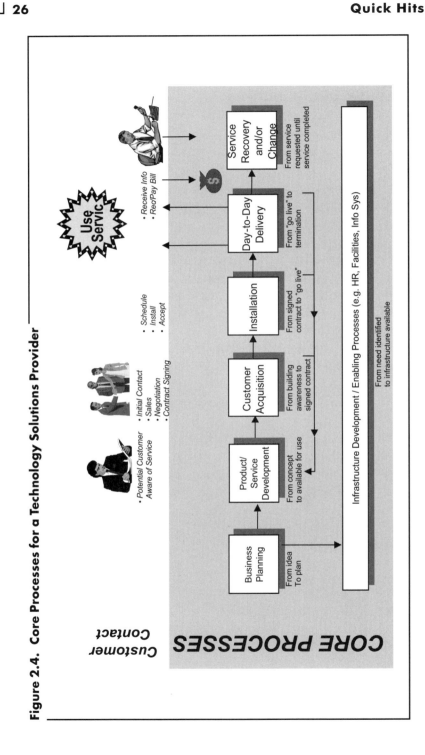

money (e.g., structuring the organization and funding projects and programs).

■ *Product/Service Development:* Perhaps this is the most critical core process for a technology solutions provider—the development and introduction of new products/services (including tailoring offerings to specific industries and channel partners).

■ *Infrastructure Development:* This core process relates to building capability—capability to meet the objectives of the business plan, including having the infrastructure prepared to sell, implement, and deliver. As such it would include: the acquisition and integration of new companies, professional people, and continual development and introduction of technological capabilities. This core process may be the first priority for high-growth companies, such as Starbucks (or Boston Chicken in its heyday) when they are opening a store a day. You might argue that their products, chicken and coffee, are not a big deal, but rather their ability to select locations and get a site up-and-running rapidly is a big deal. However, as Boston Chicken found out, infrastructure development is usually temporary as the most critical core process.

■ *Customer Acquisition:* Not to be confused with sales as a function, this core process is about how the entire organization as a whole collaborates to acquire the right customers.

■ *Installation:* While from an internal view this may not be perceived as a core process, the customer's view suggests that it is core. To the customer, it is quite distinct from the sale and from day-to-day service delivery. The transition is critical to the customer's perception of a technology solution provider's competence and capability. Also, from the company's perspective, here is where *capacity* is built (to deliver and scale up on the capability which was built, or at least defined, earlier).

■ *Service Delivery:* Generally, expectations are high for flawless performance with the service, including reporting and billing. Any company, and especially a solutions provider, is continually under pressure to perform faster, better, cheaper with the day-to-day delivery of their product/service.

■ *Service Recovery*: Lastly, when something goes wrong there is a core process around recovery, whether it be a recovery from a product failure (under warranty or not), recovery from a service failure, recovery from a billing error, or simply assisting the customer to use the product or understand your basic policies and procedures.

A Core Process Omission

Working with an executive team to define their core processes can sometimes be very enlightening, not just in what they come up with, but in what they find is missing.

A number of years ago while working with a leading Health Maintenance Organization (HMO) I had the opportunity to conduct a half-day session to define core processes. The senior executives of the company were asked to jot down on sticky notes the activities and processes performed throughout their organization.

Next I had them post their stickies on the wall, but not randomly. I had them think about their business and the logical order in which things would be done. More specifically, I said to view it as a start-up. If they all were starting over what things would happen first, second, third, etc. I divided the wall into three sections and labeled them "beginning," "middle," and "end." So, for example, all the stickies that related to planning and funding activities, defining the products and services, and so on ended up on the left side of the wall. Activities like paying claims and handling customers ended up on the right. Anyway, after the stickies were posted in rough chronological order I had them come up to the wall and do further groupings of stickies within the three broad categories.

We ended up with seven "core processes," including one for what we called "support services" or enabling processes. As we titled each of the groupings, one of the executives became very uncomfortable and said, "Something is missing. We call ourselves a *health* maintenance organization but none of our core processes has anything to do with proactively managing our *members'* health care. It has a lot to do with *patient* health care. Shouldn't we have a core process with the express intent of preventing a *member* from becoming a *patient*?" The group agreed and decided to build in a core process called "Member Health

Care Enhancement." There was agreement that "we are in the health care management business, and even though we're not doing a good job with proactive care, we should. So let's build this in as a core process, knowing full well it requires development."

Their diagram is shown in Figure 2.5.

In essence they discovered the missing core process by looking at the business from their customers' perspective. The "service promise" centered on *members'* health care and wellness, but their initial core process definitions centered on doctors, administrators, and *patients.* Their discovery put them on the road toward new thinking and new priorities.

Characteristics and Virtues of Core Process Thinking

Others concur with my view of core processes, and even go as far as to suggest it is a new breakthrough attributable to Six Sigma:

> **"By 'core process' we mean a chain of tasks, usually involving various departments or functions that deliver value (products, service, support, information) to external customers. Alongside the core processes, each organization has a number of "support" or "enabling" processes that provide vital resources or inputs to the value-producing activities. While the idea of a core process may seem pretty straightforward—and it is—it's interesting that this key organizational building block is a relatively recent idea, one of the breakthrough concepts of the Six Sigma system."[3]**

Core processes are often masked in organizations by superficial functional and political boundaries and obsolete measurement systems that cause delays, product and service defects, repair and recovery activities, and lost opportunity. Identification of your business's core

Figure 2.5. An HMO's Core Processes

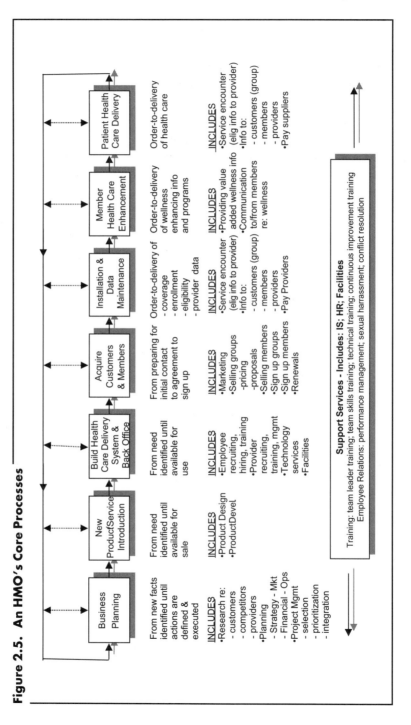

processes is a crucial first step in the race to new markets, new products, new services, and improved profitability.

As we first observed a decade ago, a *core process* can be defined as all the functions and sequence of activities *(regardless of where they reside in the organization),* management systems, policies and procedures required to meet a marketplace need through a specific strategy. It includes all functions involved in the development, production, and provision of specific products or services to particular customers. In other words, emphasis is given to workflow—not to organization charts.[4]

In essence, there are three components to our definition of a core process:

1. "Sequence of activities." Rather than viewing work as discrete, individual activities, from department to department, think of it as a river flowing continuously—regardless of arbitrary political boundaries—fed by many tributaries. In essence, the core process is a network of internal suppliers and customers throughout the organization that gets the work done.

2. "Implements a strategy." A business strategy cannot usually be implemented by one department in isolation. Strategy requires the commitment and cooperation of the entire organization. For instance, "customer acquisition" may involve finance (pricing, credit check), legal (contracting), engineering, executives—not just sales.

3. "Provides product or service to the customer." A core process includes the sequence of activities leading up to the actual delivery of the product or service to the end customer.

One problem with defining processes, organization structures, or many other management decisions, is that there is no absolute right or wrong. For example, some companies have had a long history of doing a terrific job with piecework incentives, even though the approach has long been declared dead by leading management thinkers. Management is a combination of art and science.

That said, if you use a customercentric and process-driven mindset, there could only be a few *core* processes. Somewhere between five and ten core processes is typical for any given business unit.

Customers + Processes = Strike Zones of Opportunity

With a profile of customers and a profile of core processes it becomes possible to select a "battlefield" on which to wage the war of opportunity. Expressed differently, we need to define a "strike zone"—the place to look for a surgical strike (see Figure 2.6).

For example, on the core-process side, a likely opportunity is to provide better customer service. As products and services become more complex, technological self-help solutions may not cut it. The most effective competitors may have to resort to some degree of old-fashioned personal contact. This was an assertion borne out by the First Union example described earlier and mentioned by Britt Beemer, founder and chairman of Americas Research Group Inc., in *Upside* magazine:

> **Says Beemer: "I personally believe the companies that in the '90s used technology to replace people [will] find that strategy is likely to backfire." Over the next three to five years, Beemer says, consumers "will search out those companies that offer personal contact."[5]**

I will stretch this assertion further by suggesting that it is the naïve customers who will require the "high touch" service. Therefore, the strike zone is the opportunity to cost-effectively provide personal contact service to naïve customers. Perhaps the naïve customers will be willing to pay for such service. Or perhaps the effort is worth it in order to convert naïve customers into savvy customers. On the other hand, it may be that it already costs too much to handhold naïve customers and there is an opportunity to pare those costs back (as well as those customers if they are not profitable).

In any case, the point is that the intersection of a core process and a customer segment (based on service needs) can define a strike zone. In the example just discussed the greatest opportunity for improvement *might* be found in the strike zone intersection of After-Sales Service and Naïve Customers.

Figure 2.6. Strike Zones of Opportunity

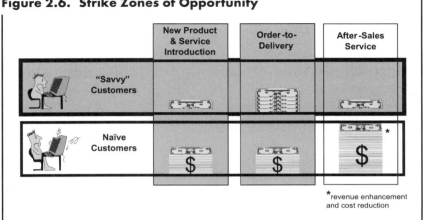

The reason I say *might*, is that the only way to be sure is to look at all the possible intersections. It might be that the customer segment could be better served with a whole new product/service offering or approach to the order-to-delivery process.

In any case there are probably a multitude of opportunities in all the possible strike zones. The point is to define the strike zone with the greatest upside and focus on it to define the surgical strike or strikes that will make the biggest difference within that strike zone.

CHAPTER 3

How to Strike

A jackass can kick a barn down, but it takes a carpenter to build one.

—Sam Rayburn, Congressman

A Plumbing Problem

Assume a strike zone or a core process has been selected—selected for further investigation and opportunity assessment. In any core process, work is requested or input to the process, and work is delivered or output at the end of the process.

A customer expresses a need for a new product or service that must be developed, or expresses interest in a product and eventually signs up to buy it; or the customer calls to request service, then receives it and pays for it. At the core-process level, a customer is key to triggering the process.

The intent of a core process is to take input (usually from a customer very early on in the process) and efficiently direct it into appropriate output. The customer's view is simple. Work is requested and a work product is delivered. The company view is different. The company becomes immersed in how work is performed and tends to lose sight of the simple customer view.

In either case perspectives on work are not unlike perspectives on a plumbing fixture (Figure 3.1). The person who approaches a beautiful sink and turns on a spigot expects to get water—warm or cold, depending on which spigot was turned. They are like the customer. However, the company's view is more like the plumber's view—an under-the-sink view of an interconnected array of pipes, hoses, valves, drains, traps, seals, nuts, and bolts.

Figure 3.1. A Simple Work Process

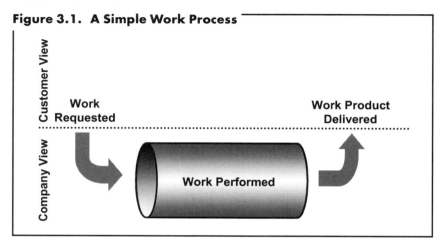

Let's look to a mortgage company for an example. Mortgage origination is a core process. It's their version of customer acquisition. For most customers the process should be very simple—request a loan and receive funds. For the company the process should be relatively simple as well—obtain the application, process the application, review and underwrite, and finalize and close.

Unfortunately, in the real world, it is not so simple. As illustrated in Figure 3.2, information is typically not obtained in its entirety up front, delays are incurred, and customers inconvenienced. And that is just what is visible to the customer. Behind the scenes each step of the process can be quite complicated and includes such detailed activities as validating employment, conducting a credit check, and preparing closing documents.

Map Out the Details

So how do we sort out the complexities of a process that engages the customer, suppliers, and various organizational entities? How do we keep our eye on the above-the-sink view and the customer's expectation of simplicity and beauty? How do we align that view with the reality of under-the-sink and the interconnected array of pipes, hoses, valves, drains, traps, seals, nuts, and bolts?

Figure 3.2. A Mortgage Origination Process

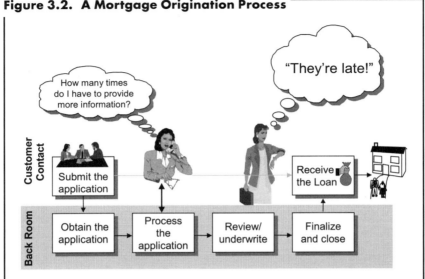

My colleagues and I look at a core process, define the key business processes within it, and then map it in detail. So, for example, our map of a mortgage origination core process would begin with the activities related to obtaining an application, and end with activities related to finalizing and closing the loan.

Typically a business process map with fifty to two hundred steps provides the detail needed to uncover the key surgical strike opportunities.

We use an approach to process mapping that encompasses all of the organizational entities involved in processing work to its completion. As described in some detail in our previous books, *Corporate Renaissance* and *Measure Up!,* a business process map is essentially a service flowchart, from the customer's perspective, which highlights:[1]

- Key customer interfaces
- Service provider or field activities (e.g., account rep)
- Critical information collection and dissemination points
- Behind-the-scenes activities, organizational interfaces, and hand-offs
- Supplier activities

Figure 3.3. Process Map of a Mortgage Process

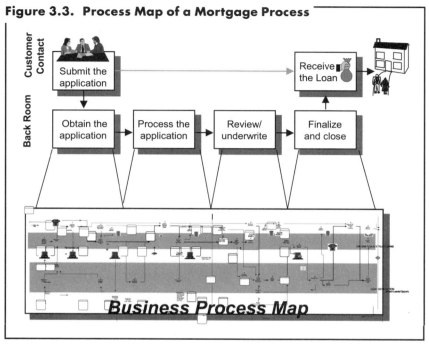

A business process map is essentially a type of flowchart. It depicts the activities and sequence required to deliver value to the customer. As illustrated in Figure 3.3, process maps are read from left to right. In a sense, these maps are like a road map in that they display a variety of possible paths in the sequence of work tasks. While we emphasize the major highways, the less traveled offshoots and back roads are also displayed. These maps present a bird's-eye perspective on the normal progression of work.

Figure 3.4 shows a framework that we use for the process maps. Perhaps most important, we depict activities performed by or with the customer on the top horizontal band. With this service orientation, these maps illustrate the customer experience across the complete life cycle of encounters. The activities within each of the bands depict the work flowing from one process step to the next.

The benefits of this form of process mapping include:

1. Building shared and consistent perception of the customer's experience with entire service

Figure 3.4. Process Map Framework

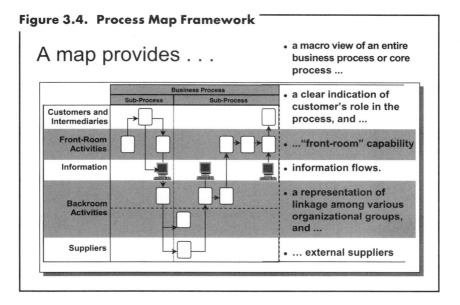

2. Identifying key interfaces with customers and channels

3. Providing basis for developing an economic model of the business

4. Identifying opportunities for improving service effectiveness and process efficiency

5. Providing framework for redesigning service system

6. Providing framework for strategic measures and controls

Most importantly, it is the process map that provides the means to identify and deliver a surgical strike. Much like the commanders on a battlefield who need maps of the terrain, which also identify enemy installations and troop movements, the process map provides guidance to the commanders of process improvement and their strike forces. In later chapters I will provide more examples of how these maps are used to uncover and deliver surgical-strike improvements.

The Nuts and Bolts of the Game

Our toy phone game has most of the characteristics of any core process—in this case an order-to-delivery core process. The customer in the game places an order by giving an index card that states the number of phones required. The customer expects to wait no longer than one minute and then expects to receive the right quantity of good phones in a little bin with the order card on top.

Unfortunately, in the early rounds of the game, the customer gets excuses—primarily excuses about late delivery and product defects.

Meanwhile the company that produces the phones is in a state of chaos. In the ten-minute chaos of Round One, no one knows what the other does. No one person knows how the product goes together. People are spread out across the room and unable to communicate very well. Therefore no one knows how the process works or should work, nor do they have a way to get it under control.

Do the participants use process mapping to sort it out? No. Why not? The customer, the process, and all activities are already right in front of them—in one small room—unlike the real world. In the real world, activities are spread across buildings, even countries. Customers, intermediaries, and vendors, as well as in-house departments throughout the company perform activities. Mapping helps make real world processes visible in one room, as in the game.

Also, in the game, all the workers in the process are engaged in diagnosing the problems, identifying, selecting, and implementing the most appropriate surgical strikes. All the expertise in working the process is involved in fixing the process. In addition, unlike the real world, the game stops while all the workers have a chance to figure out what went wrong and how to make it better. Therefore, after Round One and before Round Two, they have the expertise and the time to make sense of the interconnected array of pipes, hoses, and so on.

So, like the real world, there is a core process: It begins and ends with the customer. As in the real world, the workers are key to unraveling the intricacies of process problems, uncovering and executing the surgical strike improvements.

The only problem is when there are too many participants in the game. Too many people getting in each other's way during the rounds and too many people trying to improve the process between the rounds create the greatest potential for the game to fail and for real-world processes to fail. I will explain more about this in Chapter 4.

The Game Plan—What It Takes

Surgical strikes rely upon a wide range of elements, but are glued together by a reliable, repeatable method to identify potential strikes, choose between various alternatives, design the strikes, and deliver the strikes. In some cases, strikes are right at your fingertips. Most often, however, a simple but effective methodology is required. However, methodology does not mean "slow." A methodology can facilitate speed by ensuring no time is wasted.

We have seen companies define and deliver surgical strikes using the four phases defined below in as little as six weeks, and the Discovery Stage in as little as two weeks:

Discover: Obtain the intelligence to aim a strike; identify the key opportunity areas.

Inspire: Create the objectives and options available to achieve results.

Design: Design changes to processes, services, delivery systems, and measures.

Realize: Build the necessary elements, piloting, and delivering the strike.

While the method appears to be, and is described like, any reengineering methodology, I think you can see from the timelines that the pace is much faster. While a reengineering project would take many months, a surgical-strike initiative can be done in a few weeks. Less rigor and faster results!

The real world and the game all have something in common when it comes to improving business process performance—the Ten Surgical Strikes and targeting small actions to get big results. Plus, the best do it rapidly (weeks, not months) with four stages common in their execution:

1. A Discover Stage without overanalysis but with enough data to properly target the strike

2. An Inspire Stage, where old, new, and sometimes radical ideas are identified

3. A Design Stage to define the ideal outcome of the strike—how the new process will work

4. The Realize Stage, where they conduct the strike, quickly learning from the experience, and rapidly making modifications based on that learning

Discovery

Discovery is about understanding the terrain, and obtaining the intelligence required to know where to aim the surgical strike. Typically, discovery entails an evaluation of a key business process (e.g., customer acquisition, implementation, day-to-day operations, inquiries/services) and related workload characteristics to determine where the greatest opportunities for improvement exist.

The Discovery Stage does not have to become a science project. In most cases, the 80–20 rule applies: 20 percent of the effort provides 80 percent of the benefit! You can get the gist of the situation, with quick samples, estimates, etc. The trick is to "timebox" the effort, and do the best you can in the time available. The findings will be directionally correct. We have found that, in most cases, only two or three weeks is needed. See Figure 3.5.

The typical first step of Discovery is to work with a liaison from the company, and the process in question, to develop a plan, and then immediately start obtaining workload data and developing a detailed process map to depict how work gets done.

The next step is to quantify the process. Like a road map, a process map shows pathways and their interrelationships, but their capacities to handle traffic and the amount of traffic they typically handle are unclear.

To complete the process analysis, it is crucial to understand the workload on each path. A workload analysis is done to provide a profile of the types of work processed by the organization. The intent here is to develop a profile of the nature of the organization's work from the customer's perspective and assess the degree to which it adds value. The workload analysis also provides information regarding the volumes of work entering the process and traversing the various paths on the process map(s). The intent is to determine the characteristics of work in the process including the number, frequency, and types of work being processed, and the amount of time needed to process the work at each step. The analysis encompasses finding root causes for product and/or service defects and wasteful activities in the process. Causes for processing delays and frequency of occurrence will also be uncovered as part of the workload analysis.

These volumes, routings, and processing times are built into an Excel-based spreadsheet model. Using the model, we can develop a Pareto view of the process steps to narrow our focus on the few key steps (or portions of steps) that consume the most labor. We can then

Figure 3.5. Rapid Opportunity Assessment Work Plan

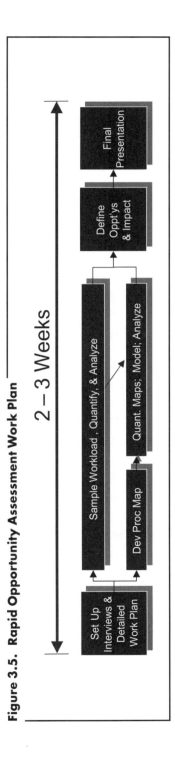

also determine the labor impact of the various improvement ideas and operating scenarios.

Finally we prepare a presentation style briefing of our investigation and our findings, which includes a profile of:

- Top labor-consuming steps

- Top steps where delays are incurred

- Value: the extent of value-added activity, versus non-value activity in the process

- Workload problems and root cause

- Suggested areas of greatest opportunity for two types of surgical strikes:

    1. Quick hits (e.g., process improvement and/or process discipline).

    2. Solutions that require more development (i.e., technological enhancements).

We do not just "throw it over the fence." All along we engage the workforce to discuss the process, help with the analyses, comment on the process map, and make suggestions. At the end of the Discovery Stage, we work with a liaison from the company to select the most viable improvement targets on the basis of additional factors such as timing, risk, degree of investment, and effort to implement. The recommended targets are described along with a presentation of the projected financial benefits.

Sometimes the quick hits are so obvious that the "Inspire" and "Design" stages can be skipped. But in most cases the really big results come from well formulated and executed surgical strikes. The "Inspire" and "Design" stages provide the means for a well-formulated strike.

Inspire

Surgical Strikes succeed with an inspired team applying inspired ideas, techniques, and technologies.

The Inspire stage is about assigning the leaders, unleashing the rene-gades, and creating the strike force for change within an organization. It is about creativity and identifying the techniques and technologies that might be employed to get the desired results. In essence, inspira-tion is about preparing the forces to succeed with the surgical-strikes approach.

A surgical strike also requires consideration of the various options regarding tools, techniques, and technologies. There is a wide spectrum of design ideas and options: Process Management Techniques, Organi-zation and Job Design Styles, Best Practices and Worker Ideas and Technology Enablers. But what is most significant is the new world of technology enablers.

While there is a whole new world of technology enablers, the basics of business to which they apply remain the same. Business processes begin with a request or order for work, and end with some form of delivered work product. Work comes in, work goes out. Technology needs to be focused on making the work flow in a more effective and efficient manner.

Sometimes the technology option is "Don't use technology." A lead-ing bank in the United Kingdom arrived at this conclusion when invest-igating the performance of their customer service operation. Nearly everyone we spoke to said, "We need desktop fax capability. Now we each print out the fax, whereupon it is picked up twice a day, and manually fed into a fax machine. Isn't this ridiculous? Shouldn't we each have the ability to send a fax directly from our computer?" In one sense, yes. But out of 400 people in the operation, only 1.5 people were involved in the faxing activities. To give every workstation desktop fax capability as well as train everyone (and continue training, because of their 35 percent turnover rate), would cost far more than having the 1.5 people manually handling the fax machine. There were far better things to do with any investment in time, money, and especially their limited IT resources. The surgical strike was elsewhere.

Conversely, technology can enable business processes, services, and products that were previously unimaginable, impossible, impractical, or at least not affordable. The key is to have technology viewed and positioned as an option to be applied only when it makes good business sense to do so.

Thomas H. Davenport, a leading authority on technologies application to business process performance, boiled down the key impact areas back in 1990. The basic concept still applies to today's focus on the application of technologies and ideas.

The following list from Davenport and James E. Short summarizes the deployment options available from Information Technology (IT):

Table 3.1. IT Capabilities in Business, Organization, and Process Design

Capability	Organizational Impact
Transactional	IT can transform unstructured processes into routinized transactions.
Geographical	IT can transfer information with rapidity and ease across large distances, making processes independent of geography.
Automational	IT can replace or reduce human labor in a process.
Analytical	IT can bring complex analytical methods to bear on a process.
Informational	IT can bring vast amounts of detailed information into a process.
Sequential	IT can enable changes in a sequence of tasks in a process, often allowing multiple tasks to be worked on simultaneously.
Knowledge Management	IT allows the capture and dissemination of knowledge and expertise to improve the process.
Tracking	IT allows the detailed tracking of status, inputs, and outputs.
Disintermediation	IT can be used to connect two parties within a process that would otherwise communicate through intermediaries.

Source: Thomas H. Davenport and James E. Short[2]

Although I have dwelt on the technology options, the "Inspire" stage is about reviewing all the options (ideas, tools, techniques, and technologies) and selecting the best fit for the opportunity at hand. The most inspired solutions, and surgical strikes, typically involve the selection and creative integration of multiple options.

Design

The Design Stage builds upon Discovery and Inspiration. The Discovery Stage identifies the target of opportunity and provides specifications for a design (e.g., cut billing inquiries in half by managing customer expectations early on). The Inspire Stage seeks to generate ideas and options with which to meet the design specification (e.g., provide a sample bill during the sales process).

Sometimes people get the specifications and the options confused. Imagine if the management of our U.K. call center said, "Design a new process using desktop fax." Worded that way, it is a design specification. To implement desktop fax would have cost more, with no appreciable effect on service. Ideally, for the most effective surgical strikes, technology solutions are an option, not a spec. For the U.K. call center the better spec might have involved cutting costs by x, or improving service by y. Such a spec would have the impact of driving a design team to select solutions to meet an objective, rather than a solution being the objective.

In the Design Stage, the strike force describes what the process could be—first as a simple sketch of the concept and then as a more detailed map of the way work will get done. The design effort also includes the development of detailed business maps, procedures, and operating policies and the design of supporting infrastructures (e.g., performance measures, job and organizational design, compensation systems). The design is then confirmed by validation through interviews and business modeling at the same time the key performance measures are defined. The design phase concludes by expanding operational involvement by testing the new process with a pilot.

Realize

The Realize Stage is no different than what we learned with reengineering: It's not easy. However, one saving grace for the surgical-strikes approach is that the changes are typically more targeted and less all encompassing. Still, for a major strike, the entire organization has to apply and institutionalize the change into its day-to-day operations.

The planning for implementation typically begins on a parallel track with the pilot, and in some cases in parallel with the earlier analysis and design work. There are two components to implementation: (1) planning and executing the logistics of converting, on a large scale, to the new mode of operation (e.g., training and facilities modifications); and (2) managing the transition. A profile of the current process, organization, and culture is contrasted with the proposed new state. The nature and magnitude of the gaps to be closed dictates the magnitude of this transformation effort.

All of the organizational, system, and people changes necessary to ensure the long-term success of the new design are identified and implemented in this stage. The cumulative impact of all these changes may stimulate or require a rethinking of how the business as a whole is defined and of its future strategy.

If the surgical strike entails a significant change to day-to-day work, the Realize Stage does not end when the pilot has proved the initial change works. In effect, the *transition* period is far more crucial. It begins after the pilot has been declared a success and ends when the organization learns, as a whole, how to incorporate the new process design into day-to-day operations.

The Cell Phone Game—from Storming to Performing

In our Process Redesign Game, there is no analysis-to-paralysis. The entire (Discover→ Inspire → Design → Realize) method is done in minutes—the surgical strikes are defined and implemented. In addition, what is unique, compared to the real world, is that the work force is the "strike force." In other words all the participants are involved in the "production operation" of building and delivering "cell phones" to the customer, and they are also all involved in fixing the process. So let's look at what happens to the "work force" and what happens to the "strike force."

The work force is in a complete state of disorientation and chaos in Round One. The Operations Manager is relegated to futilely barking orders, trying to expedite work, calm frayed nerves, all without a real understanding of the process or the product. Sound familiar? The workers do not understand how their work relates to anyone else's, how the product goes together in its entirety, who and how to ask for help, or even who's in charge. Sound familiar? The customer can't get their orders delivered; the one's that do get through have quality problems; and, to top it off, the customer can't get the attention of the Customer Service Manager. Sound familiar?

Anyway, the situation changes dramatically by Round Three. Perhaps most dramatic—the room is quiet. No barking orders, no irate customer, and a quiet work force is pumping out the work at an astonishing rate. The role of Operations Manager has evolved from a frustrated, loud, but ineffective dictator, to no role at all. The work force becomes self-managed, with the Operations Manager assisting to pump out real work.

We always ask, "Were you more stressed in Round One, Two, or Round Three?" They always say, "Round One was most stressful," even though they delivered as much as ten to twenty times the output in Round Three. When change is effectively accomplished by the people who have to live with the change, it can be a real win-win—for the company and the employee.

Regarding the game participants' role as a strike force, my experience is all over the map. While most groups quietly and constructively work together; others break up into disconnected, uncoordinated subgroups while others allow one strong personality to dictate a course of action.

We have run sessions in companies where everyone knows each other, and at conferences/seminars where the participants are meeting for the first time. People meeting for the first time tend to be polite and work well together. My recollection is that the most dysfunctional groups are within companies, and that the higher the levels of management, the more dysfunctional. You can learn a lot about a company's management style by having the management team go through this game. I remember one vice president, in a game with those directly reporting to him, who gave up listening to his people after a mere five minutes and got up to start moving the tables himself while telling everyone how it was going to be. One of his people whispered to me, "Now you see the way it really is around here!"

Most of the time, the strike force works well together and gets the job done. We show them their performance (the scorecard), and then have them first discuss what did not go well and why (Discover), before diving into possible solutions (Inspire), and deciding how to do it in the next round (Design). Focused and empowered, they get the job done (Realize).

The next chapters will discuss each of the ten key surgical strikes, how they are identified, what specific actions are taken, and what quick-hit results are derived.

CHAPTER 4

STRIKE 1: UNCLOG THE WORKPLACE

[The biggest risk of all] is that [the] lean, fast-acting management style that's made the company a winner will turn into a fat-assed bureaucracy where managers spend all their time writing procedures, forming committees, attending meetings, decorating their offices, building empires, and protecting their tushes instead of making things happen.
—WILLIAM G. MCGOWEN, FOUNDER AND CEO,
MCI COMMUNICATIONS

Reengineering and downsizing got intermingled and confused for good reason. As companies embarked on reengineering projects, they found too many people for too little work. So they downsized. In such cases, downsizing was a quick hit, but it was not reengineering.

An injustice occurred when reengineering was solely equated with this kind of downsizing. Done well, reengineering is about designing efficient processes to better serve customers. In most cases I have seen, big downsizing moves were made prior to such reengineering not as a result of reengineering.

The tragedy is not so much in the downsizing, but in the gross overstaffing that led to the downsizing in the first place. Downsizing is an admission of management failure. There may have been a failure to continuously match workforce levels with workload demands. Or there may have been a failure to think ahead and build new businesses, new products, and new sales opportunities in which to absorb workers freed up from other parts of the company.

So with a lack of forward thinking, and finding themselves with too many people and too little work, management faces two choices: (1) Quickly find value-added work to do and put the underutilized people to productive use, or (2) downsize, by cutting people and payroll. Although I am not fundamentally here to advocate or make a case for layoffs and downsizing, there are times when option 2 is the right move.

As the old expression reminds us, too many cooks spoil the soup. People can (and do) get in each other's way. Numerous meetings, phone calls and messages, e-mails, and the like can provide the appearance of productivity but in fact are actually just clogging the workplace. Although sometimes well intentioned and often done in the name of involvement and "buy-in," the real workflow can be brought to a crawl.

Busy but Not Productive

Let's look at an oversimplified example of how people can be busy but not productive.

Picture a large dinner table with four people on each side and one on each end. Now assume one of the people on the end says, "Pass the salt, please." Now assume the salt shaker is at the opposite end and that everyone, to feel useful, participates in moving the salt from one end of the table to the other. The salt would take a long time to meander its way through a total of nine hand-offs.

Now assume, at another table, one side of the table is busy eating and only one side of the table participates in moving the salt. The total hand-offs are reduced to five and the time is cut in half. Plus the people on the other side continue to eat uninterrupted!

Figure 4.1 illustrates the difference. Table 1 involves everyone in passing the salt, while Table 2 uses a more direct route.

So what's the point? The point is that many organizations behave like Table 1. Enlightenment and involvement, while well intended, has been allowed to deteriorate into inefficiency and delay. People are busy, but not productive.

Figure 4.1. Passing the Salt

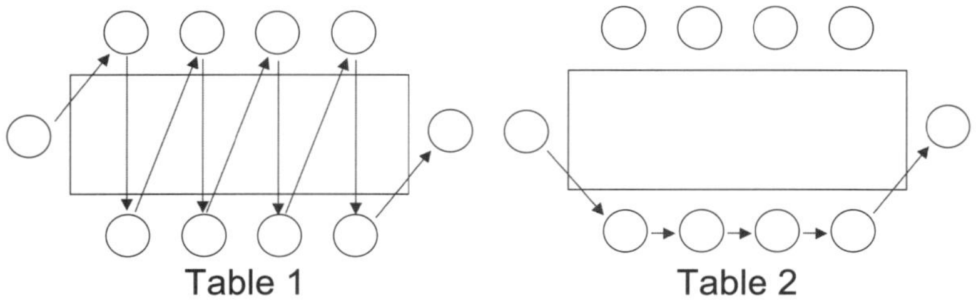

Table 1   Table 2

The complexity and confusion of Table 1 is nothing compared to the flows of work within real companies. In real companies the nonsense and the workflows are much more complicated, intertwined, and obscured from view. Sometimes it is very difficult to sort out the work from the nonsense, but when the nonsense is painfully obvious, there are simply too many people involved.

Unfortunately, such bureaucratic bloat appears to be a natural human tendency that gets addressed sporadically rather than continuously.

So How Did We Get Here?

The idea of bureaucratic bloat is not new. People have been observing and complaining about bureaucratic nonsense for years. Recently my mother had a visitor from the U.K. Having heard about my work in helping businesses improve process performance, he brought along a copy of a book written and published in the U.K. in the 1950s. The book, by C. Northcote Parkinson, is *Parkinson's Law or the Rising Pyramid*, a well known classic of management theory.[1] In the first chapter there is an amazing account of how bureaucracies are formed. I have included it here, nearly in its entirety; because I couldn't say it better myself:

> **Work expands so as to fill the time available for its completion. General recognition of this fact is shown in the proverbial phrase "It is the busiest man who has time to spare." Thus, an elderly lady**

of leisure can spend the entire day in writing and dispatching a postcard to her niece at Bognor Regis. An hour will be spent in finding the postcard, another in hunting for spectacles, half an hour in a search for the address, an hour and a quarter in composition, and twenty minutes in deciding whether or not to take an umbrella when going to the pillar box in the next street. The total effort that would occupy a busy man for three minutes all told may in this fashion leave another person prostrate after a day of doubt, anxiety, and toil.

Granted that work (and especially paperwork) is thus elastic in its demands on time, it is manifest that there need be little or no relationship between the work to be done and the size of the staff to which it may be assigned. A lack of real activity does not, of necessity, result in leisure. A lack of occupation is not necessarily revealed by a manifest idleness. The thing to be done swells in importance and complexity in a direct ratio with the time to be spent. This fact is widely recognized, but less attention has been paid to its wider implications, more especially in the field of public administration. Politicians and taxpayers have assumed (with occasional phases of doubt) that a rising total in the number of civil servants must reflect a growing volume of work to be done. Cynics, in questioning this belief, have imagined that the multiplication of officials must have left some of them idle or all of them able to work for shorter hours. But this is a matter in which faith and doubt seem equally misplaced. The fact is that the number of the officials and the quantity of the work are not related to each other at all. The rise in the total of those employed is governed by Parkinson's Law and would be much the same whether the volume of the work were to increase, diminish, or even disappear. The importance of Parkinson's Law lies in the fact that it is a law of growth based upon an analysis of the factors by which that growth is controlled.

The validity of this recently discovered law must rest mainly on statistical proofs, which will follow. Of more interest to the general reader is the explanation of the factors underlying the general tendency to which this law gives definition. Omitting technicalities (which are numerous), we may distinguish at the outset two motive forces. They can be represented for the present purpose by two almost axiomatic statements, thus: (1) "An official wants to multiply subordinates, not rivals" and (2) "Officials make work for each other."

To comprehend Factor 1, we must picture a civil servant, called A, who finds himself overworked. Whether this overwork is real or imaginary is immaterial, but we should observe, in passing, that A's sensation (or illusion) might easily result from his own decreasing energy: a normal symptom of middle age. For this real or imagined overwork there are, broadly speaking, three possible remedies. He may resign; he may ask to halve the work with a colleague called B; he may demand the assistance of two subordinates, to be called C and D. There is probably no instance, however, in history of A choosing any but the third alternative. By resignation he would lose his pension rights. By having B appointed, on his own level in the hierarchy, he would merely bring in a rival for promotion to W's vacancy when W (at long last) retires. So A would rather have C and D, junior men, below him. They will add to his consequence and, by dividing the work into two categories, as between C and D, he will have the merit of being the only man who comprehends them both. It is essential to realize at this point that C and D are, as it were, inseparable. To appoint C alone would have been impossible. Why? Because C, if by himself, would divide the work with A and so assume almost the equal status that has been refused in the first instance to B; a status the more emphasized if C is A's only possible successor. Subordinates must thus number two or more, each being thus kept in order by fear of the other's promotion. When C complains in turn of being overworked (as he certainly will) A will, with the concurrence of C, advise the appointment of two assistants to help C. But he can then avert internal friction only by advising the appointment of two more assistants to help D, whose position is much the same. With this recruitment of E, F, G, and H the promotion of A is now practically certain.

Seven officials are now doing what one did before. This is where Factor 2 comes into operation. For these seven make so much work for each other that all are fully occupied and A is actually working harder than ever. An incoming document may well come before each of them in turn. Official E decides that it falls within the province of F, who places a draft reply before C, who amends it drastically before consulting D, who asks G to deal with it. But G goes on leave at this point, handing the file over to H, who drafts a minute that is signed by D and returned to C, who revises his draft accordingly and lays the new version before A.

What does A do? He would have every excuse for signing the thing unread, for he has many other matters on his mind. Knowing now that he is to succeed W next year, he has to decide whether C or D should succeed to his own office. He had to agree to G's going on leave even if not yet strictly entitled to it. He is worried whether H should not have gone instead, for reasons of health. He has looked pale recently, partly, but not solely because of his domestic troubles. Then there is the business of F's special increment of salary for the period of the conference and E's application for transfer to the Ministry of Pensions. A has heard that D is in love with a married typist and that G and F arc no longer on speaking terms—no one seems to know why. So A might be tempted to sign C's draft and have done with it. But A is a conscientious man. Beset as he is with problems created by his colleagues for themselves and for him created by the mere fact of these officials' existence he is not the man to shirk his duty. He reads through the draft with care, deletes the fussy paragraphs added by C and H, and restores the thing to the form preferred in the first instance by the able (if quarrelsome) F. He corrects the English—none of these young men can write grammatically—and finally produces the same reply he would have written if officials C to H had never been born. Far more people have taken far longer to produce the same result. No one has been idle. All have done their best. And it is late in the evening before A finally quits his office and begins the return journey to Ealing. The last of the office lights are being turned off in the gathering dusk that marks the end of another day's administrative toil. Among the last to leave, A reflects with bowed shoulders and a wry smile that late hours, like gray hairs, are among the penalties of success.

A Magnificent Navy on Land

Parkinson goes on to show how the principle applied to the British Navy of the early 1900s.[2]

> The strength of the Navy in 1914 could be shown as 146,000 officers and men, 3,249 dockyard officials and clerks, and 57,000 dockyard workmen. By 1928 there were only 100,000 officers and men and only 62,439 workmen, but the dockyard officials and clerks by then numbered 4,558. As for warships, the strength in 1928 was a mere fraction of what it had been in 1914—fewer than 20 capital ships in commission as compared with 62. Over the same period the Admiralty officials had increased in number from 2,000 to 3,569, providing (as was remarked) "a magnificent navy on land."

These figures are more clearly set forth in Table 4-1:

Table 4-1. Admiralty Statistics

Classification	Year		Increase or Decrease %
	1914	1928	
Capital ships in commission	62	20	−67%
Officers and men in R.N.	146,000	100,000	−31%
Dockyard workers	57,000	62,439	+9%
Dockyard officials and clerks	3,249	4,558	+40%
Admiralty officials	2,000	3,569	+78%

What we have to note is that the 2,000 officials of 1914 had become the 3,569 of 1928; and that this growth was unrelated to any possible increase in their work. The Navy during that period had diminished, in point of fact, by a third in men and two-thirds in ships.

That Was Then, and This Is Now

So what's changed? Apparently not much.

Look at the following March 1998 report and press release about the U.S. military from the Project on Government Oversight (POGO):[3]

> Our military has almost twice as many officers per enlisted personnel than at the end of World War II. In short, officer inflation in the U.S. military has reached an all-time high. In 1945 there was one officer for every 11 enlisted personnel; now there is one officer for every six enlisted personnel. Some specific examples:
>
> ■ Army: In 1945, the number of Army generals per active Army division was 14. In 1986, at the height of the Cold War, the army had 24 generals per division. Now, as we face no major threat, there are 30 generals per division.
>
> ■ Navy: At the end of WWII there were 130 Navy ships per admiral. In 1986, at the height of the Cold War, there were 2.2 ships per admiral. Now, as we face no major threat, there is an average of only 1.6 ships per admiral.
>
> ■ Marines: In 1945 there were 469,925 Marines commanded by 81 generals; by March 1997, 79 generals commanded a mere 173,011 Marines.
>
> ■ Air Force: In 1945 there were 244 aircraft per general in the Air Force. In 1986, at the height of the Cold War, there were 28 aircraft per general. Now, as we face no major threat, there are only 23 aircraft per general.

In the business world, there is the same inclination to bloat the bureaucracy. AT&T is probably the poster child for bureaucratic bloat, and its saga continues. The November 2000 issue of *U.S. News and World Report* had this to say on the breakup of AT&T into four pieces: " 'The four new entities will likely perform as poorly as they do now,' says Ken McGee, an analyst at Gartner, a consulting group. 'The same problems—a less than lean workforce, slowness to market, and ponderous bureaucracy—likely will plague each company.' "[4]

Over the last decade or more, AT&T has been described as in trouble and hard to fix as a result of its "meeting-intensive culture." Too many people, too many chiefs with too much time, leads to too much bureaucracy—too many meetings, presentations, useless memos, e-mails, reports, time for interpersonal disputes, and political high jinks.

In response to the leading headline of the week "AT&T Offers Buyouts to 77,800 Managers," an article in *Fortune* delved into the key question: " 'What have these people been doing?' Good question. . . . The company divides its employees into two camps: 'occupational,' which basically means hourly paid, and 'management,' which is all others. So not all those 'managers' AT&T is proposing to buy out do any managing."[5]

Nor did many do any real work. Many of those "managers," with no employees to manage, went from meeting to meeting to pontificate on issues and action items, with no one truly accountable to get any real work done. When real work had to get done many of these managers hired outside consultants and contractors to the tune of roughly $1 billion annually in the mid-1990s. The net result was more people, more confusion, obfuscation, and hopelessly clogged processes.

For AT&T, and for many organizations, the pipe occasionally gets hopelessly clogged (Figure 4.2). Like a clogged septic system, the hidden flow meanders around a maze of sludge, blockages, twists and turns, and occasionally backs up and bursts out in a repugnant and glaring manner.

So what can be done? Unclog the workplace.

Figure 4.2. Strike 1—Unclog the Workplace

Work Requested   Work Product Delivered

In our Process Redesign Game: You can't fix what you can't see. In our process redesign game, and in the workplace, too much confusion and too many people obscure the flows of work and related problems. Much like a cloudless day is needed for reconnaissance planes and satellites, a clear view is needed to get a true perspective on work processes. Sometimes the sole act of clearing the view will clear up the process. In the game, if there are too many people involved, it bogs down, takes too long, and performance suffers. The larger the group, the more difficult it is to produce the toy phones, and the more difficult it is to bring the group to consensus on how best to change the process in the time available.

The game performs best with about a dozen people. However, on a number of occasions we have been asked to incorporate as many as twenty people into the game. We did this by developing some phony-baloney jobs. We add an extra material handler or two, a few more process engineers, an order taker, and another inspector or two. With this many people crowding the workplace, chaos ensues. The operators aren't sure who to ask for help. The managers don't know who does what or even how to begin to find out. The inspectors become too specialized, don't see the big picture and understand the product's construction, and therefore can't help improve quality.

After the first round of the game, where the poor-performance baseline is established, the group has a chance to discuss problems and fixes. When there are too many people it is not unusual for two or three subgroups to emerge and have isolated discussions. Bringing those subgroups back together and driving to consensus is nearly impossible in the time we allow. Therefore as the time draws near to make changes to the process and begin Round Two, a dominant subgroup takes over. Then a subgroup is either "laid-off" or given some menial jobs for Round Two. If they stay for Round Two, performance inevitably suffers; sometimes performance even gets worse than it was in Round One. Again, too many people will lead to too much confusion and performance will suffer.

Routine Maintenance . . .

In the real world some companies do something about the tendency to bloat and others do not. Companies, like General Electric, are known for continuously paring, pruning, and realigning their workforces, in good times and bad.

Other companies, through either benign neglect, or over optimism about the future, obtain, gain, and retain too many employees for far too long. At some point it hits a breaking point when it become painfully apparent that the business can no longer sustain it. Then what? Put out the fire.

. . . Or Radical Cleanup

Assume your house is on fire. Assume the firemen arrive quickly and save half your house. Would you fault the firemen for saving only half your house?

Now assume your company is caught in a financial inferno. Wouldn't you want it put out as fast as possible by someone who knows what they are doing? Assume the "corporate firemen" arrive and save half your company. Would you fault the "firemen" for saving only half your company?

The answer for many of us is "yes." We condemn the turnaround specialists—Albert Dunlop for what he did to Scott Paper, and Rick Miller for what he did at Wang Laboratories. But, they were only the firemen. To their credit they put out the fire and left something standing. (Although, in the case of Dunlop, some suggest he robbed the house while putting out the fire—by taking $100 million in compensation for eighteen months' work.)

So if the turnaround specialists are the corporate firemen, who is to blame for the fire? In a house fire, usually the homeowner is to blame, not out of deliberate arson, but rather out of benign neglect. A homeowner may accumulate and neglect the oil soaked rags, paper, and other clutter that can catch fire and, at the same time, not repair frayed electrical wires.

Likewise, it is the benign neglect on the part of corporate owners, directors, and their management that leads companies to a financial firestorm. They provide the fuel for a financial firestorm with an undisciplined accumulation of products, services, people, and other assets, along with a basic neglect and lack of aggression regarding their competitive position. For larger traditional firms, this situation typically occurs slowly and unintentionally. For other entrepreneurial ventures (the dot-coms), this progression is quite rapid. Whether such a situation results from mismanagement or at best an educated gamble that just didn't play out, the time comes to unclog and clear the view.

So while on national television the laid-off Scott Paper employee of many years berates Albert Dunlop for his troubles, his wrath is misguided. It is likely the benign neglect (and abdication of responsibility) on the part of the owners, directors, and previous management to aggressively manage the business (and not just "ride the runaway horse") that is to blame.

Finally, these corporate firemen are attacked for their short tenures and nearsighted goals, but that's their job. Like the firemen who put out a house fire, they're done when the fire is out.

When All Clogged Up . . .

Whether it's routine maintenance or radical cleanup of a clogged up process the mission is the same: Identify the clogs and clear the flow.

Sometimes the situation is extreme. I remember working in one division of one of the nations largest companies and thinking they should have everyone count off "one," "two," "one," "two," etc. and then simply lay off all the "twos." Sure, some good people would be caught up in the random count, but the net effect would still be a leaner more focused operation. There would be a lot less time for the nonsense (absurd meetings and memo wars) that I observed.

> **The Game:** Random downsizing (before reengineering) is not unlike what happens in our game when there are too many people. Although the critical workers stay (the five operators who actually construct the phones), for the others there is no real serious thought that goes into who stays and who goes. The game simply gets easier to operate with fewer people clogging up the workflows and the change process.

In a very bloated situation, where speed is of the essence, it may not matter very much who goes. But it does matter from which areas of the business—the critical functions should not be cut to the same degree as the noncritical functions. For example, if the customer-service operation has expanded to meet the demands of a bigger installed base of product and customers, an arbitrary cutback could be disastrous. However, if administrative and corporate-headquarters support functions have grown disproportionately, that is where the opportunity lies.

. . . Focus the Hit

Is your revenue per full-time equivalent employee (FTE) going down? That is the basic question. The ratio will show trouble when headcount growth exceeds revenue growth, or when revenue declines faster than employee attrition. This ratio provides some measure and check on the degree of corporate bloat. (Remember: Your FTE count will have to include your employees plus any significant contracted or outsourced FTEs.)

If there is bloat it probably is not evenly spread around the business. So where is the greatest source of change? Has customer service grown as the installed base has grown? Has SG&A (Sales, General, and Administration) grown significantly greater than revenues?

We worked with a technology solutions company where we found the headquarters SG&A had doubled from 12 percent of revenues to 24 percent of revenues in a year-and-a-half. It was a familiar story, especially in the zeal of the "new economy." Rapid growth and related revenues were projected, hiring was done, but the degree of growth in revenue did not happen, and did not appear to be forthcoming in the near future. So what to do? Should they cut the support staff across-the-board by nearly 50 percent to get back in line with revenues?

We were asked to look for the key opportunities to scale back SG&A expenses, without compromising their drive to be a full-service industry leader. We triangulated on the problem—looking at SG&A from three different vantage points: (1) industry benchmarks; (2) relative growth by function; and (3) degree of customer-valued costs.

Industry Benchmarks

In general, across all industries during that year we found SG&A expenses to be running at 17 percent of revenues. So with a one-and-one-half year move from 12 percent to 24 percent, our technology solutions firm had gone from well below average to well above average. To get to an industry average SG&A ratio would require a reduction of 25 percent in SG&A costs with flat revenues, and a 20 percent reduction if revenue grew as projected.

Further investigation into specific competitors and similar companies corroborated the feasibility of operating with a 20 percent to 25 percent lower SG&A expense.

Relative Growth by Function

We looked at the specific functions within the SG&A category. As illustrated in Table 4-2, the relative growth rates varied a great deal among the various functions:

Table 4-2. SG&A Salaries (000s)

Salaries	Avg Mth Yr 1	Avg Mth Yr 2	% change
Ops Support	$ 122	$ 207	70%
Acct'g	$ 541	$ 734	36%
Admin	$ 911	$ 847	−7%
Gen'l Sales	$ 44	$ 42	−5%
Health Industry Sales	$ 234	$ 158	−33%
Tvl Industry Sales	$ 32	$ —	−100%
TeleCom Industry Sales	$ 274	$ 354	29%
FinSrv Industry Sales	$ 102	$ 136	33%
Tech Industry Sales	$ 50	$ 44	−12%
Training	$ 164	$ 292	78%
HR	$ 375	$ 618	65%
Client Serv	$ 190	$ 424	123%
Quality	$ 213	$ 271	27%
Facilities	$ 45	$ 232	416%
Launch	$ 77	$ 372	383%
TeleCom	$ 48	$ 317	560%
Purchasing	$ 40	$ 85	113%
Mktg	$ 323	$ 422	31%
Legal	$ 154	$ 131	−15%
IR	$ 44	$ 96	118%
Technology	$ 280	$ 1,659	493%
TOTAL	**$ 4,263**	**$7,441**	**75%**

Here, like most situations, an across-the-board 20 to 25 percent cut did not make sense. And it wasn't simply a matter of whacking back the high-growth areas. For example, a conscious strategic decision had been made to invest and grow the sales to the telecom and financial services industries at the expense of the travel and health care sectors.

The biggest opportunity was found in the ambitious growth of the technology development, which was also the primary contributor to the growth in purchasing and human resources (HR). They hired HR people to hire technology people. They hired purchasing people to buy equipment for the new technology people.

Unfortunately the technology bubble had burst. So while some of the growth was still warranted to fulfill the company's ambition of becoming a more full-service firm, the bulk of the growth was excessive.

Significant and justified cutbacks in the technology group, HR, telecom, facilities, and product launch would yield a 24 percent reduction in overall SG&A expenses.

Customer-Valued Costs

But we weren't done. We needed to know how much of the SG&A work was amorphous overhead, and how much was really in direct support of this company's clients or specific internal projects. To find out, we surveyed everyone so we could figure out how much support various clients were receiving. We found that 27 percent of the SG&A labor was really directly attributable to client work. This component was not pure overhead, but potentially value-added service, and certainly should be examined more closely before becoming part of a labor cutback.

Assuming the services were value-added from the client's perspective, here was an opportunity to charge the clients for the services being provided, and actually increase revenue per employee. This company was able to do so in most cases. For those cases where their client refused, the support was withdrawn. (Herein lies a good definition of "value-added." An activity adds value if a customer is willing to pay for it.)

Triangulate and Strike

The three views of SG&A provided clear guidance toward two surgical-strike actions. The first was a targeted layoff of 20 percent of the SG&A labor. The second was a revenue-enhancing move to charge appropriate fees for consultations and other professional services.

The point is that good in-your-face data was needed to drive good decisions. A combination of the data, along with the pleading and politicking, enabled the right decisions to be made. Without the data, the pleading and politicking alone could have grossly distorted the actions taken. As I recollect from a conference I attended some years ago, the hard-charging CEO of a Fortune 500 company said something to this effect: "If you don't bring facts and data, you're just another *%$# with an opinion."

Strike 1: The Tip of the Iceberg

Strike 1 is about downsizing—identifying and eliminating obvious bloat. Sometimes such downsizing is a legitimate and essential strike. One may argue whether the decisions that lead to overstaffing are excusable or inexcusable. But when an organization grows beyond its ability to be funded and paid for, something must be done. If something isn't done—and fast—you're going down. While a fast strike to reduce staff may enable you to scrape by, the more intractable problems and opportunities lie underneath the surface. Strikes 2 through 10 are about uncovering those big opportunities.

Strike 1: Unclog the Workplace

Strike 1 is essentially a significant and rapid downsizing that may be warranted in cases where:

- Employee growth has significantly exceeded revenue growth, and/or
- Revenue per employee greatly lags that of your competitors

If warranted, Strike 1 typically needs to focus on:

- Specific areas (functions, departments, or processes) in the company where headcount growth has far exceeded revenue growth and the growth for other areas, *and*
- The areas of extraordinary growth that are not justified to that degree by today's strategic objectives

Strike 1 is a beginning, not an end. The elimination of excessive bloat, and related confusion, is what allows the organization to see their work and how it flows. With such visibility, more precise and more significant surgical strikes can be identified and carried out.

CHAPTER 5

STRIKE 2:
ELIMINATE WORK

It's what man has aimed at all his life—getting out of work.
—J. IRWIN MILLER, CEO, CUMMINS ENGINE

In the dinner table analogy from the last chapter everyone was involved in passing the salt. There were too many people clogging up the process. One solution is to disengage a number of people and streamline the hand-offs. However, before streamlining any process, it helps to consider whether or not the work itself is even necessary.

Years ago I used to put salt on everything without tasting it. My wife removed the saltshaker from the table. I got used to food without adding salt and never use it today. So now I make no requests for salt and therefore no hand-offs of the saltshaker.

In the real world of work it is also useful to consider how much of the work should be done at all before streamlining the means by which it is done. All too often the incoming work is taken for granted. Like my salt habit, it goes on day-after-day, week-after-week, year-after-year, because that is the way it has always been done. Sometimes the incoming work is irrelevant, or worse, it can even be destructive. Why streamline a process to handle work you shouldn't be doing at all?

In our Process Redesign Game, we have the customer issue an order to build the toy phones. Each order is issued on an index card. The card has an order number. Typically the game begins, an order card is issued and the team starts to build the toy phones. The Credit Checker is supposed to see if the order number matches a list of poor credit numbers. If so, they should reject that order and get a new good-credit order from the customer. However, in the confusion of Round One, it is not unusual for the credit check to either not be done, or to be done at the time the order is supposed to be delivered to the customer. If an order with poor credit is delivered to the customer, it does not count. A lot of work will have been done for nothing.

Typically, by Round Two the team eliminates the dedicated credit checker and has the person who first takes the order from the customer check the credit. If the credit is bad, the order is rejected right away and a new good order is issued. The process never begins without a good order from a good customer.

In the real world it is not so simple. There are incentives to accept bad orders. For example, many sales incentives are based on the dollar value of the order, not the profitability of the order. In such cases, no attempt is made to distinguish bad from good on a number of dimensions. For instance, there are good customers and bad customers. Some customers understand how to use the product or service with little guidance; they pay promptly, and speak highly and publicly about your firm. At the same time there are others that buy less, yet demand more service, are never satisfied and say so publicly. Likewise there are bad products and good products. The application of activity-based costing has been particularly effective at identifying the true costs of delivering each product or service. In many cases such studies have led to products being re-priced or discontinued.

However, the processing of "bad" work is not just related to dealing with the wrong customers or money-losing products. In addition to these "bad" work orders, there is rework—work that is performed but should never have occurred had something been done right in the first place.

In our Process Redesign Game, the customer gets annoyed when they receive their shipment of products late, and/or they are built incorrectly and have to be rejected. The customer then has to

> issue complaints, repeatedly explain their requirements for on-time delivery, inspect every unit delivered, and repeatedly explain how to build the product properly. In Round One the management team spends more time dealing with a disgruntled customer than they do working to produce and deliver a good product on time.

In the real world we see the same situation despite years of TQM, reengineering, and Six Sigma initiatives. An inordinate amount of time and money is spent on service recovery and problem resolution without addressing the root causes. For instance, we see call centers work diligently to become more effective (resolve the issue during the first call) and efficient (short call-handling time) at handling billing inquiries. We ask, "Why get better at billing inquiries when a well-designed bill could eliminate the inquiries altogether?"

Strike 2 is about identifying and not processing work that really should not exist in the first place. There is a saying, in process improvement, that says, "Eliminate the unessential, and streamline the essential." Usually it is intended to refer to work activities and tasks. In this case, why worry about specific tasks if the work itself should not exist. Eliminate the unessential work. As Figure 5.1 shows, don't let unessential work get to the process in the first place.

Figure 5.1. Strike 2—Eliminate Work

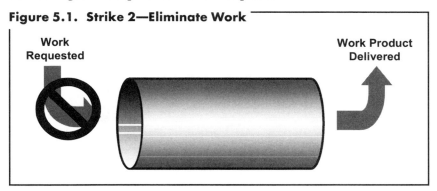

So there are really three forms of work that should not be accepted or processed at all:

- The first is all the work volume related to undesirable products and customers.
- The second is the volume of work related to service recovery and problem resolution.

■ Third is the work volume related to other non-value-added work processes.

In the interest of this book's primary focus on process, I will briefly touch on the first and primarily focus on the last two—eliminating rework and other entire non-value-added work volumes and processes. Chapter 6 will drill down further to focus more on the non-value-added activities and individual steps within a work process.

I will begin with a look at eliminating bad customers and bad products. The impact of such a strike is substantial. Think back to the core-process view. Eliminating bad customers and bad products will eliminate work volumes in a number of core processes.

Eliminate Bad Customers

"For banks, a typical bad customer makes frequent branch visits, keeps less than $1,000 in the bank, and calls often to check on account balances. The most profitable customers keep several thousand dollars in their accounts, use a teller less than once a month, and hardly ever use the call center. And while favored customers generate more than $1,000 in profits apiece each year, the worst customers often cost the bank money—a minimum of $500 a year. What's more, the top 20 percent of typical bank customers produce as much as 150 percent of overall profit, while the bottom 20 percent of customers drain about 50 percent from the bank's bottom line, according to Market Line Associates, an Atlanta bank-consulting firm."[1]

A recent article in *The Wall Street Journal* had this to say about eliminating bad customers: "After years of casting a wide net to lure as many consumers as possible, banks and many other industries are becoming increasingly selective, limiting their hunt to 'profitable' customers and doing away with loss-leaders. Wielding ever-more-powerful computer systems, they are aggressively mining their vast databases to weed out losers, or at least to charge them more, and to target the best customers for pampering."[2]

"Profitable" can be defined in a number of ways. Certainly if a customer does not have money, or is unwilling to spend enough of it on your company, they are "unprofitable." In other cases it is not so clear.

For example, two customers may spend the exact same amount but only one might be profitable. In our work on process improvement we see service encounters, and related process steps and activities, provided for one customer that we do not see for another.

In Chapter 3, I described a "Value-Needs Profile" that showed how customers could be categorized by their service requirements. Some customers were naïve about the product (a home mortgage in the example) and naïve about using technology (e.g., the internet to conduct the loan process). This Value-Needs Profile creates an interesting dilemma. The 10 percent totally naïve customers are likely to be the highest cost to serve, yet the lowest revenue. On the other hand, the 25 percent totally savvy customers will bypass the "guidance" steps, therefore cost less to serve, and at the same time be likely to bring more revenue (assuming savvy and experience means bigger bank accounts, and higher mortgage values). In this situation it may make sense for a bank, especially a self-professed "e-bank," to not encourage applications from the naïve segment.

On the other hand, a high-service traditional bank may want to cultivate that segment of naïve customers—and price its services accordingly. In this case the savvy customers might be bad customers for the traditional bank in that they would likely become annoyed at the extra handholding for extra cost. Furthermore, they might have a longer-term view and intentionally provide exceptional service to the lower revenue customers to build loyalty. The lower revenue customers will likely become higher revenue customers.

So the definition of good and bad customers may have less to do with the customers themselves and more to do with the strategy of your company. Customers may be "bad" if they are a bad fit with your company's strategy.

So what's the surgical strike here? Basically it is to identify customer segments based on criteria related to profitability, strategic fit, and service needs. Then initiate actions that will cultivate the desired segments and eliminate the undesired segments from becoming customers in the first place. Or if you already serve bad customers, then initiate actions to have them do less with you and hopefully drive them to your competitors.

So what are some of these actions? *The Wall Street Journal* article mentioned earlier describes "Einstein," First Union Bank's system to identify and segment each customer in real time for the call center reps, in this case Ms. Hathcock.

> **When it comes to answering yes or no to a customer who wants a lower credit card interest rate or to escape the bank's $28-bounced-check fee, there is nothing random about it. The service all depends on the color of a tiny square—green, yellow, or red—that pops up on Ms. Hathcock's computer screen next to the customer's name. For customers who get a red pop-up, Ms. Hathcock rarely budges; these are the ones whose accounts lose money for the bank. Green means the customers generate hefty profits for First Union and should be granted waivers. Yellow is for in-between customers: There's a chance to negotiate. The bank's computer system, called "Einstein," takes just fifteen seconds to pull up the ranking on a customer, using a formula that First Union declines to detail of minimum balances, account activity, branch visits, and other variables.**[3]

One caution, there are risks with this and other customer-discrimination strategies. What if the declined customer is the son or daughter, or even a close friend, of a very affluent customer? What if the declined customer is an up-and-coming businessperson? What if the declined customer is a poor but influential or government official? An automated selection criterion, employed by remote and impersonal contact center reps, has the risk of inadvertently mishandling some people and perhaps alienating some potentially desirable customers.

In the business-to-business marketplace there are similar dilemmas. Your company may make money by doing business with one part of a customer corporation while losing money on another. Yet the two accounts are intertwined, and dropping the money-losing business may not be an option. Likewise, a new loss-leader account may be a deliberate strategy to gain a foothold in a huge corporation. (I have heard this loss-leader argument, and seen it tried on numerous occasions, particularly by solution providers and consulting firms. In my experience it either doesn't work—no additional sales—or a precedent is set and the customer expects and demands a similar discount with all future sales. In either case the loss-leader approach is a failed strategy.

Eliminate Bad Products

Like bad customers, there are "bad" products and services. Some products and services, when all costs are accurately tabulated, are likely to be losers while others are winners. And many times the distinction is lost with traditional accounting. Hence the advent of activity-based costing (ABC) over the last decade.

With traditional accounting, an overhead rate that covers support costs is evenly distributed among all products. In other words each product may have the same fixed percentage added on to account for its share of corporate overhead.

In Chapter 3 we showed a case in which roughly a quarter of the corporate staff could be directly attributed to support of particular products and particular customer accounts. When we drilled down to specific products, we found the degree of support varied greatly from product to product. In Figure 5.2 you can see Product D: Its cost doubles when all support costs are included. This product then becomes a candidate for re-pricing or discontinuation. In this case it was discontinued.

Conversely, Product B, a heavy seller, was now accurately recognized as the company's highest margin product. It did not consume much corporate support.

One of the best and quickest ways to look for problematic products is to look at the phone calls from customers. Are the product-related call volumes commensurate with product sales and/or products in use (the installed base)? Or, like Product D, do some products consume more than their share of phone calls? Or, even more important to look at, as in Product D above, do some products consume more than their share of phone call *time*? In other words, the number of calls might seem in line, but those calls may be very difficult and time-consuming. It is the time that really matters.

Figure 5.2. Pareto of Product Costs by Product

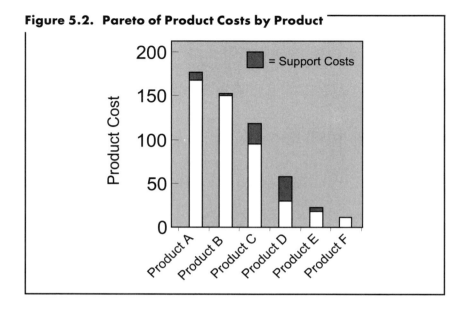

Eliminate Failures and Failure-Related Recovery

Many businesses spend an inordinate amount of effort on processing work that they should not get at all. Then they want to streamline those processes—in essence to become more efficient at processing re-work. Nowhere does this show up more than in the customer service center, where a focus on call times and call closure distracts attention from eliminating calls.[4]

Eliminate Those Pesky Customer Contacts

Customer contact centers, call centers, help desks, and the like are a mainstay of customer care regardless of industry. Yet for most customers, a call for assistance represents an encounter of last resort, mostly because the product or service did not perform as expected in the first place. For example:

■ The anxious mortgage applicant calls to find out the status of their loan, since they have not heard anything for two weeks.

■ The purchaser of a new software package calls for help when they find the program does not work on their system.

■ The patient calls their HMO about the status of their medical claim when their doctor says he has not been paid.

As customers we've all been there—calling a company for information and inquiry- or problem-resolution. All too often, we then complain about how long we're left on hold, how many times we have to call back, or that we have to wait for them to call us. Once we get through we are frustrated about how long the call takes and that our request for service cannot be completed.

In response to this cry for service, managers have recognized that a focus on "abandonment rates," "time to answer" and "first-time call resolution and closure" is critical. Despite best intentions, companies are discovering that these and other measures should not be the first priorities for most service and support inbound call centers.

Many Calls Are Unnecessary

After analyzing numerous call centers, and thousands of individual phone calls, we can safely say that many calls are unnecessary (most in some situations). The key question becomes "Should we get the call at all?" So before redesigning how calls are managed, a couple of key questions need to be answered. First, how many calls would be eliminated if something else was done right the first time? Second, how many calls would be eliminated if something were done differently?

The answers to these questions can be found, but not easily. A rigorous root-cause analysis of numerous phone calls is required to pinpoint the real solutions.

Figure 5.3 depicts the root causes for inbound phone calls to the customer service center at a leading health maintenance organization. This company was shocked to find out that 68 percent of all calls were non-value-added, and should not have occurred all.

In this example, 36 percent of phone calls are related to a lack of complete, accurate, and timely information updates from suppliers and

Figure 5.3. Phone Unit Root Cause Breakdown for a Leading HMO

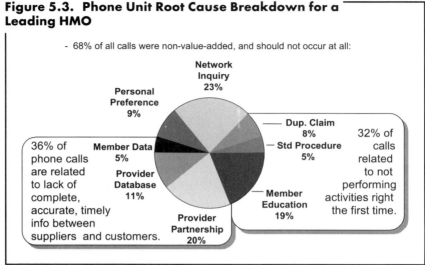

- 68% of all calls were non-value-added, and should not occur at all:

Network Inquiry 23%

Personal Preference 9%

Dup. Claim 8%

Std Procedure 5%

32% of calls related to not performing activities right the first time.

36% of phone calls are related to lack of complete, accurate, timely info between suppliers and customers.

Member Data 5%

Provider Database 11%

Member Education 19%

Provider Partnership 20%

customers. More specifically, the providers' (doctors and hospitals) data was not up to date or accurate, creating 11 percent of the phone calls. Another 20 percent of the phone calls could potentially be eliminated if there were a closer partnership between the HMO and the provider group. For example, the doctor or the doctor's administrator could have prevented the phone call had they provided their patient with better or timelier information. On the right side of the pie chart, 19 percent of the phone calls would not have occurred had the HMO done a better job educating its members.

For this HMO, the potential for improvement was enormous. As it turned out, the root cause for phone calls was the same as the root cause for problem claims. In other words, if a claim were submitted with errors a lot of work was required to straighten it out, and it was highly likely that one or more phone calls would occur because of that problem claim. Furthermore, a claim that took over thirty days to process would likely generate a duplicate claim to be filed and related phone calls.

Great Gains Result When Root Causes Are Attacked

This HMO found that they could serve 82 percent more members with the same staff level by doing a better job up front in educating their doctors (and their administrators) and members. With the databases up to date and claims submitted properly, the claims and calls could be processed quickly and accurately. The result would be fewer claims (few duplicates), fewer suspended or problem claims, and fewer phone calls. (Interestingly, "time per call" will rise as the simple calls are eliminated.)

The gains depicted in Figure 5.4 are not a fantasy. The numbers do not reflect the elimination of all problems, but that over time, half of the problem claims and calls could be eliminated. So while 68 percent of calls were non-value-added, it was assumed that only 32 percent would be eliminated.

Figure 5.4. Great Gains Result When the Root Causes Are Attacked

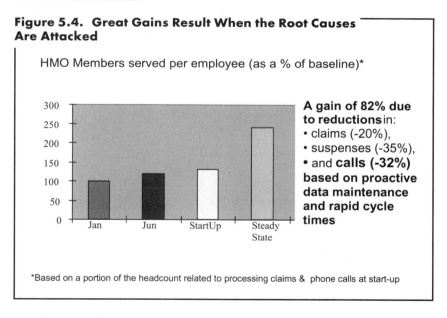

HMO Members served per employee (as a % of baseline)*

A gain of 82% due to reductions in:
• claims (-20%),
• suspenses (-35%),
• and **calls (-32%) based on proactive data maintenance and rapid cycle times**

*Based on a portion of the headcount related to processing claims & phone calls at start-up

The same phenomenon occurs in industry after industry:

■ The majority of billing inquiries to a leading telecommunications company would not occur if the phone and related services were installed right in the first place.

■ The calls to the mortgage company about status would not occur if expectations were managed up front, and the process were faster in delivering the commitment letter.

■ Likewise, for the software company, managing customer expectations and providing clear initial instructions would eliminate the bulk of the calls.

Recently we worked with a new bank that was signing up thousands of new customers each week. We found that each new customer, on average, called the contact center 3.25 times in the first five weeks. The bulk of those calls were because the customer was confused about "funds availability." In other words, the customer needed to understand the time lag from time of deposit to an ATM until the funds were available for use, and the difference in time lag between cash deposits, in-state checks, and out-of-state checks. Their expectations were not effectively managed at initial sign-up. We then developed and piloted a one-page letter describing the rules around funds availability. Not only did it bring clarity to the customer, it brought clarity to the sales staff that spent time enrolling the customers. Calls dropped to 1.25 in the first five weeks. The approach was rolled out across the country, freeing up nearly 20 percent of the contact center staff.

An effective and efficient process for customer care, and elimination of service recovery, comes from a detailed understanding of the facts regarding volumes and types of calls, time-per-type of call, root cause of those calls, and a rigorous feedback mechanism. Excellent service delivery means eliminating the need for excellent service recovery.

Eliminate Non-Value-Added Nonsense Work

Sometimes there is work, along with processes and activities, that adds no value, but their existence has gone on so long no one questions them. So what do you look for? The key here is the definition of "non-value-added." If "value" is something the customer is willing to pay for, then non-value must be everything else. Here are some definitions:

Non-value-added:[5]

■ *External failure:* product or service error and/or correction that is visible to the customer

■ *Internal failure:* in-process failures and fixes prior to being visible to the customer

- *Set-up:* preparation of work for a subsequent activity in the process without any transformation

- *Inspection/Control:* internal review of work without any transformation

- *Move/Store:* relocating or storing work without any transformation

I have already spent a fair amount of text on external failure as found in customer phone calls and service recovery activities. Let's look at examples in other areas.

Eliminate Internal Failure

Not that long ago a leading European auto manufacturer had to perform some additional work to as many as 10 percent of the cars after they arrived in the United States. To get this work done, a "prep center" was established to examine the new cars and correct any defects. Even with the prep center, upon delivery to the dealers, the dealers found additional errors in workmanship and had to do their own prep.

All this activity was rework—work that was required to make up for work not done or not done right by the factory. But it was not a quality problem (not an *external failure*), from the customer's perspective (assuming the car was delivered on time with no defects). The prep-center rework and dealer rework related to an *internal failure* and was essentially a cost problem—the cost to get it right before the customer saw it.

This company embarked on an effort to identify and prioritize the defects. They determined root causes and took corrective action at the factory and with the product designers. A few critical defects created the bulk of the rework activity. Some surgical-strike quick hits were conducted to fix the problems at the source, dramatically reducing the need for a prep center.

Eliminate Inspections

When a process works well, inspections can become unnecessary. But sometimes they remain as an artifact of a previously bad process. We saw this situation at a health care insurer, where we were asked to help cut claims processing costs. However, when we looked at the claims process we were surprised. As a matter of fact, their claims process was first class—a "lights-out" operation. If the claim was submitted electronically, or scanned and uploaded, with no errors, it would be adjudicated by the system with no human intervention. So why were there so many people in the claims department?

Unfortunately only 20 percent of the submitted claims were automatically adjudicated. The rest were "suspended" and routed to a claims processor for manual adjudication. The department existed to rework suspended claims.

So we randomly selected and investigated the root causes for nearly three hundred suspended claims. As seen in Figure 5.5, the root causes for the suspended claims were found outside of the claims process/organization.

Figure 5.5. Root Causes for Suspended Claims

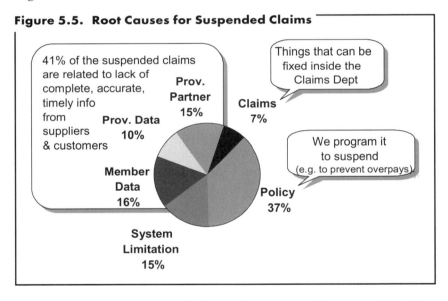

Two things were particularly striking. First there was little that could be done within the confines of the claims department to become more efficient. Second, the biggest single reason for manual intervention was self-inflicted. During the early days of implementing the new claims system, the risk management people in collaboration with the system developers, placed some "triggers" to suspend certain types of claims. This was done because they were afraid the new system might automatically pay out some high-dollar claims when they could have been rejected. However, we found the system would have worked correctly. Well after the system was implemented no one reviewed its performance and removed the triggers. Nearly the entire 37 percent could now be automatically adjudicated, thereby eliminating a quick intervention by a claims processor for each of these claims. This quick hit cut the need for claims processors by 15 percent.

After eliminating the unnecessary inspection, we went on to reduce the big failures. We found that by taking the 15 percent freed-up staff and having them work with doctor's administrators, we could get claims submitted without errors. To be more specific, we found the bulk of errors were related to the wrong Taxpayer ID number being associated to the claim. In this case, the mission was to work with the administrators to cut the 41 percent of suspended claims with errors in half. These tended to be the problem claims and would result in freeing up nearly half of the claims processors.

Eliminate the Unnecessary Movement of Work

We spent a few days reviewing the performance in the call center of a large bank. Their data suggested the bulk of calls were related to account inquires and the like. To understand the calls we decided to listen to calls. We didn't trust their data.

We listened to a couple hundred calls over two days and developed our own profile of the work. See Figure 5.6.

We actually found that the single greatest group of calls, and related call time, corresponded to transferring the caller to the right person— essentially an operator function. Our sample showed that nearly 45 percent of the calls were simply received and transferred elsewhere, and it consumed 33 percent of the reps' time. Their data did not count transfer calls. They only measured and kept records of the calls handled by the reps.

Most of the transferred calls we observed were fairly straightforward and simple, as in: "Please transfer me to extension 6328" or "May I speak to Bill Jones." We found the bulk of these calls could be handled via a combination of technology solutions. In other words, the technology can enable direct extension transfer, with a "ring back" to the operator if there is no answer. Also a customer could either enter the extension number, or push "0" to get an automated directory (e.g.,

Figure 5.6. Profile of Calls to a Bank's Call Center

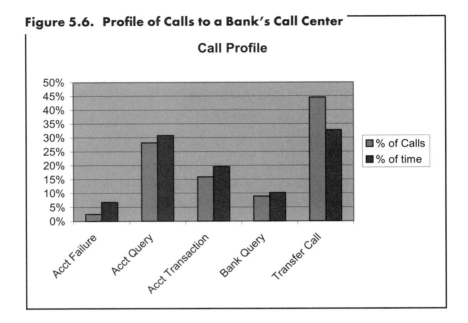

enter the first five letters of the last name). The use of voice mail and enabling the callers to dial extensions directly would allow for fewer contacts with the reps (routing, message taking, callbacks). Assuming 50 percent of these routing calls would be eliminated from human handling, the savings were significant: 22 FTEs (Full Time Equivalent people).

Eliminate the Unnecessary Movement and Storage of Work

Sometimes work is moved around and stored with no value-added benefit. A few years ago we were asked to look at streamlining and automating the records management department of a leading magazine subscription service.

We began with a look at the basic workload. We found that they stored over a million paper records of subscription orders each year. So input volume exceeded 1 million records. We than looked at output volume—the number of records retrieved each year. We found that only 0.3 percent of the records were retrieved and out of that only 0.1 percent were useful. So what was the risk of not having the records?

There was a slight chance that the company could not prove the existence of a subscription and would have to eat some subscription costs. We looked at these costs and found it to be far more costly to maintain the records.

Perhaps more fascinating was our investigation into why so many records were sent to records management in the first place. It turns out that people sitting in their cubicles had three choices of what to do with any document. They could file it themselves. They could throw it out. Or, they could send it to records management. What would you do? Certainly the most practical and safe decision was to get it out of the cramped cubicle and send it to records management. And that is what nearly everyone did.

In the end, the entire function did not need to exist. Streamlining and automating would have been a complete waste. Again, I am reminded to "eliminate the unessential, and streamline the essential."

Strike 2: Just Say No

Strike 2 is about eliminating workload in the first place. All too often the incoming work is taken for granted. It is processed week after week, year after year, because that is the way it has always been done. Sometimes the incoming work is irrelevant, or worse—destructive. Why streamline a process to handle work you shouldn't be doing at all? Why get better at billing inquiries when a well-designed bill could eliminate the inquiries?

Strike 2: Eliminate Work

If appropriate, Strike 2 typically needs to:

- Eliminate some customers: Uncover and stop doing business with undesirable and unprofitable customers, and/or
- Eliminate some products and services: Uncover and stop offering undesirable and unprofitable products and services, and/or
- Eliminate non-value-added nonsense work: Uncover and stop doing work with no value
  1. Eliminate failures and failure-related recovery

2. Eliminate inspections

3. Eliminate set-up, movement, and storage

Strike 2 is about eliminating the need to have a process. If there is no work to do, there is no need for a process. The next strikes are about pinpointing targets of opportunity within processes.

CHAPTER 6

STRIKE 3: STREAMLINE THE WORKFLOW

There is less in this than meets the eye.
—TALLULAH BANKHEAD, ACTRESS, ON A MAETERLINCK PLAY

The last chapter described how Strike 2, Eliminate Work, could negate the need to even look at the process—no workload, no process. However, in most cases Strike 2 is a partial hit—some work may disappear, but not all of it. So if only some customers are turned away, or some products discontinued, a process still exists to process the rest. However, when we drill into the process we can ask some of the same questions we do about the workload. In this case we ask about value-added and non-value-added steps and activities. Strike 3 is about eliminating the unessential steps and streamlining the essential steps in a process.

In our Process Redesign Game, we start Round One with five Assemblers—people at workbenches actually building the toy phones. We have two Inspectors, two Material/Information Handlers, one Operations Manager, one Customer Account Manager, a Credit Checker, and one or more Process Engineers.

The process begins with the Customer Account Manager accepting an order card from the Customer. The Customer Account Manager gives the card to the Operations Manager. The Operations Manager then frantically tries to figure our how his team can fill the order. In the meantime the Assemblers yell for parts and subassemblies from the Material Handlers, and when they have completed their subassemblies, they yell for more. At Workbench 5, Final Assembly and Inspection, the completed toy phones are placed in a bin and delivered to the customer by the Customer Account Manager.

Typically chaos ensues. No one gets the parts they need on time. Communication is totally ineffective—a lot of accusations, blame, and misunderstanding. And, the customer is left getting very little of the product they ordered, and most of what they do get is built incorrectly.

In between Rounds One and Two the team figures out a new way of working. The workbenches are pulled together and the raw materials are placed on the workbenches. Now there is no need for Material Handlers, the parts are there and the Assemblers can push the subassemblies one at a time from workbench to workbench, since they are literally touching each other.

In Round Two the face-to-face close proximity of the workers enables constructive communication and learning regarding the proper way to build the toy phone. By the end of Round Two it is not unusual to have a dramatic improvement in the quality of the product. After Round Two, and prior to starting Round Three, the team typically decides either to lay off the Inspectors or have them engaged in assembly.

Furthermore, the Operations Manager may get the order directly from the Customer, and do the credit check immediately, negating the need for a dedicated Customer Service Rep and a Credit Checker. Since the Assemblers have the bulk of the product knowledge they typically control the redesign effort negating the need for the Process Engineers. All these positions are either put to productive use, building toy phones, or let go.

In the end, the ratio of value-added activity (the assembly steps) goes from under 40 percent to 80 percent or more by "eliminating the unessential." The output per person typically quadruples by "streamlining the essential." And the time a toy phone is in process declines from twenty minutes to a matter of seconds.

The objective is the same in the real workplace—streamline the workflow by reducing process steps and time. See Figure 6.1.

Unfortunately, the real workplace is not as simple as the game. In the game the entire workflow, workforce, workplace, plus the customer, is visible and self-contained in one room. In the real world this is not the case. So tools and techniques are needed to make these things visible in one place, which will enable the key surgical strikes to stand out.

Figure 6.1. Strike 3—Streamline the Workflow

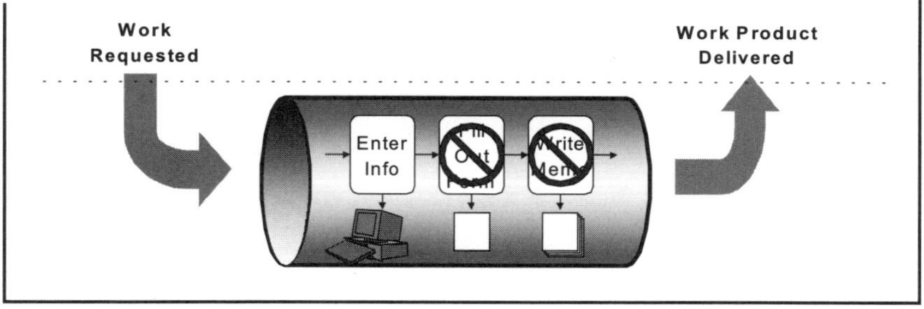

Profile the Workload Within the Process

To guide our priorities for the analytical work within the process and to focus the development of specific surgical strikes, we develop a workload profile. This profile goes beyond the workload evaluation described in Chapter 5. There the intent was to discover and eliminate workload that should not be done at all. Here we assume the workload needs to be done. Before diving into the details of how the work is done, we want to understand the types of work, key differences, and respective impacts on the process.

Let's revisit our experience with the bank's call center. To develop a profile of the calls, we depend upon real-time observations and detailed notes regarding a sample of calls. We do not count on existing systems and reports to give us the whole story. For example, time-per-call data from the switch tells us nothing about the type of call; reporting systems are likely inaccurate, while, in addition, no system has told us what goes on within the call time.

Although the bank provided us a list of over twenty types of calls, we listened to calls and grouped the calls into five types. (And remember from Chapter 5, the bank neglected to include "call transfers" and they were the biggest single group of calls.)

1. Call Transfers (operator/receptionist functions)
2. Bank Query
3. Account Query
4. Account Transaction
5. Account Failure

The first two, for the most part, do not require access to the caller's account and do not require that the caller be validated. Again, call transfers simply refers to all the calls where the rep's task is to route the call to another area (branch, service center, etc.) at the request of the caller. In most cases the caller is asking for the transfer by name ("Connect me to John Smith") or by number ("Connect me to extension 9999"). A bank query is a request for general bank information that is not account specific. ("What are your interest rates?" or "Where is your nearest branch?").

The last three are account-specific. The request for service requires access to the customer's account information. Account Queries include the requests for information only, such as Account Balances and Entry Details. ("Did the check clear?" or "Was my paycheck deposited?"). Account transactions are the requests for some work to be performed beyond providing information only (e.g., pay a bill, or transfer money from one account to the other). These transactions require essentially the same process steps and the same processing time (labor content).

Finally, the account failures are those service encounters where the customer is complaining about an error with their account (e.g., a bill was paid incorrectly or "The cash machine ate my card").

Since the greatest opportunities for call center performance improvement will involve labor savings, we looked at labor content per call type. A sole focus on call volume could be misleading. Difficult calls, for example, may take a tremendous amount of time. Therefore, we enhanced our initial profile of call types with more observations and timing of calls.

The observations to develop call times are based on listening to calls and taking detailed notes regarding the nature of the call, how it was processed, and timing of each portion of the call. The overall time-per-call results are shown in Figure 6.2.

Our study showed that (at least based on time consumption) the failure-related calls are likely to have the most complicated process (the most steps and the greatest variety of paths containing alternate if-this-then-that routings). On many occasions it is best to develop a process map for the most complicated workload, and then the simpler work just becomes a few additional steps and a lot of bypass paths.

This is where we build upon the process mapping approach I described in Chapter 3. The level of detail varies greatly with the type of process. However, for us one common theme seems to be with the number of horizontal bands (to distinguish organizational entities) and

Figure 6.2. Time Per Call by Type to Bank

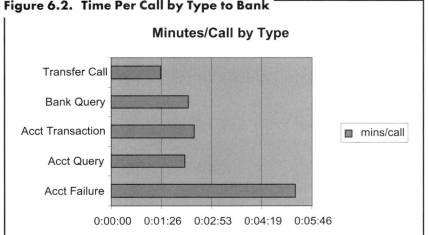

the number of process steps. We tend to keep the organizational bands to no fewer that five and no more than eight. Any more than that invites a "spider web" of complexity.

For most processes the maps contain no fewer than 50 steps and no more than 150. More important is the definition of a step. In a high volume, short processing time, transaction environment, a step may represent a portion of a person's overall task. For example, when we mapped how a phone call is handled, Step 1 was "Answer Call, Determine Nature of Inquiry," and Step 2 was "Authenticate Customer (if needed)," and so forth. These steps represent a breakdown of the tasks performed by one rep within the few minutes of handling one call. At the other extreme is when we look at low volume, lengthy, project-oriented processes, that encompass many people, such as new product development, sales processes, and client launch processes. In such cases, each step (e.g., "Prepare Requirements Document") may take weeks, many people, and numerous person-days. The nature of the process in question will dictate the depth and breadth of the process map.

Also, don't believe the documentation. Develop the process map by asking people who do the work. Flow charts, procedure sheets, training materials are usually outdated and wrong. Inevitably they don't represent how the work is really done.

With a map of how the work moves through the process, the next step is to quantify it.

Quantify the Process Itself

Like a road map, a process map shows pathways and their interrelationships, but their capacities to handle traffic and the amount of traffic they typically handle are unclear. To complete the process analysis, it is crucial that we understand the workload on each path. Essentially this means quantifying how much work is routed to each path. In addition, assuming the work arrives at a particular step, we need to quantify the amount of time needed to process the work.

Usually we conduct interviews with people who do the work, and get their estimates of approximate routing percentages and processing times for each step of the process. Recently, the only exception has been in working with call centers. There we get detailed and accurate call-handling times by inserting start and stop times into our spreadsheet as we listen and take notes on our laptop computers.

In both project-oriented processes and high-volume transaction processes, workers' estimates have proven close enough. We validate the estimates a couple of different ways. First, we get estimates from two sources. Second, we use today's work volumes and the process time estimates to calculate the current staff level required. To do this we multiply the volumes times the process time and divide the total by 0.7 to account for an assumed 70 percent utilization of the employee conducting the work as shown on the map. (Our process maps follow the direct flows of work and do not account for an employee's time in staff meetings, training sessions, or anything else not depicted on the map.) In almost every case the calculated total is close enough. On the few occasions where the calculated number of employees is too low, some key part of the process is typically missing. The employees may have neglected to say how much of their time is consumed with a re-work activity or some other activity that was not identified in the process map. So the employees' time estimates and the model also provide a way to validate the completeness of the process map. (See more about utilization in Chapter 7: Strike 4: Reclaim Lost Time—Utilize Capacity and Expand Capability.)

A computer-based spreadsheet model is then built to help us pinpoint priories and evaluate the improvement potential. Remember the intent here is not to build a staffing model per se, but rather to show the relative weighting and importance of each step in the process and to assess the relative impact of making surgical-strike improvements.

The model (Figure 6.3) contains a step-by-step calculation of labor required. Each step's calculation is based on: a work driver—the type of work processed by the step (e.g., calls, and applications) and their respective volumes; plus the estimated processing time; and a field to define the job function that performs the step.

The model also calculates the approximate number of FTEs required at each step of the process. For each step in the process, the model multiplies: the volume of work by the routing percentage of work by the time to process the call. The total required time-per-step calculation is then factored for a variety of factors (e.g., utilization) to obtain a realistic headcount requirement.

In summary, the workload profiles, process maps, and ultimately a detailed process model provide the means to: (1) generate improvement ideas; (2) target the priority steps for improvement; (3) quantify the impacts of various improvement ideas across all steps.

Initial Ideas

As the map is being developed and quantified we see opportunities. Some steps are obviously non-value-added "move" steps, "set-up" steps, and inspections. We question whether such steps are needed, although early on it is sometimes difficult to tell if an idea is significant or not relative to other ideas and priorities that will show up later. However, once the model is working it becomes possible to see the labor savings potential of various ideas.

For example, the map portion in Figure 6.4 shows that if two steps are no longer needed, an additional 1.2 minutes become available (per unit of work processed at that step):

In a process with 2,000 units per day of work going through these steps, the savings are roughly 7 full time equivalent people. The rough calculation is:

1.2 minutes × 2000 units = 2,400 minutes per day

One person works for 480 minutes per day, but at 70 percent utilized = 336 minutes available

2,400 minutes per day divided by 336 minutes available per person = 7 FTEs

Figure 6.3. Spreadsheet Process Model

- **The model contains:**
  - All steps in the map
  - A description of each step from the map
  - A "work driver" for each step and work volumes
  - Percentage of work routed to each step
  - Labor time estimates
  - Organization and skill set to whom the work is assigned

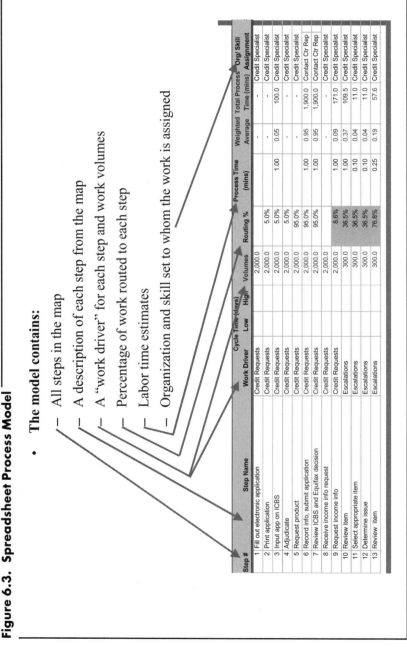

Step #	Step Name	Work Driver	Cycle Time (days) Low	High	Volumes	Routing %	Process Time (mins)	Weighted Average	Total Process Time (mins)	Org/ Skill Assignment
1	Fill out electronic application	Credit Requests			2,000.0			-	-	Credit Specialist
2	Print application	Credit Requests			2,000.0	5.0%		-	-	Credit Specialist
3	Input app on ICBS	Credit Requests			2,000.0	5.0%	1.00	0.05	100.0	Credit Specialist
4	Adjudicate	Credit Requests			2,000.0	5.0%		-	-	Credit Specialist
5	Request product	Credit Requests			2,000.0	95.0%		-	-	Credit Specialist
6	Record info, submit application	Credit Requests			2,000.0	95.0%	1.00	0.95	1,900.0	Contact Ctr Rep
7	Review ICBS and Equifax decision	Credit Requests			2,000.0	95.0%	1.00	0.95	1,900.0	Contact Ctr Rep
8	Receive income info request	Credit Requests			2,000.0			-	-	Credit Specialist
9	Request income info	Credit Requests			2,000.0	8.6%	1.00	0.09	171.0	Credit Specialist
10	Review item	Escalations			300.0	36.5%	1.00	0.37	109.5	Credit Specialist
11	Select appropriate item	Escalations			300.0	36.5%	0.10	0.04	11.0	Credit Specialist
12	Determine issue	Escalations			300.0	36.5%	0.10	0.04	11.0	Credit Specialist
13	Review item	Escalations			300.0	76.8%	0.25	0.19	57.6	Credit Specialist

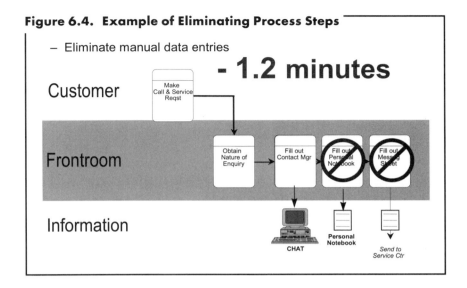

Figure 6.4. Example of Eliminating Process Steps

Prioritize Opportunity Areas

Before embarking willy-nilly on an idea-generation, brainstorming exercise, you will find that the model has proven very effective at focusing such an effort. The map and model work to provide two profiles: (1) a profile of where value is lost (non-value steps and time), and (2) a clear hierarchy of the labor-consuming steps.

Where Value Is Lost

At a Fortune 100 company we worked with their Voice and Video Service Management Group ("the group"). The group was responsible for managing all internal voice and video communications infrastructure within the corporation. Their scope ranged from handling changes in individual phone lines up to major installations of internal call centers. The group also managed the internal help desk for all corporate communication and information technology needs.

The group found themselves increasingly unable to provide quality service in a reasonable period of time. In fact, internal ratings showed that fully one third of this multi-billion-dollar corporation rated the group's performance as "fair to poor."

The group assigned a project team to evaluate the current process to determine how much of what they did really added value to their customers. In this case, the group's customers were the company's employees themselves. After agreeing upon this definition, the project team was able to draw an as-is process map from their customer's perspective.

The project team completed a six-hundred-plus-step map, and built a process model. In this case the team noted a "process value" category next to each step. The project team was then able to construct a value analysis. The analysis clearly showed how many steps and how much time was consumed by non-value-added work (Table 6.1).

With the data presented in this way, the team made some interesting discoveries. Fully one-third of the process time was spent on setting up or moving work around. Another 55 percent of the time was spent either checking for or fixing failures. More than half of actual time spent on work related to the failure of that work. Only 15 percent of what was going on in the process related to what the customer wanted: inexpensive communications support provided quickly and accurately.

Even more telling was the percentage of cycle time data. A telephone order spent only 6 percent of its time moving to completion. The other 94 percent of the time, the order sat at the bottom of someone's in-basket awaiting processing. After analyzing the data in the table, the team concluded that there was much potential in redesigning this process. There was much that could be improved.

For instance, through a combination of reducing specialists and their segregated job tasks, and teaming of remaining specialists, the team concluded that two-thirds of the moves and set-up steps could be eliminated. Those unnecessary steps, more specifically the excessive use and handling of work orders, work-tracking forms, e-mails, follow-up e-mails, and the related prepare, send, receive, and review steps, could go away.

The value-analysis is directional. While not highlighting specific surgical-strike actions, it provides guidance and direction as to where such strikes are likely to be found.

The Labor-Consuming Steps

After calculating the FTE requirement for each step, it is easy to sort the list of steps in descending order (from high labor steps to low labor steps).

Table 6.1. Value of Process Steps

<table>
<tr><th colspan="9">PROCESS VALUE ANALYSIS</th></tr>
<tr><th>Category</th><th>Move</th><th>Set-Up</th><th>Control/ Accuracy</th><th>Internal Failure</th><th>External Failure</th><th>Value Added</th><th>Delay</th><th>Total</th></tr>
<tr><td>*Sample activity descriptions from the map*</td><td>Retrieve Deliver Transmit</td><td>Batch Sort Prepare Assign</td><td>Review Verify Check Clarify</td><td>Correct Request Get More Info Document Errors</td><td>Reissue Rework Resubmit Fix</td><td>Produce Install Initiate</td><td></td><td></td></tr>
<tr><td># STEPS</td><td>194</td><td>108</td><td>139</td><td>65</td><td>39</td><td>113</td><td></td><td>658</td></tr>
<tr><td>% OF STEPS</td><td>30%</td><td>16%</td><td>21%</td><td>10%</td><td>6%</td><td>17%</td><td></td><td>100%</td></tr>
<tr><td>% OF PROCESS TIME</td><td>20%</td><td>10%</td><td>20%</td><td>30%</td><td>5%</td><td>15%</td><td></td><td>100%</td></tr>
<tr><td>% OF CYCLE TIME</td><td>1.2%</td><td>.5%</td><td>1.2%</td><td>1.9%</td><td>.3%</td><td>.9%</td><td>94%</td><td>100%</td></tr>
</table>

We did this with our bank and found that twelve steps consumed 90 percent of the labor. Therefore, for the improvement ideas and "surgical strikes" to be effective and significant, these steps must be im-

Table 6.2. Ranking of Labor-Consuming Steps

Step #	Step	FTE	Cum FTE	Cum FTE %
4	Answer Call: Determine Nature of Inquiry	31.7	31.7	28%
5	Route Call	13.1	44.8	39%
12	Provide Basic Bank Info (e.g., Interest Rates)	9.0	53.8	47%
38	Select Payee; Enter Amount & Pay Date	8.3	62.2	55%
15	Obtain Password (e.g., Mother's Maiden Name)	7.8	70.0	61%
16	Obtain Time & Amount of Recent Transaction	7.8	77.8	68%
24	Retrieve "Balance" Screen	6.1	83.9	74%
87	After Call Work	4.9	88.8	78%
67	Deal with Account Failure or Complaint	3.9	92.7	81%
13	Obtain Name	3.9	96.6	85%
25	Provide Balance	3.7	100.3	88%
21	Select "Account"	2.4	102.7	90%

pacted. Table 6.2 demonstrates that one step on the Bank's Process Map, "Determine Nature of Inquiry," consumed 28 percent of the call center's labor content.

Generate Ideas and Assess Impacts

Look at the Steps That Consume the Most Labor

With the facts in hand, a facilitated half-day session with people from throughout the process can go a long way toward identifying the key surgical strikes. Perhaps more important, participation by those within the process at this stage will go a long way toward making the strikes their idea. If it's their idea, it is more likely to be accepted and implemented successfully.

One caution—if your company is in a lay-off mode, the participation idea may not be a good idea. It is only a good idea when it can be truthfully stated that the freed-up workers will be redeployed to productive work (and negate the need for additional hires).

Anyway, in the example shown above, obviously the first place to look for opportunities is within Step 4: "Answer Call: Determine Nature of Inquiry." Twenty-eight percent of the reps' time is spent on this one step. In our session with call center staff a number of ideas were generated, such as:

"Enable the customer to hit '1' if bank inquiry only, or '2' if account inquiry, etc. Enable the rep to see what number they hit and cut the determination time dramatically."

"Provide a new script so the rep can cut-to-the-chase with the customer more rapidly."

At the end of the discussion we settled on a combination of suggestions and then estimated the potential impact. In this case we conservatively assumed only half the customer calls would effectively use the new approach. And for those that did use the new approach, the "Answer Call: Determine Nature of Inquiry" time would be cut in half.

In other words, we found a surgical strike that would result in a savings of eight FTEs.

Look at Ideas That Impact Multiple Steps

Sometimes the biggest gains are not simply found in the step that consumes the most labor. Sometimes the impact of an idea is on a combination of steps. In our example, about 17 percent of the total labor time is used to validate the customer ($\cong$20 out of 114 FTEs modeled). The validation process consists of three steps:

Step 13: Obtain Name

Step 15: Obtain Password

Step 16: Obtain Date, Time, and Amount of Recent Transaction

Our brainstorming session identified a few surgical-strike ideas. First was to develop and encourage the use of personal identification numbers (PINs):

> "Have the customer enter a single PIN and the system will validate the customer, prior to transferring the call to the call center rep"

> "Use the system to provide a 'Screen Pop' of the customer's account information to the rep upon transfer of the call from the system to the rep."

The session, and subsequent evaluation, calculated the savings to be sixteen FTEs. This estimate was based on an 80 percent reduction of the current $\cong 20$ FTEs involved in the three "Validate Customer" steps. While these technologies, and customer interface practices, can have a dramatic impact, perfection was not assumed. We assumed 10 percent of callers would "forget" their PIN number, and still require the current validation process, and that 10 percent of callers would bypass the automated system validation and go straight to the rep for all transactions.

Look to Automate Simple Information Requests

In many businesses the customers contact the company for basic information. For instance, the FedEx customers check a Web site or phone in to find out the status of their package. At FedEx the request and the answer are automated—no human intervention is needed. In our banking contact center example, 10 percent of total labor time (12 out of the 114 FTE's modeled) was used to answer queries related to basic account information:

- Step 21: "Select Account"
- Step 24: "Retrieve Balance Screen"
- Step 25: "Provide Balance"

The surgical strike opportunity was to enable and encourage the customer to more readily obtain their account balance through the Internet and the automated phone system without human intervention.

The savings was estimated to be 8 FTEs. This estimate was based on the current ≅12 FTEs involved in account inquiry being reduced by 60 to 80 percent. We recognized that not all customers will use such a system and tempered the estimated benefits as follows:

- 10 percent to 20 percent of customers will bypass the automated system and go straight to the rep

- 10 percent to 20 percent of queries will still go to the rep because they know they have follow-on questions beyond the simple account inquiry

Overall Impact

In summary, the impact of a few surgical strikes through various technologies and process improvements can be dramatic. In our banking contact center example, a 44 percent gain in process productivity resulted from improvements in the following areas:

Improvement Area	Capacity Gain
Determine Nature of Inquiry	8 FTEs
Customer Validation Process	16 FTEs
Account Inquiry Activities	8 FTEs
	32 FTEs

In this case the thirty-two people were freed-up, but not laid-off. With a relatively high turnover rate and rapid growth these people were readily absorbed into the organization.

To convince others of the need for the surgical strikes, a clear picture of the benefits is needed. One approach that has proven very effective is simply to show a picture of the impact. We use the process map and show the steps that will be eliminated and how a new path will get around the deleted steps. The following process map (Figure 6.5) illustrates just how dramatic such a picture can be. In this case a company that installs, maintains, and services over 100,000 pieces of equipment in over 15,000 locations had many possible ways to accept an order (for new equipment, a change in equipment, or for service). The company had grown through acquisitions, so it was not unusual

Figure 6.5. Opportunity to Eliminate Numerous Process Steps

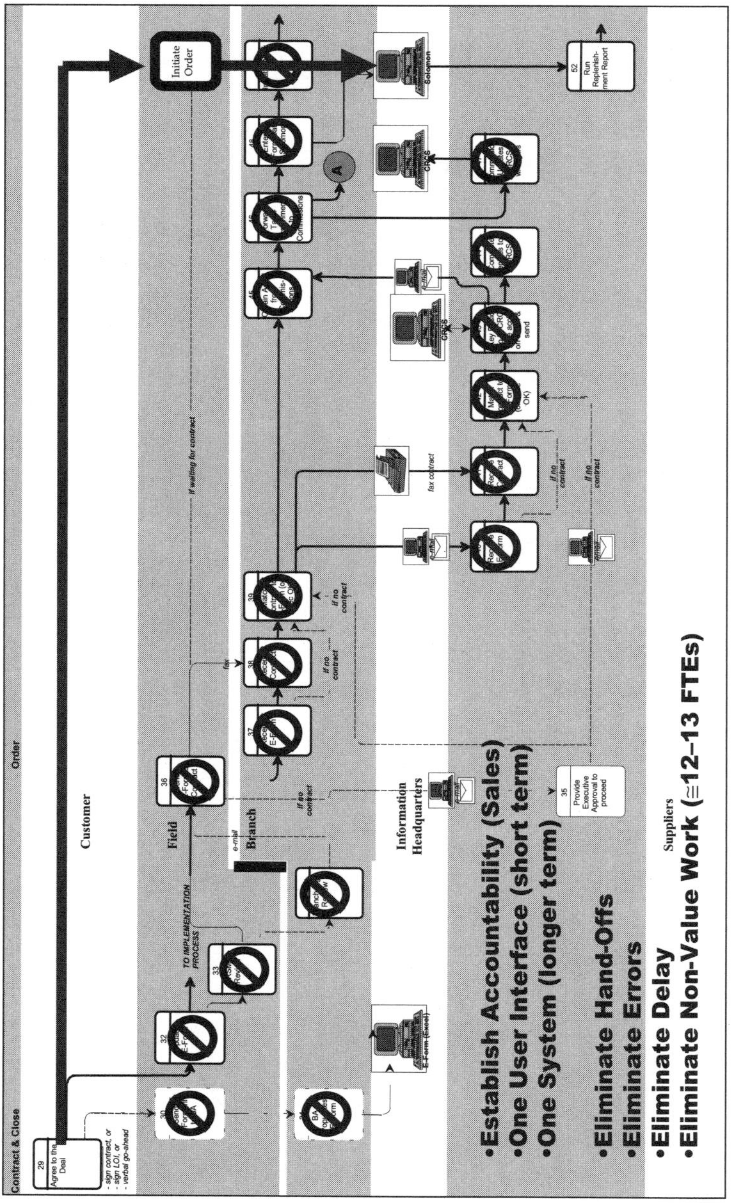

•Establish Accountability (Sales)
•One User Interface (short term)
•One System (longer term)

•Eliminate Hand-Offs
•Eliminate Errors

•Eliminate Delay
•Eliminate Non-Value Work (≅12–13 FTEs)

to have a multitude of order-entry processes. The company was surprised to learn the degree to which the processes could be simplified.

In this case we showed how revamping the order-taking process and related system could cut out all of today's complexity. In the short term, a front-end Web-based order entry system could be developed and standardized for everyone to use. The data could then be automatically routed to the existing systems. In the long run the company needed to standardize on one system. The impact was huge: 19 out of 23 steps eliminated along with an administrative bureaucracy of 12–13 FTEs. This capacity was previously hidden, since they are spread around the country in pockets of .3 people here, .5 people there, and so on. The time was freed-up, enabling these people to assist the sales people bring on more accounts rapidly (faster turnaround time on quotes, proposals, and orders).

Cut Cycle Time

Speaking of sales and order taking, here is an area where it may be more important to focus on cycle time rather than labor time. The more competent and rapid you are at selling your product, and turning the sales into dollars, the more revenue you will reap in a shorter time (improved cash flow).

Whether you call it cycle time, turnaround time, or elapsed time, the start to completion time for any unit of work is not always the same as labor time. For example, when a leading property and casualty insurance company looked at the time to request and receive insurance coverage, they were struck by a key ratio: the ratio of labor time over elapsed time. At best, for only 2.5 percent of the elapsed time was the application being processed; 97.5 percent of the time the application was waiting to be processed.

The sum of the process times for each step amounted to two hours at the most. In other words, it takes only two hours of labor to completely process (enter application info, gather supporting info, underwrite, notify customer, etc.) an application for insurance coverage. Yet, the elapsed time from request to completion could be as much as a month. So even if we assume a best-case view, ten business days at one eight-hour shift per day, the available time is eighty hours. Two hours of actual hands-on processing time is only 2.5 percent of that time. The greatest opportunity in this area is to reduce the turnaround time, by reducing the numerous delays created by paper- and mail-driven hand-offs. See Figure 6.6.

Reducing the turnaround time will not only enhance customer satisfaction, it will reduce costs. For instance, within this new business group, providing status information was the second greatest consumer of labor time. Approximately 8 percent of the group's time was spent on providing status. If the process were more expedient (a few days max), then these calls would not occur at all.

Recently, for example, a company in the medical device industry discovered its product returns were taking upwards of three to four weeks to be processed through its decontamination chambers. This delay represented the lurking liability and risk that a problem might not be found as soon as it should, and/or the regulators could find them not in compliance. After some interviews, mapping, and analysis, it was determined that the bottleneck occurred because the product-return packaging was too big to fit in the decontamination chamber on the regular cycle. All incoming returns had to be processed by hand, in a cycle performed intermittently, as needed when the pile of returns became unwieldy (or someone complained loudly enough). By switching to a standard box two inches smaller in overall dimensions, all returns are now processed on-line in standard cycles. This minor fix, which cost pennies per return, cut decontamination cycle times of three to four weeks to hours.

There are a number of ways to reduce cycle time, but a couple of key principles stand out. They are just as relevant today as when I first wrote about them in my earlier books: *Measure Up!* And *Corporate Renaissance.*[1]

Establish One-at-a-Time Processing

I have been preaching this (and the next) principle for years, but continue to see work moved in batches, creating unbelievable delays. Years ago I worked for a company that took thirty days to get their own invoices out to their customers. It turned out that the invoices were not processed individually, but rather in batches of twenty-five that moved from desk-to-desk. Batch processing can add up to huge delays. For instance, assume that the first processing step receives twenty-five

Figure 6.6. Mapping the Opportunity to Reduce Cycle Time

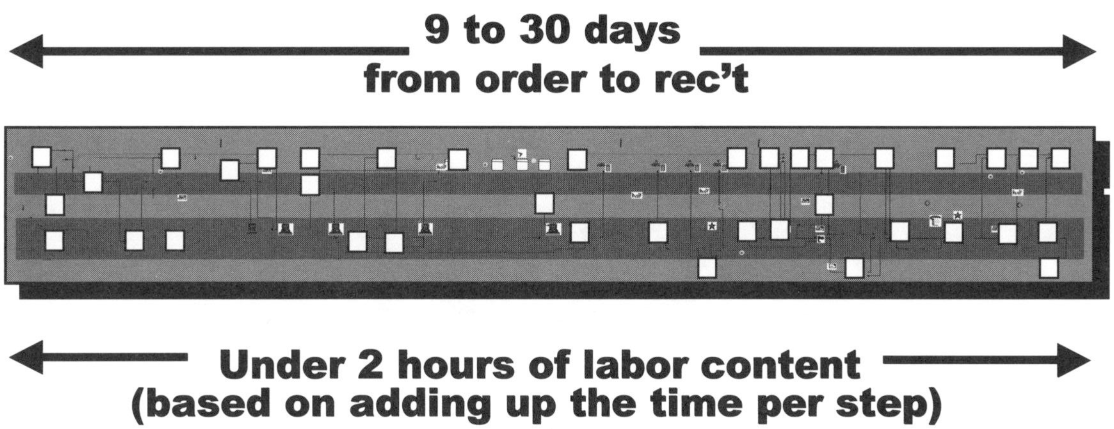

9 to 30 days
from order to rec't

Under 2 hours of labor content
(based on adding up the time per step)

invoices and takes five minutes each to process. Assume the second step also takes five minutes per unit. If the units are processed as a batch of twenty-five at both steps (i.e., all twenty-five units are completed before they're sent to the next desk), it will take two hundred fifty minutes, or just over four hours before they reach step 3. Processed individually, the first unit would reach step 3 in ten minutes, and all twenty-five units would reach step 3 in one hundred thirty minutes, or just over two hours. Imagine the implications for batch processing across dozens of steps (Figure 6.7).

Figure 6.7. Cycle Time Benefits of One-at-a-Time Processing

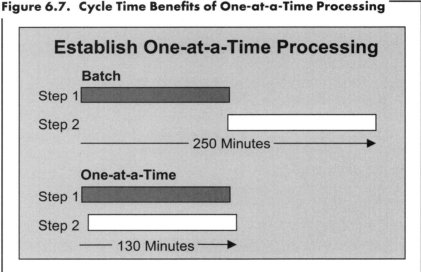

So whether you eliminate batch processing, or cut out hand-offs and move steps, a focus on cycle time reduction is critical to improving process performance. Mistakes are found sooner and corrected before more work is produced with the same errors. Also, a rapid process will dramatically reduce the need for progress updates, and the status inquiries, e.g., "Where is my order?"

Cycle time reduction is particularly important in lengthy project-oriented processes, such as new product development, software development, and installation of major solutions at a customer site. The longer a project is in the works, the more time there is for reconsideration, second-guessing, and changes to the initial request and specifications. The longer the process the more likely the initial requests and specifications are sketchy. We have seen, on numerous occasions, where a software enhancement is requested based on speculation about what will be needed a year hence. The request is put in as a placeholder in order to capture some of the resources and capacity that will be required to do the work. Unfortunately, when the work starts, the first step is to figure out what the request is really all about. This investigation, and redrafting of the specification, creates delay and so forth. To break the cycle of lengthening lead times and poorly constructed requests, one dot-com company in Seattle instituted a team-based process. The new process eliminated hand-offs among various specialists and could turn around a software change in weeks rather than months. Then it became possible to reject sketchy requests, and only work on requests that were complete and detailed. Their mantra became, "You get what you ask for—fast." There was little time for second-guessing and scope creep (expanding the initial request and asking for more features), the request was done before they could rethink it!

Minimize Sequential Processing

Another way to streamline and shorten the flow is to reduce the dependencies created when one step feeds the next. Sequential processing can create two problems that lengthen throughput time. First, the operations are dependent on each other and therefore gated by the slowest step. Second, no one person is responsible for the work as a whole or has a whole job.

Assume a four-step loan-application process that requires twenty minutes of labor to complete the (Figure 6.8). In the sequential process, each individual gets one-quarter of the work, or five minutes per application. But let us assume that the third person always takes six minutes per application. The slowest step becomes the gate and limits output of completed applications to ten per hour. In real situations the problem might not always be a particular person every time but rather a floating bottleneck created by fatigue, product, or mix. Sequential processing permits this kind of bottleneck to occur. While sequential processing is an inevitable part of processing work, in many cases it is not essential. Sequential steps can at times be replaced with parallel processing. In the example, if each of the four people completes the entire application process, output per hour could be increased by 15 percent. The slowest person could still work at the same pace and take 20 percent more time, but this would not affect the others' productivity.

Figure 6.8. Productivity Benefits of Parallel Processing

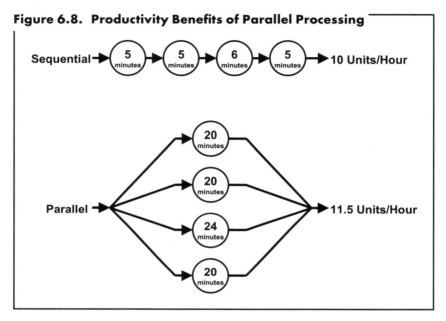

We see the same situation with some manufacturers, where material preparation and/or kitting is a part of the manufacturing process. As a distinct step the preparation process unnecessarily creates an additional sequential step. It is often possible to store components at the workbench and give the assembler the capability to pick (and prepare) the parts as required at their workbench.

From the standpoints of human factors and quality, parallel processing may be beneficial. Each worker can take pride in building a whole assembly and therefore will accept responsibility for productivity and quality. It then becomes possible to eliminate another sequential step: inspection.

Also, controlling the flow of work and its quality is difficult with many sequential and independent steps. For example, even if at each step everything goes right 99 percent of the time, in a fifty-step sequential process the odds are that only 60 percent of the time will the entire process perform correctly. In order to depend on the process as a whole, each step must be designed to work correctly 100 percent of the time. One means of improving quality of process is to consolidate activities into fewer parallel steps.

Cut Value-Added Time (Not Steps)

With an overemphasis on eliminating non-value activities, one big danger is to neglect the opportunities within the value-added activities. Even though an activity adds value and should not be eliminated, there are plenty of instances in which the time to perform the activity can be reduced.

In Our Process Redesign Game: The Assemblers quadruple their output by getting much more proficient (through learning) and much more efficient (through changing the assembly method and sequence). After the first round, everyone realizes the toy phone is not as simple as it first appears. The pieces are not symmetrical. One side of each part has a single row of prongs; the other side has a double row. The top side is made up of more prongs than the bottom side. Therefore the parts have to be oriented properly in order to fit together properly. They also discover that sequence matters. When we first start the game, Workbench 5 has to take apart some work performed at a previous step in order get their part in place. Workbench 1 puts on the antennae when there is no way to line it up properly, because the part it has to be lined up against is added later in the process. The location of the antennae then gets repositioned later (or shipped to the customer as a defect). When the group gets together, they discover the problems and develop a new sequence in which to put the parts together. The new sequence does not require any dismantling of previous work.

Through Proximity, Communication, Learning, and, Ultimately, Proficiency

Although I will cover the means to proficiency (proximity, communication, and learning) in more detail when we get to Strike 10, the ultimate impact is proficiency. Proficiency leads to spending less time to do the same amount of work. In Round One of the game no one really understands how the toy phone goes together. After training and education on the intricacies of the assembly, combined with process changes, performance improves dramatically in Round Two.

For your work environment there are some key questions:

- Do all employees know how to do their jobs properly?

- Does everyone know how the entire product or service comes together for the customer?

- Does everyone know how their job and their job performance relate to others in the workflow?

- Do they know the measures of success?

- Do they know how to identify improvement ideas?

- Are they encouraged to work on improvements with their colleagues?

- Does everyone know who to go to with questions and suggestions?

- To what degree are they empowered and rewarded to make improvements?

We have seen the best and most productive work environments when a seemingly informal peer-to-peer on-the-job training approach exists. Over time a process typically evolves and changes. At some point it doesn't resemble the documentation or the formal training. People forget what they learned on Day 2 of a multiweek training program, but they don't forget what they see and do everyday on the job. And they are more likely to listen to their peers' assessment of what's important and how to do their work.

Through Orienting the Work

In the game, the assemblers learn to have the parts oriented and placed so as to facilitate easy and correct assembly. For example, they place all parts with the two-prong side on the left, and the single prong on the right. That way they can pick it up and readily put it together with another part, rather than spend time during assembly with each-and-every-part figuring out the left from the right side. If the parts aren't lined up right, the toy phone is not likely to come together right.

The same situation occurs in real companies with data entry situations. If the paper form is in one format (the customer's phone number is at the bottom left), and the data entry screen is in another format (the customer's phone number is in the upper right) the chance for error increases dramatically. Aligning the form to look like the screen, or vise versa, cuts errors.

Through Sequencing the Work Steps

The order in which things are done makes a big difference both in cycle time and labor. In the game, the participants completely redesign the process to enable easy and error-free assembly. In the workplace, sequence matters as well.

We saw that in our software-development example where getting the request and related specification right up front saved a lot of time and effort downstream.

Through Automation

In some cases a value-added activity can be eliminated, at least from human intervention. For instance, in a bank, one of the credit department's value-added activities is to make a decision—accept or reject a loan request. In many cases an application is entered into a system (a setup step), and then it is automatically processed through credit bureaus and decision models, enabling the system to make the decision immediately.

Strike 3: On the Straight and Narrow

Strike 3 is about recognizing the most direct route from Point A to Point B is a straight line, and that anything else just gets in the way. Yet most workflows look like Round One of the game, a convoluted crisscrossing maze of confusion. The trick is to determine points A and B and then straighten and shorten the flow of work between them. Eliminating hand-offs, approvals, and anything else that doesn't add value will shorten the flow.

Strike 3: Streamline the Workflow

Strike 3 starts with facts and data about the process. There are typically four steps to getting the facts:

- Define the workload.
- Map the process.
- Quantify the process.
- Identify the key priority areas for action.

Strike 3 actions typically encompass:

- A focus on the few process steps that consume the most time (labor time and cycle time).
- The elimination of non-value-added nonsense process steps.
  1. Eliminate failures and failure-related recovery activities.
  2. Eliminate inspection steps.
  3. Eliminate setup, movement, and storage steps.
  4. Reduce labor time and cycle time to perform the value-added steps:
     a. Through proficiency.
     b. Through orienting the work.
     c. Through sequencing the work.
     d. Through automation.

Strike 3 is about pinpointing targets of opportunity within processes. The next chapter gets at opportunities to improve utilization of capacity that is lost outside of the work process.

CHAPTER 7

STRIKE 4: RECLAIM LOST TIME

Utilize Capacity and Expand Capability

I may be fat, but I'm not lazy.

—DETROIT AUTO WORKER

The last chapter focused on improving the processing of work. However, there is enormous capacity and capability lost "off-process." This chapter will focus on surgical-strike opportunities to reclaim lost time—time spent not processing work.

The actual processing of work makes up only a portion of a workday. Time is lost for two main reasons: (1) time is lost while waiting for work to do; and (2) time is lost when doing other things. In the first case you have a worker without work to do, and a worker without work to do is a terrible thing to waste. In the second case you have work, but without a worker available to do it.

Figure 7.1 tries to clarify the terms I will use and to point the way toward areas of investigation.

We typically find any workforce spends around 30 percent of their time on activities other than the direct flows of work. Even for people considered "direct labor," it is not unusual to find 30 percent of their workweek spent waiting for work to do, combined with off-process activities such as company meetings, staff meetings, training, special

Figure 7.1. The Utilization of a Workday

projects, as well as some additional lost time due to extended breaks and long lunches. Even in project-oriented "knowledge work" processes, such as new product development, we find that 70 percent utilization applies.

In either case (as mentioned in Chapter 6) we arrive at the 70 percent utilization by quantifying the flows of work through a process map, assuming today's process, with today's process times, and today's volumes. Invariably, by multiplying the processing times (minutes per unit of work) by the work unit volumes and dividing by the working minutes per person, we come up with somewhere around 70 percent of the actual headcount. Sometimes it is a little worse—like 50 percent to 60 percent. So where does the time go, and how do we reclaim the lost time?

We have come to realize that lost time is a management problem, not a worker problem. For the most part, people want to be productive and are frustrated when they are not fully utilized. To reclaim the lost time requires a perspective on the entire flow of work and how people fit into that flow—a management perspective (Figure 7.2).

Strike 4: Reclaim Lost Time is about getting work to a worker. The work and worker have to be available—and together—or nothing gets done. As my call center friends put it, the intent is to "keep butts in seats" handling calls.

Figure 7.2. Utilize Capacity

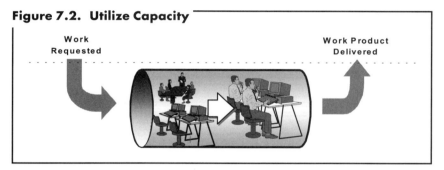

Reclaim Lost Time by Eliminating the Wait for Work

As mentioned above, there are two cases with opportunities to reclaim lost time: (1) There are cases where you have a worker without work to do; and (2) in other cases, you have work but are without a worker available to do it. First I will focus on the former, reclaiming lost time by eliminating the wait for work.

Relieve the Bottleneck

In many cases an idle worker or a busy worker is simply the victim of process flow. Some steps in the process take more time and others take less. The steps that take more time per unit of work become bottlenecks and never run out of work. The steps downstream from the bottleneck are nearly always waiting for work. The steps upstream can overproduce and swamp the bottleneck, so they eventually stop and let the bottleneck catch up.

Understanding the bottleneck and balancing the flow through it is the essence of Eli Goldratt's Theory of Constraints, which was eloquently articulated in a fictional account by him in his book *The Goal*.[1] Although his theory originally was intended to be applied to manufacturing processes, it applies to all processes (described in more detail in subsequent works by Goldratt). Again, this is a basic workflow principle that I have promoted for some time, including my earlier books: *Measure Up!* and *Corporate Renaissance*.[2]

The point is that it makes no sense to pass more work through any step in a process than the bottleneck-process step can handle. For instance, in Figure 7.3, Step 3 displays a capacity to output 200 units per day. However, the fifth step can only handle eighty units per day.

Figure 7.3. Manage Flow to the Bottleneck

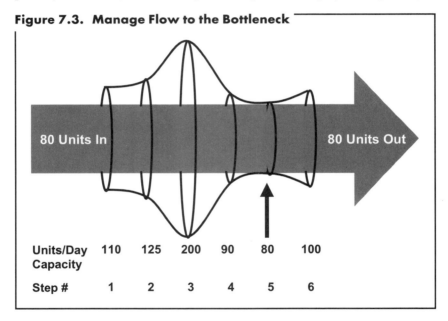

Units/Day Capacity	110	125	200	90	80	100
Step #	1	2	3	4	5	6

While every other step can handle more than eighty units, it's ineffective to do more than eighty. To do more than eighty will result in an accumulation of work prior to the fifth operation and, therefore, a reduction in throughput time. The output of the department as a whole is gated by the bottleneck and as a whole it is only capable of eighty units/day.

In reality, bottlenecks are not usually fixed. The mix of work, the size of the batches of work, and the time it takes to change over to do new work all have a major impact on the bottleneck. The key is to be aware of the importance of the bottleneck and recognize that the process as a whole is regulated by it.

With this awareness, something can be done about it. In this example, assume the last step, with a capacity to do a hundred units, can help Step 5. By not waiting for work and by helping Step 5 instead, assume its capacity drops to ninety units, but that Step 5 now has capacity to do ninety units. Now Steps 4, 5, and 6 all become the new bottleneck of ninety units per day—a 12.5 percent increase in overall output!

Now assume the excess capacities at Steps 1, 2, and 3 are put to good use helping Steps 4, 5, and 6. No longer will Step 3 be waiting for work half of the time, but rather will be contributing to improving the department's overall output by more than 30 percent (beyond the original 12.5 percent increase)!

Some suggest another solution to this type of imbalance. They assign a worker to do Step 3 for a half-day, then something else for the other half of the day. This solution may appear to be an efficient way to deal with the imbalances, but it may be destructive. If Step 3 produces defects, the problem may not be caught early on. A lot of work may pile up that will require disposal or rework, and then lead to greater effort and delay than was originally "saved."

Use Generalists Rather Than Specialists

One of the major obstacles to relieving the bottleneck is the need to change the rules and the culture. Assume that each of the six positions has been defined as a specialist of one sort or another. Assume Step 3 is the highest grade level—the position to which people aspire. To the person that reaches that Step 3 position, the other positions and tasks are beneath them. It is perceived as an insult to be asked to perform lesser work, yet such flexibility would go a long way toward relieving the bottleneck and greatly improving process performance.

Some companies are changing the rules of engagement. In insurance companies, banks, software companies, manufacturers, distributors, call centers, we have seen a similar outcome from process analyses and improvement efforts. They have all come to the conclusion that their overemphasis on labor classifications, job descriptions, and specialists contributes to out-of-balance workflows. The slide in Figure 7.4, from a technical services company (which could have come from any one of the industries mentioned above), says it all.

Figure 7.4. From Specialists to Generalists

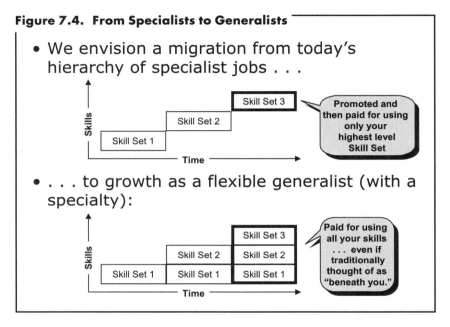

Companies are moving from job growth as "steps," to job growth as "building blocks." No work is beneath anyone when it comes to helping the overall performance of the enterprise.

Proximity Counts—Get People Together

As much as possible, locate people next to each other to foster immediate, informal communication. If it is hard to see who needs help and when they need help, then the flexible generalist remains a nice concept and the bottleneck remains as well.

Years ago I worked on a work cell design for the assembly and testing of circuit boards. In the design it was very clear when bottlenecks occurred: circuit boards would start piling up in front of the bottleneck operation. Workers from non-bottleneck areas could come over and help out until the bottleneck was relieved. No sophisticated scheduling and tracking system was needed, just the simple visual cue of work piling up.

> **In our Process Redesign Game,** we start Round One with five assemblers, each putting together two components. However, some components are much more difficult than others to assemble. Workstation 1 and Workstation 5 are particularly difficult. To make matters worse, Workstation 1 sometimes fails to see the difficulty and simply makes errors and passes the defective units on. If detected, it is at Workstation 5, which is already a bottleneck. So in addition to doing a difficult task, Workstation 5 is burdened with rework. So instead of pumping out the desired ten units per minute, Workstation 5 may only have capacity to do *one* unit per minute in Round One. So regardless of how many units the other workstations can process, the net effect to the customer is one unit per minute.
>
> In Round One everyone is a specialist. No one knows anything but his or her own job. Even if they want to help, the workers are somewhat isolated at their respective tables across the room from the others.
>
> In Round Two the tables are usually right next to each other with no space between them. During the round when one worker has trouble keeping up, the workers on either side help out. Furthermore, the "off-process" staff (material handlers, inspectors, managers) will jump in and help out. Bottlenecks are relieved as they crop up.

Schedule Work

This principle hasn't changed since I first wrote about it in the late 1980s.[3] However, back then my emphasis was on manufacturing efficiencies. Since then I have seen the principle applied with great success in a variety of environments such as product development and customer service. Both labor time and throughput time are a direct result of scheduling or lack of scheduling. The order in which various units of work are processed can make a big difference.

For instance, assume an administrative operation where mail is received and acted upon. Some mail takes longer to act upon than others. If a large portion of time-consuming mail is acted upon at once, then the mail that could be rapidly processed is delayed. If the work arrives randomly, then intermittent surges and troughs of work will result.

Also, like manufacturing, the sequence and timing of work can make a difference especially with regard to throughput time (Figure

7.5). For example, assume "Job A" takes ten minutes to process at Step 1 and five minutes at Step 2 of the process. Also assume "Job B" only takes five minutes at Step 1, but it takes ten minutes at Step 2.

Schedule 1 depicts starting "Job A" first. "A" takes ten minutes before transfer to step 2, then "Job B" can begin. It is twenty-five minutes before both jobs are complete. Also, if there is no other preceding work, the worker who performs Step 2 is idle for ten minutes awaiting his first job.

Schedule 2 displays what happens if "Job B" is started first. Both jobs are completed in twenty minutes. Just by sequencing the jobs differently, throughput time is reduced by 20, and Step 2's labor time is cut by 20 percent (assuming the "wait time" is idle time).

Figure 7.5. Scheduling for Faster Cycle Times

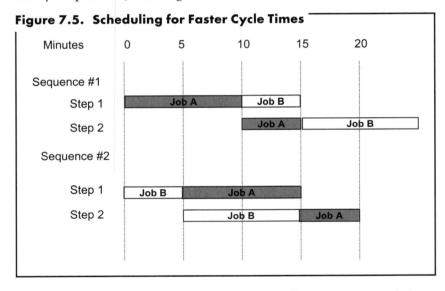

In reality, scheduling is not simple, especially in project work (e.g., new product development) and administrative operations. At any given time, for any given step in the process, the processing time is likely to be unpredictable (within a range). Also, there are multiple types of work and numerous steps (with some workers as generalists and others as specialists to handle those steps). Scheduling is difficult, to say the least. However, the scheduling issues of timing and sequence are real and a little thought and planning can go a long way. Focus on the potential bottlenecks and schedule to the bottlenecks. The rest will likely take care of itself.

Schedule Workers

Sometimes fluctuations in workload occur predictably, sometimes they don't. Scheduling is so important to workforce utilization that I will devote Chapter 9 and Strike 6, "Manage Fluctuations in Work Volume," to effectively matching the capacity to do the work with a fluctuating workload.

However, since it has a direct bearing on overall utilization, I will discuss it briefly now. Perhaps the best examples of utilization measurement and improvement are found in manufacturing operations and call center operations. These are two environments where utilization is a priority and it gets a lot of attention. Companies pride themselves on their techniques for managing utilization performance.

For example, my firm worked with TeleTech, one of the leading customer-care solutions firms. They primarily handle inbound customer contacts (phone, e-mail, Web) for a number of leading Fortune 1,000 companies. As experts in managing contact centers, they consistently demonstrate an ability to exceed utilization and productivity levels of the typical in-house operation.

As I will show, there are a number of aspects of utilization to be managed. Improving any one of them may represent a significant surgical strike. (However, on other occasions a significant surgical strike may require all aspects of utilization and productivity to improve simultaneously. In those situations an in-house quick hit is not possible. The only way to get everything at once—and fast—is to outsource. Outsourcing as a surgical strike is discussed in Chapter 8, "Redistribute the Work").

One aspect of utilization to be managed in many environments, and especially the contact center, is "scheduling efficiency." Scheduling efficiency refers to balancing workforce availability with inbound calls' peaks and valleys. They use a combination of flexible planned/scheduled staffing levels and techniques that enable last-minute adjustments (e.g., the opportunity, at the worker's discretion, to go home early without pay if volume is down).

For one leading financial services firm, TeleTech found they could improve scheduling efficiency from 87 percent to 90 percent. In a year when wage increases amounted to 3 percent, or so, this one savings was enough to cover the entire labor increase for the contact center employees for a year. And this was just one component of their utilization management process. Let's look at the other components.

Unavailable Time: Use It or Lose It—Time Is Money

The workforce spends a lot of time on activities other than the direct flows of work or even simply waiting for work. Even for people considered "direct labor" (involved in the direct flows of work), we have seen cases where as much as 50 percent of their work time is spent on other things. As I have been describing, there can be a significant surgical strike in improving utilization. Earlier, I showed how time is lost while waiting for work, and what can be done about it. Now I will describe how time is lost when a worker is "not-at-their-desk" and how utilization improvement can be very significant.

After working with TeleTech to conduct numerous opportunity assessments within call centers, the findings have been strikingly similar across companies and industries. Table 7.1 shows a typical impact summary and the specific magnitude of savings possible for a leading financial institution by focusing on utilization:

Table 7.1. Call Center Improvement Opportunities and Staffing Impact

Staffing Calculations	Before		After	
	%	minutes	%	minutes
Avg Paid Min/Day/Person		480.0		480.0
Scheduling Efficiency	87.0%	417.6	90.0%	432.0
In-Chair Occupancy	85.9%	358.7	89.0%	384.5
Telephone Occupancy	75.9%	272.3	80.0%	307.6
A—Time Utilized to Handle Calls		272.3		307.6
B—Call Time (avg. minutes)		6.0		5.6
C—Calls per Day per Person (A/B)		45.4		54.9
D—Call Volume per Day		10,000		10,000
E—Employees Required (D/C)		220		182
Impact				−17.3%

As you can see, the cumulative impact is significant. So how does TeleTech do it? What are these opportunities and how do they apply to your business? Let's now look at the "occupancy" factors.

In-chair occupancy refers to the portion of the workday a customer service rep spends in their chair. So the issue is—if they are not in their chair, where are they? Table 7.2 shows where the time goes and where it can be improved:

Table 7.2. Where Time Is Spent During a Workday

IN-CHAIR OCCUPANCY—BASELINE WORKDAY		
	Current Practice **Hours**	**Proposed Practice** **Hours**
Scheduled Workday	8.00	8.00
Work Time (− 1.00 for lunch)	7.00	7.00
Break Periods	−0.33	−0.33
Team/Meetings/Briefings	−0.22	−0.12
Training/Evaluations	−0.12	−0.12
Unproductive Time	−0.32	−0.20
In chair to Handle Calls	6.01	6.23
% In-Chair Occupancy (In chair/Work Time)	86%	89%
Net Additional Minutes to Handle Calls:	+ 13	
Net Productivity Improvement:	3.60%	

There were two areas of opportunity. One was found in reducing the start-of-shift meeting duration. The customer care outsourcer's experience and expertise has led to a formularized time bound meeting agenda that works in any contact-center environment. Likewise their combination of carrot-and-stick incentives has proven able to cut down on unexplained "unproductive time."

In this case the break periods and other categories were appropriate for the environment. However, in many cases the training time requires adjustment (up or down). Some companies do not spend enough time on training, and pay for it later with poor performance (e.g., service to the customer and/or efficiency and utilization). Other companies spent too much time. For example, one firm trained their new hires in a classroom for eight weeks, and then no one could remember anything by the time they got out, and they learned on the job anyway.

Telephone occupancy refers to the time that the rep talks to the customer or performs associated after-call work. It is expressed as a percentage of the in-chair occupancy. So here the measure indicates the in-chair time spent actually handling customers and any follow-up work. In a traditional call center, the measure is easily obtained from the telecom switch (which records every call's source, destination, and its duration). It provides summary data on how much time a call takes and when the rep signals they are available to take the next call (accounting for after-call work).

In the financial services company, we found a telephone occupancy of 76 percent. TeleTech's routine practice has repeatedly shown 80 percent to be a conservative and realistic level of performance with calls of a similar workload profile. A combination of their training, tools, measurement, and management techniques provide the ingredients for such results.

However, sometimes simply recognizing the extent of the opportunity and looking for a simple solution can achieve a quick hit. Especially in smaller companies where call centers are relatively small and not a primary part of their business, we sometimes find the greatest opportunities. For instance, in a cable television company's call center we found telephone occupancy at 20 to 30 percent. First and foremost, the company's call volume had steadily declined over the year but no action was ever taken to reduce staff. Staff was available to take calls that were not forthcoming. Second, partially because they had the time, each call center rep would jot down notes and update the tracking system after a call was concluded. Some minor tweaks to the system enabled the reps to more easily update the system during the call— eliminating the note taking and the bulk of the after-call work.

Call handling efficiencies—in addition to the workforce utilization opportunity, we sometimes find a marked difference between the observed time per call, and the time per call extrapolated from the switch data. I have listened to numerous calls by sitting with a rep and plugging in a headset to their workstation. The average time per call, as recorded by the switch, is longer than when a rep's activities are observed directly. I am sure we intimidate the rep; the rep knows that short call times are encouraged, so they act quickly to wrap up the call when we are right there listening and observing. However, the difference still suggests an opportunity to reduce call time, and increase the number of calls that can be handled. (You have to listen carefully to the content of the call. Sometimes in the rep's zeal to end a call, the customer is left dissatisfied or with questions. They will likely call back and create another call. That second and perhaps longer call might have been avoided by staying on the first call a little longer and answering a few lingering questions.)

There is nothing as effective as actually listening to calls with the rep, and watching the rep perform any after-call work, to ferret out the opportunities. They can tell you if the call you heard is typical, or an exception. The rep can clarify what you are hearing and be quite insightful as to the potential improvement opportunities.

Utilization—It Applies to You

While the utilization factors described here are specific to a call center environment, they provide insight into the right questions for any process. So what is the relevance to professional work environments and less factory-like administrative work? The questions for such environments are the same:

■ *How much paid work time is spent "utilized" and processing work?*

Typically we can account for this utilized time by quantifying a process map and building a process model (as described earlier in Chapter 6). Essentially we come up with the utilized time and then factor it to account for unutilized time and extrapolate a staffing level. If we find a 70 percent or more utilization we look for the greater opportunities to be within the process. If less than 70 percent we further investigate the unutilized time.

■ *How much paid work time is spent waiting for work?*

If we need to investigate further, the first thing we do is find out how much time is simply spent waiting for work. We look at the bottleneck issue, the scheduling issue, and the related issues of worker flexibility and proximity of workers to each other. On many occasions we have found the surgical strike is in this wait time, but goes beyond the bottleneck and related worker flexibility issues. It relates to managing to fluctuations in work volumes, and that will be covered in detail in Chapter 9, "Manage Fluctuations in Work Volume," and Strike 6.

■ *How much paid work time is spent off-process and unavailable?*

This question can be specifically reworded to suit a particular environment such as how much of a product-development person's time is not spent on the process of developing products. How much of a salesperson's time is spent on something other than the sales process?

Sometimes we investigate unavailable time and find our process map is incomplete. For instance, time spent analyzing process failures, their root causes, and fixing the source of problems should be on the process map. It should be a critical part of the day-to-day process and be built in as a hard-wired part of the process.

On other occasions we find "unavailable time" is put to valuable use on another process. For example, we looked at a new product development process in a software company. We mapped and quantified the development process and could account for only 50 percent of the development engineers. As we investigated, we found that the time unavailable to the development process was spent elsewhere. Time was spent helping the sales process (by helping with technical analyses and developing proposals). Time was spent installing the software at customer sites, and occasionally assisting with support services.

So sometimes an investigation leads to an explanation and no surgical-strike opportunity. On other occasions the surgical strike can be significant such as excessive training time where the training is ineffective.

All this discussion of availability and utilization can be confusing. Plus, as we saw with the customer care example, every industry has its own view and its own terminology. Nevertheless, the point is to question where time is lost, why it is lost, and what can be done about it.

Customer Chaos Is No Excuse for Poor Utilization

I can't tell you how many service organizations, with which we have worked, blame poor utilization of their workforce on their customers. As one operations manager said about years of poor labor utilization, "We can't do anything about it. Our customers' behavior is erratic and unpredictable." With two sentences this operations manager had dismissed any potential to even think about improving the utilization of her workforce. Her view was tainted by years of failed attempts with various planning and scheduling techniques. But that is where she went wrong. Planning and scheduling weren't the answer. The answer was found in accepting chaos, becoming a part of it, and becoming good at it.

The best explanation, and most pragmatic solution to maximizing utilization with chaotic customers, was described by *Wired* magazine about Cemex—Mexico's large cement company:[4]

> **Here's how the cement business worked in Mexico's second-largest city, Guadalajara, only a couple of years ago:**
>
> A builder telephoned in an order a day or so ahead, two days in advance for big jobs. He specified a time, knowing it was basically theoretical, depending on an endless array of variables—weather, traffic, a missing receipt, the number of other orders the plant had to try to fill. Trucks got lost—up to 140 might be on the road at a time—walkie-talkies conked out, ill-financed projects shut down with their foundations half poured. Penalties or not, on delivery day half of the customers canceled or rescheduled their orders. The bottom line: tons of costly cement rumbling around town with nowhere to go, even as builders were lucky to get delivery the right day, let alone the right hour. "You tried to stay on top, but something would always get by," recalls Alejandro Contreras, a veteran dispatcher with the local subsidiary of Cementos Mexicanos—Cemex for short. "When the phone rang, it was usually someone who was upset. You had to sit there and take it—let the customer blow off steam—then try to negotiate a solution. Hijole! Oh, man! When the phone rang, sometimes I wanted to just not answer it."

Here's how things worked in the same city one afternoon this March:

In an air-conditioned operations room on the top floor of a two-story office, Contreras and Oscar Suárez are manning their stations. The ambiance is ops-room generic, with five screens—including a 19-incher with a glowing map of the city—and half a dozen phone sets.

It's half past twelve, and Contreras is fielding a request: a load of ready mix in 40 minutes for a new gas station. No hay problema. A satellite-linked GPS system pinpoints three Cemex trucks on the road, one of them right in range. Still talking, Contreras does a quick check on the customer's billing status. Then he taps a few keys, the instructions go out to the onboard computer in a truck near the site, and the concrete is on its way.

Over on Suárez's side, Alarma flashes onscreen in white letters: a delivery is due in 30 minutes, but the customer hasn't called to confirm. Suárez glances at the city map, then goes back to some paperwork: If the builder calls, there's a truck available. If he doesn't, the plant will automatically be notified to cut back the rest of the day's production. Any dispute? The customer's welcome to come by and listen to a Teac digital recorder play back not only his original phone conversations with the dispatchers, but—like a cockpit voice recorder—everything said in the operations room. On the other hand, if a truck is more than 20 minutes late, it's 20 pesos (about U.S. $2.50) off for each cubic meter, about a 20 percent discount. To promote the offer, Cemex has even printed miniature pizza boxes labeled with a slogan that pokes a little fun at the local Domino's franchise: ''Now, the concrete is faster than the pizza.''

There are probably stranger places to see the latest in complexity theory in action, but delivering cement in Mexico is a pretty good start. Cemex is a company on a high-tech roll that has carried it in scarcely a decade from a sleepy perch in northern Mexico to its place as the world's third-largest cement company. Its 20,000-plus people, 486 plants, thousands of vehicles, and fleet of freight ships move more than 50 million tons of the stuff annually in 60 countries—including places that make Guadalajara look like Geneva. And in doing so, Cemex is confounding ideas about the lines that supposedly separate the info haves of the world from people like Alejandro Contreras and Oscar Suárez.

The mission in Guadalajara was to build a system that could surf the complexity by making each ready-mix truck as independent as possible—in effect, an autonomous agent cruising the city, waiting for orders. Instead of stationing an order taker at each plant, Cemex would have just one central ops room for the whole city. Most important, instead of struggling hopelessly to keep to a fixed schedule, the goal would be to keep enough options open to handle any likely request. Says Massey: "If I can predict where the orders are coming from and can maintain random distribution of trucks, I should always be able to have one close to where it's needed. If I can have a chaotic distribution of vehicles, then I'm really trying not to control chaos, but to use it to my advantage."

The result is three integrated systems: one for taking orders, another for checking a customer's financial profile, and the last for tracking software the ops room dispatchers use. And the whole thing is accessible from any of the 30 PCs spread throughout the Guadalajara headquarters—sales, accounting, maintenance—as well as through Cemex's global WAN by any staffer armed with the right passwords.

Does it work? That is, does it work every day, in the field? Francisco "Paco" Rivera, a Cemex programmer and troubleshooter visiting the Guadalajara ops room, jacks in his IBM ThinkPad and calls up Cemex's South America network. In the first half of March, the company's low tech Venezuela operation made 771 deliveries, 34.4 percent on time. By contrast, in Guadalajara in March of last year—with the system barely six months old—97.63 percent of 1,365 deliveries were on time, within 10 minutes of the promised hour. This year, with business creeping back toward normal and the number of deliveries doubled, the on-time percentage is even higher—98.15 percent.

Expand Capability

As we saw in Chapter 4, idle time creates problems. Too many people together with too much idle time leads to an internal focus, personality clashes, and corporate politics to the detriment of a focus on customers.

However, most of the surgical-strike opportunities lead to freeing up capacity. It is a strategic choice as to what to do with that freed-up capacity. The easy answer is to downsize and institute lay-offs. The harder, perhaps more beneficial choice, is to productively utilize the freed up capacity.

Even if the choice is layoffs, it is impossible to have everyone 100 percent utilized on direct process work. There will always be time, on someone's part, available to do something else. The trick is to define what that "something else" is and make it a productive endeavor.

Three things come to mind that companies have done to productively capture what would have been unutilized time: (1) enhance the process, (2) enhance the customer experience, and (3) enhance sales and expand the customer base.

By expanding capabilities that add value, customers will place more orders, refer more customers, and generate more work—a vicious circle of success:

Figure 7.6. More Value → More Demand

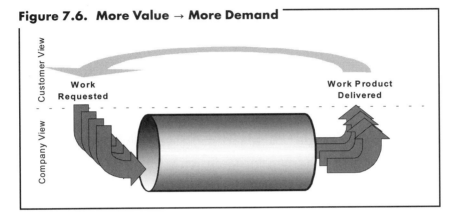

Enhance the Process

As underutilized time is found and people are freed up, there is an opportunity to create improvement teams and find more improvement opportunities. Surgical strikes do require some time and effort to achieve. The identification of surgical strikes, as described in this and the previous chapters, is born out of quality improvement programs, reengineering, Six Sigma, and the like. It takes some effort to gather facts, conduct the analyses, and design solutions. Typically there is a team, or even teams, of people dedicated to such initiatives.

Dedicated improvement teams can always use help. Here is one area where intermittently idle talent can also be put to good use—assisting your process improvement teams. Collecting data, summarizing data, and the like can typically be done as time permits. So for a person who has a few minutes, or an hour or so, here and there while waiting for work, the time can be put to good use.

Enhance the Customer Experience

A customer that has a good experience with your company is more likely to buy again, buy more, and tell others to buy from you. The value of customer loyalty and retention is not insignificant. The book, *The Loyalty Effect*, by Frederick Reichheld, suggests, "A shift in retention of as little as 5 percentage points—from, say, 93 to 98 percent—seems to account for more than a 20 percent improvement in productivity."[5]

Sometimes it's an over-the-top service encounter that makes a great customer experience. With some time and some empowerment on the part of those closest to the customer, an act of superior service can go a long way. For example, in an *Inc* magazine article, Larry Harmon, president of De Mar Plumbing, recalls the value of extraordinary service when he went out his way to meet a service commitment:[6]

> **We won a bid on a residential air conditioner and budgeted $100 for installation with a crane. But then we got some real heavy rains, the kind Southern California's famous for. On the day we were supposed to do the work, the ground was too wet to get the crane in, and there was no asphalt to drive it onto near the house. But since we had promised the customer we'd complete the job that same day, we hired a helicopter for $500. Let me tell you, it was freezing and foggy, and then it started raining. But we got the air conditioner installed, videotaped the work, and gave a copy of the tape to the customer. The customer offered to split the extra $400 expense with us, but I wanted to stick to our bid. So we covered it. Well, that customer showed the videotape at his New Year's Eve party, and we got three new leads and one sale from that. The sale was a five-ton unit, and our profit was $2,400. So for an initial $400 investment in customer service, we figure our return was 600 percent.**

Sometimes it's the small things that make a great customer experience. For instance, service companies look for opportunities to make the intangible tangible. Hotels provide candies on the pillow, and fold the toilet paper into a point, to show they have taken care of your room while you were out. Some car dealer service departments are visible through glass walls to the waiting room and they deliberately let you see paper floor mats in your car to show their concern for your car's cleanliness. What does your company do that could be made more visible and tangible for customers?

The best hotels think ahead and prepare for helping customers with problems. They have a game plan to open your car door if you lock your keys inside by accident. They have umbrellas to loan, toothpaste, and other incidentals to give you if you forgot yours. Have you thought through the things that go wrong and how to prevent them? And when things do go wrong, how to react?

Here again, freed-up time can be used to benefit the customers as well as your company. Teams, with help from people with some freed-up time here and there, can work to enhance the customer's experience. Teams can put themselves in the role of customers and figure out things that are likely to go wrong someday, and pre-define corrective actions. Teams can figure out how to make visible the invisible things the company does behind the scenes on behalf of their customers.

Done well, such actions can lead to more customers and more sales per customer. Sometimes these teams come up with very direct revenue enhancing ideas.

Enhance Sales and Expand the Customer Base

Companies, particularly conglomerates, may have a great opportunity to cross-sell products and services across divisions. One leading financial services conglomerate realized a huge opportunity by linking a couple of their subsidiaries into a seamless process for the company, and a seamless service flow for the customer. My partner John Feather, at Corporate Renaissance, facilitated a process redesign team within their life insurance company. The original intent was to streamline the life insurance company's death claims process. However, they found a much greater opportunity. This excerpt from John's article, in the Institute of Industrial Engineers monthly magazine, describes the approach and the finding:[7]

> **The individual insurance group of a Fortune 500 insurance company knew that its process for settling death claims had been suffering from too many**

hand-offs, lengthy cycle times, a high cost structure, and numerous complaints from beneficiaries.

In 1997, they decided to do something about it. A design team was assembled to tackle the systemic problems and redesign the process. In just six months they designed a process that could:

- Reduce cost by 28 percent
- Reduce cycle time by 56 percent
- Eliminate many of the cross-functional hand-offs
- Enable once-and-done processing
- Increase value-added time to a world-class status

A more important feature, however, was the increased asset retention potential in the hundreds of millions of dollars.

The process design team, working in conjunction with an internal technology development team, accomplished this by linking the death claims process to other business units in order to allow for cross-selling additional company products such as financial investment services. This system was developed after the careful analysis of customer data and process data by the two teams.

During the analysis phase, it was discovered that the time to process a death claim was significantly longer than what the customer wanted. It was also found that hundreds of millions of dollars were flowing out of the company because linkages did not exist to allow for cross-selling of additional company products (e.g., annuities and mutual funds).

The redesign team began by creating sub-teams of two people each to conduct data collection and analyses in three areas:

1. Evaluation of the existing death claims process (process map of the existing workflow and measure of value-added time to the beneficiary)
2. Opportunity analysis and quantification (e.g., cycle time analysis)
3. Beneficiary segmentation and requirements analysis (needs assessment by beneficiary age profile)

The intent here was to find out where the gaps existed between the existing process and the expectations of both the beneficiaries and the agents. The team was careful to perform the analysis on an order-of-magnitude basis. Once they determined what was needed, the team was split up into three subgroups to complete the three individual components of work.

One subteam was responsible for mapping the flow of work within the existing Death Claims process. The process map, which is a visual depiction of the activities from the point at which a claim was received until it was paid, encompassed approximately 200 steps. The value-added time of these steps to the beneficiaries was measured at only 18 percent!

Another subteam was responsible for analyzing the length of time (cycle time) that it took to process the claim. One year's worth of claim data was analyzed on a representative sampling basis.

The third subteam was responsible for completing focus groups with beneficiaries and agents. The focus groups yielded critical information on ideal turnaround time, expectations on initial contact, and the level of assistance required to complete the claim. It was here that a major discovery was made regarding beneficiary expectations.

The prevailing perception was that the beneficiaries did not want to be contacted after a death. To a degree this was true, with most beneficiaries responding that they would like to have some time to pass before being contacted. When asked how much time was appropriate, many of the beneficiaries responded that investment advice was expected approximately 30 days after a death.

After paying off the funeral bills, many beneficiaries were at a loss on investment strategies. It was at this point where beneficiaries most often sought advice from brokerages houses.

The design team saw this as a great opportunity. The money was already sitting in an account under the auspices of the corporation. How could they design a process that would meet the needs of the beneficiaries and manage to retain approximately hundreds of millions per year in assets?

The Process Owner for Death Claims, said at the time, "The potential of the process efficiencies in the backroom were wonderful, but the real eye opener was the cash retention capability that was already sitting right there in our accounts."

He was right. The new process design had 50 percent less steps than the original process and the value-added time more than tripled. Also, after extensive analysis, it was found that approximately 65 percent of the claims would be classified as "low administration" and would be processed within 2 days.

However, the important part here is that for the first time the life insurance division was not thinking about the payment of the claim as being the end. The post-payment interaction represented an opportunity to create a follow-up with the beneficiary after 30 days for the purpose of re-investment of funds with other divisions. The investment services division would manage the information and work with the agents to pursue the "leads".

The life insurance division would provide the agents with tools, training, and best practices information on how to assist with the claim and also the follow-up with the beneficiary. Also, a new incentive program would be linked to the process to ensure more effective follow-ups.

The net impact was the potential for the corporation to retain nearly 1 billion dollars under management!

Expand Capabilities and Reap the Rewards

As seen in the examples, expanding your capability to serve customers can have a huge upside. So while the easy solution to capitalizing on freeing up excess capacity is layoffs, the greater gain is in putting that capacity to productive use.

In our Process Redesign Game, we start Round One with thirteen employees and the opportunity to fill ten orders and deliver a total of sixty toy phones. Alas, in Round One the process gets jammed up and the business is lucky if they can deliver ten phones. The customer is annoyed with poor delivery (the orders are unfilled), poor quality (phones that are delivered are defective), and poor service (the process is in such a state of confusion they can't get the attention of their customer service rep).

As the game progresses through Round Two, quality and delivery improve dramatically; the service is responsive. There is even time for dialogue about forthcoming orders, constructive communication about the few remaining quality problems, and the potential for more work.

The potential for more work is realized when we open the floodgates in Round Three. We say, "Because your quality and delivery is so good, along with your attention to service, we want more of your product." We allow the customer to place as many orders as the operation can handle. Typically instead of the ten orders and sixty phones delivered in a round, the workforce delivers somewhere around fifteen orders and nearly a hundred phones.

However, here's the kicker. During the middle of Round Three the customer requests a few customized phones—phones for the hearing-impaired that require an extra earpiece. With the process humming and in control, the request is easily assimilated. So not only are one hundred phones delivered, but ≅15 of them are customized.

However, some groups get in trouble. They see that employees are costing them money and they lay them off between Round One and Two. They get the desired improvements in Round Two, but then do not have the capacity to excel with quantum leaps in output that we see other groups get in Round Three.

Strike 4: Reclaim Lost Time

Strike 4 starts with facts and data about the where time is spent. There are typically a few categories of lost time:

- Wait time
- Unavailable time
- Utilized time
- Unutilized time

Strike 4 actions typically encompass:

- Reclaiming lost time by eliminating the wait for work.
  —Relieve the bottleneck.
  —Use generalists rather than specialists.
  —Get people together.
  —Schedule work.
  —Schedule workers.
- Putting unutilized time to work
- Expanding capabilities
  —Enhance the process.
  —Enhance the customer experience.
  —Enhance sales and expand the customer base.

Strike 4 is about opportunities to improve utilization of people's time by finding and eliminating time that is wasted and by ideally putting that freed-up time to good use.

CHAPTER 8

STRIKE 5: REDISTRIBUTE THE WORK

One does what one can, not what one can't.
—AGATHA CHRISTIE, EXPLAINING WHY SHE ONLY WROTE
MYSTERY NOVELS

Who says you have to do all the work? Could the customer do some of the work? Should you outsource some of the work? Are there intermediaries in your business and its processes that could do some of the work more effectively and efficiently? Are the "right" employees doing the "right" work? If someone else or another organization can do some of the work more effectively, why not have them do it? Shifting a portion of the work process from one group to another can be a significant surgical strike.

Strike 5, Redistribute the Work, is about capitalizing on targets of opportunity to shift work, and the related processes, to or from other organizational entities—whether customers, suppliers, or intermediaries. For example, if we view the process like a pipe through which work flows, a significant surgical strike may be found by cutting the pipe and having others perform a portion of the process (Figure 8.1).

Figure 8.1. Customers and Suppliers—Part of the Process

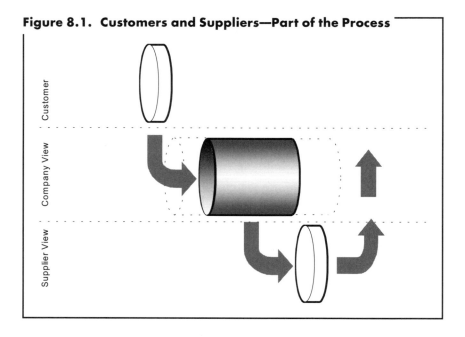

Put Your Customers to Work

There are numerous opportunities to have customers perform part of the process themselves, and be pleased to do it.

Banking provides one of the best examples of customer self-service. It works for the customer and it works for the banks. The benefits are huge and are roughly quantified in a book called *The Service Profit Chain*: "John Reed, CEO of Citibank, estimated that the costs of serving a customer totally by credit card and automatic teller machine were twenty-five times lower than through a Citibank branch. And if the relationships could be maintained by phone and computer, costs would only be 25 percent of those incurred by credit card."[1]

However, the banking example has been overused. There are many business articles and books on service excellence, customer focus, and e-business. They all seem to come with a description of the now decades-old and tired bank teller to automatic teller machine example. Then the nearly decade-old migration to direct banking (on-line and telephony based) is rehashed. Great examples, great results, but I have little to add.

Customers Weigh In

Instead I will focus on an example from a project we did nearly ten years ago at one of the premier high-contact consumer service companies: Weight Watchers International. First, a little background. For forty years Weight Watchers' highly ethical and effective program has helped millions of people around the world to lose weight. Now each week, more than one million people attend approximately 39,000 Weight Watchers meetings that are led by over 14,000 classroom leaders who themselves have successfully completed the program and are inspiring role models. The Weight Watchers brand is widely recognized throughout the world with retail sales of over $1.5 billion in 2000, including sales by licensees and franchisees.[2]

We worked for their North American company-owned operation that encompasses approximately 2,500 North America meeting locations, each with multiple meetings per week. These numbers are important. A small surgical strike action can get huge results. If the customer experience is improved and staffing is made more productive in one meeting location, it has application across many more.

We were engaged in a project to do exactly that—improve the customer experience and make the staff more productive within the meeting room environment. The directive was clear—not only with its insistence on not sacrificing the customer experience for the sake of saving money, but especially on its insistence that the customer experience comes first. As the Weight Watchers' project manager Judy Donnenfeld pointed out, "Our service is emotionally charged, with a high degree of empathy and interaction among members and service providers. Retention of existing customers, referrals of new customers, and ultimately their revenue is highly dependent upon a great one-hour experience each week."

So basically we were asked to make the meeting experience better for both the employees and customers—and to save money. So what did we do? Like any surgical-strike initiative, we used the four-step approach described in Chapter 2: Discover, Inspire, Design, and Realize.

Discover the Facts

The first step was to go to approximately twenty Weight Watchers meetings in both retail strip mall locations and third-party locations (e.g., church basements, civic centers). We observed those meetings with an expected attendance of enough members to justify three or more staff service providers. During those meetings, we documented the arrival patterns of members, the tasks performed and their sequence, along with the time spent conducting each process step (average times and degrees of variation).

In this way we documented the step-by-step experience of the member. At the same time we documented the step-by-step experience of the service providers. At first we saw a two-step process: a check-in and pay station and then a weigh-in station. However, as we observed the pay station we realized the two service providers were not doing the same thing. A member would approach the first service provider to obtain their card. The card contained a record of the member's status (meetings attended and a record of their weight at each session). The first service provider would retrieve the member's card from a card file. Then the member would pay the second service provider for the meeting. So we found there was a three-step process leading to the meeting itself. There was a "get card" check-in, then a pay step performed by two receptionists, plus the weigh-in performed by a weigher. Prior to the start of the meeting, the leader would also assist with weigh-in.

The basic three-step process and its deviations are depicted below:

Figure 8.2. 3-Step Check-in Process

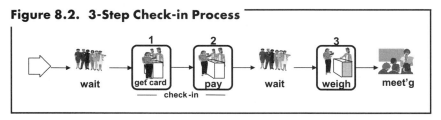

In addition to the process flows being defined, we quantified the flows. We looked at the arrival patterns. The arrival patterns varied, within a predictable range, from meeting to meeting. As you might expect, we found that fifteen minutes before and five minutes into the meeting is "crunch time" and that two-thirds of the attendees arrive during this period.

We also established the processing times for the "get card," pay, and weigh-in steps. Here we found the need to distinguish new enrollees from current members. The time to enroll a new member was longer than the time to check-in a current member. Even within such groupings we found quite a bit of variation, but within predictable ranges. One other interesting observation—the "get card" and "pay" time was roughly a half-a-minute longer in New York than in New England. It appeared that the New Yorkers were chattier.

Inspired by Insight

With the facts in hand, my colleague James Jennings was able to build a simulation model. We used the model to conduct analyses, and find areas of opportunity. We knew the process; we knew the arrival patterns (and degree of variation); and we knew the processing times (and degree of variation). A model could be built to rapidly simulate many more meetings than we could possibly view in person. Plus a computer-based dynamic simulation model could provide detailed information on the length of the lines and waiting times for both the reception desk (get card and pay) and weigh-in.

We created the simulation model and observed the high variability in processing time per member at both reception (get card and pay) and weigh-in created long wait times for members. As we saw in person, not only were these lines and the wait time undesirable for those in the line, but also for those early arrivals in the meeting room. Those in the meeting room were inconvenienced either by a delayed start while trying to get everyone through the lines and into the meeting or by interruptions as members entered the room after the meeting started. We could see that a focus on reducing wait times for the members would enhance the member experience for all members.

For the size meetings and related staffing levels we observed and modeled, we found that at the high end as much as six and a half minutes could be spent waiting in line. Compared to Disney World this may not seem like much, but as a part of a weekly service experience it was viewed as less than desirable. We also we noticed that the current members waited over 33 percent as long on average as new enrollees. Here was a classic case of slow-to-process work, holding up the fast-to-process work. Our model was based upon appropriate specified staffing levels for the expected number of members attending. If the members came in greater numbers than expected the service experience could be significantly worse.

There are two ways to reduce the wait times, add staff or reduce process time. In this case adding staff was not an option. So we had to find ways to reduce the time to process members, particularly at the non-value-added experience at the reception desk (the get card and pay steps). If we had to reduce process time, how much time was needed? The model helped us here as well.

Here is a simplified example of how the model helped us. I have not used the real data and model, since it is more complex and difficult to follow.

So for the example, assume that 60 percent of the members arrive during the critical 15 minute peak time period just before the meeting time. In a thirty-five-person meeting, twenty members arrive during that peak time. If 25 percent are prepaid, then fifteen people arrive at the registration desk over fifteen minutes. For the sake of the example assume one person arrives each minute for fifteen minutes. But also assume the reception process takes 1:06 minutes per person. Since members arrive faster than they can be processed, a line forms, and the wait times increase as shown in Figure 8.3.

Figure 8.3. Members Arrive Faster Than They Can Be Processed

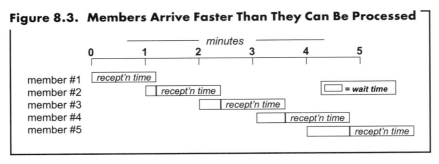

Now assume an improved reception process now takes 0:54 seconds per person (see Figure 8.4). Each arriving member is served immediately, there is no wait time, and six seconds becomes available to the service provider.

So while this example is oversimplified (e.g., most people show up in the five minutes preceding the meeting, some members are prepaid and can skip the payment step), it does show the degree to which a small improvement in process time can have a great impact. In reality the model showed us the complexity of managing a three-step process with multiple possible flows and a wide variation in processing times per step. In the sequential three-step process, the second step's per-

Figure 8.4. Members Processed Faster Than They Arrive

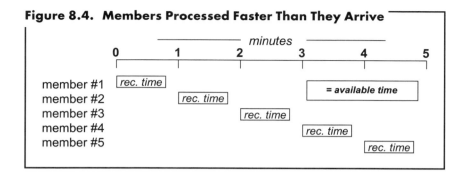

formance depends upon the first, and so forth. Plus, the differing types of members (e.g., new enrollees and current members) and the additional routings (lifetime and prepaid members) increase the variation and complexity.

Fortunately, the simulation model has a way of making the complexity manageable. Once built and shown to be accurate with the current process, the model allowed us to alter process times and see the impact. We then knew how much time we had to shave off of each step or what would happen if we eliminated a step.

Design a New Way

We found a few very simple changes could have a huge impact.

The first was to have the customer do some of the work. In this case the members could retrieve their own card. There was no need to have a dedicated receptionist pulling each member's card and handing it off to the member. We found that the act of finding and pulling the card was twice as fast as making the payment. So, the card puller was already inactive half the time, and the time they were active did not add any value. We also found that the members were twice as fast as the card puller in finding their card anyway (probably because a member knows their name, how to spell it, and where to find it quickly in an alphabetical listing). So we suggested that the box of cards be placed out in front of the desk, so the member could retrieve their own card while in line—if there was a line. This combination self-service process would free up one service provider to either assist with collecting the payments or assist with weigh-in, or not come in at all. The correct answer was "all of the above." We needed some of the freed up capacity to assist with processing to keep the lines down, but not all of it. So we were also able to change the staffing plan and have a lower staff-to-member ratio for various meeting sizes than previously possible—and still provide a better service experience than previously possible.

But we had to make some other changes as well. A two-step process (pay and then weigh) was still undesirable. We looked at combining the steps into one stop. The one-stop "pay-and-weigh" process is greatly simplified and, even with a high variability in the processing time, the performance at one step does not impact another step (downstream or upstream).

The basic one-step process is depicted in Figure 8.5.

Figure 8.5. One-Step Check-In Process

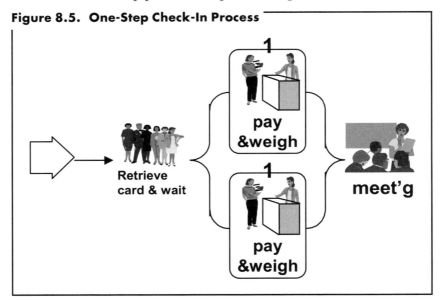

With a one-step process, the wait times can be dramatically reduced. There would be 87 percent less wait time on average for current members and 66 percent less wait time for new enrollees.

So while the one-step process has the longest processing times (with the combined steps), the one-step process has the shortest wait times. There is no idle time on the part of the service providers at the pay-and-weigh stations until the members have all been processed.

Realize Benefits

In summary, the new approach could be applied to a number of meetings in certain locations with the appropriate attendance levels. For those locations, the surgical strike of having customers retrieve their own cards, combined with the surgical strike of "eliminating sequential processing" by creating a one-stop process, enabled significantly better service for the customer (less waiting in line, more attention at weigh-in, meetings start on time with fewer interruptions). The new process also enabled the employees to focus more time on value-added work (weigh-in and counseling with customers), and less on administrative tasks.

Years later, Judy Donnenfeld mentioned that "members still pull their own cards and many locations still use the one-step weigh-in process. So those solutions have stood the test of time."

So for years Weight Watchers was able to handle more members per meeting with same staff. In other words, they were able to lower staffing-per-member ratios and save money. Again, this drive for cost-effective performance was driven as much by customers as their parent corporation. Lower costs enable lower prices. The price of admission to a Weight Watchers meeting is intentionally low so as to help as many people as possible. This is a business with passion and purpose beyond the dollar.

Technology-Enabled Self-Service

I deliberately wanted to emphasize a low-tech example of work being done by the customer instead of the company. At Weight Watchers, having the customer obtain their own card before approaching the service provider was simple and relatively easy to roll out across multiple locations throughout the world. There was no dependence upon technology.

All too often high-tech solutions end up as high-cost pipe dreams that take too long to build and too long for customers to accept and use. However, like the ATM, there are some great examples of technology that enables the customer to do work previously done by companies' employees. Most I would not consider a surgical strike in that they don't meet the definition of low-cost, low-risk targeted actions, and are more likely to represent more sweeping process design projects and slow customer acceptance.

However, as the cost of technology continues to decline, and the publics' readiness increases to adopt new technologies, the technology-based surgical strikes become more likely. This trend toward more technology-based customer self-service was highlighted in *Newsweek*, along with the emphasis on creative use of existing technologies—not radical new inventions: "Companies are always looking just over the horizon for the next great innovation. But often the best ideas come from a smart new spin on devices that are right under our noses—like checkout scanners and magnetic-card readers—that can change many routines of life. Think of it as the lagging edge of technology."[3]

Unfortunately the article went on to describe how slowly customers adopt and use the new technologies:

> It's a slow process: research showed that it often took seven years from the time a company began installing a high-tech innovation—like a fancy database that disburses customer information throughout a company—to the time it began to pay dividends.
>
> Banks placed the first ATMs inside branches, eliminating their best feature (24/7 access); once inside, customers went straight to tellers. . . . But labor-cost reductions have proved elusive, partly because even today, 15 percent of customers still don't use ATMs.
>
> The same slow cycle has played out at gas stations. . . . It took more than 20 years for the self-service gas station to catch on.

The article also suggested that sometimes it's not the customers that are slow to adapt; it is the corporation holding back.

> [B]y the 1980s the gasoline companies had another potential breakthrough: computerized "pay at the pump" systems that would let folks use credit cards to buy gasoline without ever entering the gas station's office. That technology worked just fine, but gas companies proceeded very slowly. After all, if

> people could avoid going inside, they wouldn't buy the coffee, cigarettes and gum that are key to many stations' profits. Even so, Mobil—now ExxonMobil—plunged ahead, and sales inside its stores actually increased as shorter lines made more people willing to shop. "It drove more business into the store who knew?" says ExxonMobil executive Mike Goldberg. But the slow rollout meant the devices didn't fully catch on until the mid-1990s.

So while there is a lot of evidence that technology-enabled self-service can reap big benefits, the odds of a reasonably inexpensive and quick "surgical strike" are long to say the least.

Hire Some Help

Another option for shifting work out of your organization is to hire some other company to do it—in other words, outsource it. And sometimes it can be done rather quickly—a matter of a few months. The trick is to outsource work that someone else can do better and more efficiently, and work that is not a part of your company's core competency. For nearly any company candidates for outsourcing might include, hardware, software, services, human resources functions, financial and administrative activities, strategic procurement, report generation, benefit administration, and payment systems. For some product development oriented companies (in pharmaceuticals, software, and electronics) the actual manufacturing is something best left to others. Likewise for customer care operations with some technology driven companies (telecom, cable television, and computers products), their focus is on designing, marketing, installing, but not necessarily handling direct customer contacts.

One caution—you need an organization with which you can work seamlessly. If outsourcing is not well managed, the hand-offs of work and information can create huge problems—more than offsetting the initially perceived benefits of outsourcing. But more about this in Chapter 11, "Strike 8: Link and Learn—Unclog the Flows of Knowledge."

So why would it ever make sense to outsource? Simply because there are tasks that others are better equipped to handle from both a capacity and a capability perspective.

Let's think about how contract manufacturers make money, even with their promise to do it cheaper than their clients can. Basically, a contract manufacturer can buy a sophisticated specialized piece of equipment and/or specialized skilled labor, and use it to process work for multiple client companies. Therefore they keep the people and equipment utilized and get better skilled at using the equipment. Conversely, a client company might use the same equipment infrequently and never get good at it or not buy the equipment at all.

Business Week described how a contract manufacturer in the computer industry could "invest in a $1 million vibration chamber for making sure industrial gear can take a good shaking. Such equipment can help the contract manufacturer meet its customers' marketing promises and avoid costly returns in case the gear isn't up to snuff."[4]

So not only are there efficiencies to be gained by using an outsourcers' capacity, but the outsourcers may have capabilities that are way too expensive to be justified solely for in-house use.

Hire a Builder

One of the biggest successes in recent years has been the growth of contract manufacturers in the electronics industry. Companies like Flextronics, Jabil Circuit, Inc., Celestica, Inc., and Solectron build circuit boards and final assembles for major brands, such as: IBM, HP, Cisco, Erikson, Nokia, and Mitsubishi. They get the work, not simply because they are more efficient, but because they are also flexible and responsive.

The Wall Street Journal described the cost efficiency of these contract manufacturers, with Selectron as the example:[5]

> **By keeping assembly lines running twenty-four hours a day, Solectron spreads the costs of its buildings and machines across more products. As a $3 billion-a-year purchaser of electronic components, Solectron gets low prices and precisely scheduled**

> deliveries that minimize inventory. Every efficiency
> and every expense is meticulously recorded; profits
> are tracked weekly for the entire company. "We
> measure the hell out of things," says Jim Daly, man-
> ager of the complex-systems division.
>
> It has to. Solectron operates on much thinner
> profit margins than its customers do. On average, it
> spends almost 90 cents to make products it sells for
> $1, compared with 66 cents for HP and 35 cents for
> Cisco. It relies on high volume and low overhead.
> "If they can build a unit and charge us $5, it may
> cost them $4.80," HP's Mr. Faraci says. "But they
> turn it over so many times a month that it's a good
> deal for them."

The article goes on to stress the importance of the company-to-company relationship, including the importance of Solectron's proximity (5,600 employees in California) to Terayon (at the time, a start-up cable modem company), in the outsourcing arrangement:

> To manage growth, Solectron often turns away
> business. Its executives say they choose clients care-
> fully because of the effort they put into each rela-
> tionship. For Terayon, that means daily huddles
> with some or all of the eight Solectron managers on
> the account. Solectron employees know Terayon's
> production schedule, revenue targets and plans for
> new modems.
>
> For a young company still learning its business
> and tweaking its designs, the help is more valuable
> than any savings from manufacturing overseas,
> says Dennis Picker, Terayon's COO. "We might be
> able to get a slightly better price in Asia," he says,
> "but the proximity is worth its weight in gold."

Hire a "Backroom"

Financial service companies hire firms to do all kinds of backroom processing. For example, according to their Web site, Fiserv provides nearly all the operations support a bank could need:[6]

> **The Fiserv Custom Outsourcing Solution is a custom-tailored suite of information technology systems and services for financial institutions that is offered through a single-provider relationship.**
>
> **The Fiserv Custom Outsourcing Solution combines a set of solid, efficient core accounting systems with a flexible selection of advanced technologies that enhance your customer relationship management, contact and experience management, service delivery, e-commerce activities, channel integration, branch and platform automation, back office operations, and enterprise-wide data warehousing.**
>
> **Our solution can also include a variety of related services such as Web design, production and hosting, item and EFT processing, bill payment operations, plastic card fulfillment, lease servicing, and a broad range of deployment, training, and consulting services.**
>
> **For our largest client, we process the work of 577 branches and 3.3 million accounts on a daily basis.**

So you might ask, as we did when working with a bank similar to their largest client, what's left for the client bank to do? In a sense not much is left for the client to do, at least in terms of operations. In such cases, their core competency is viewed as marketing and enlisting prospective customers for banking services. Once a prospective customer submits an application for a bank account and/or loan, the service bureau such as Fiserv or PNC Financial Services Group, Inc. takes over the processing of the work. However, these are the extreme cases.

In many other instances these service bureaus can perform your back-room processing for one product or one portion of the backroom proc-ess. It's not all or nothing.

So How Significant Can a "Backroom" Outsourcing Strike Be?

We recently worked with an emerging national bank that found a sur-gical strike in outsourcing the processing of home equity loans. While home equity loans were not the core of their current business, it was already a little out of control. There were too many people involved, too many specialists and hand-offs, and the loan applications took too long to accept or reject.

The bank could either straighten out the process itself, or simply hire a service bureau to do the work. Given their immediate strategies, other priorities and initiatives, it was determined that an outsourcing solution made sense. They really couldn't devote enough attention to the home equity loan area this year, and it needed attention. The ser-vice bureau had already figured out the home equity loan process and had a lot of volume in it. Adding this bank's volume would be rela-tively simple.

For the bank, waiting would only make things worse. The home equity loan business was forecast to grow to be a significant piece of business. In four years they forecast a need for nearly 500 people to handle the workload from home equity loans.

Table 8.1 is one small portion of the cost-benefit summary that went into their decision making. It suggests a major saving, not from the outsourcing of handling applications, but from handling the servicing of the loans over time as the customer base builds.

So while they could save over 12 million dollars in their fourth year of the outsourced operation, the surgical strike for the short term (this year) would amount to just over a million dollars—still a significant strike for them at this stage of their growth.

Hire a Care Provider

Customer care activities are points of contact between a company and its customers. (The top band in one of our process maps represents

Table 8.1. In-House Versus Outsourcing Costs for a Bank's Home Equity Loan Process

	In-House FTEs	Total Cost	Acquisition Cost per Origination	Servicing Costs per Average Loan
YEAR 4 PROJECTIONS				
In-House Solution	500	$32,000K	$190	$120
Outsourcing Solution	100	$20,000K	$260	$ 20
Difference	− 400	− $12,000K	+ $ 70	− $100

these points of customer contact.) Everywhere the customer comes in contact with the company is an experience for the customer—good, bad, or indifferent. In our core process view, the customer participates in the customer acquisition process (marketing, sales), the order fulfillment process (order taking, distribution, and installation), plus all the after-sales service encounters (requests for information, status, questions, problems resolution, service inquiries, billing inquiries, and complaints).

An IDC study showed customer care to be a top priority (in this case for technology companies). They said that 46 percent of respondents to their survey ranked customer care "as one of their top three concerns, including 11 percent who ranked it as their top concern."[7]

Many companies in many industries that share this concern have come to the conclusion that the handling of their customer contacts (phone, mail, Web) can best be done by others with expertise and a dedicated focus on customer care. A Jupitermedia Corporation report states:[8]

> Domestic outsourcing [of customer care] continues to increase, particularly in the telecommunications, financial services, and high-tech sectors. The largest domestic outsourcers by revenue (i.e., Convergys, TeleTech, and West Communications) reported combined revenues of more than $1 billion in the first quarter of 2001. Most of the largest outsourcers re-

ported at least a 20 percent growth in revenues
over the same period in 2000.

IDC studies have forecast continued growth in customer-care-services outsourcing. According to Brian Bingham, Manager of CRM & Customer Care research, "The ideal of improved customer relationships is one of the key drivers behind the rapidly growing customer interaction services marketplace." IDC expects this market to grow by nearly 19 percent compounded annually between the period of 2001–2006.

So why is outsourcing of customer care so popular? The reasons are basically three and probably in this order: (1) cost reduction; (2) superior customer service; and (3) flexibility (outsourcer is better able to ramp up fast, and/or adjust to workload fluctuations). We saw a specific example of the potential benefits of customer care outsourcing in the previous chapter where TeleTech looked at the potential of saving over 17 percent of the customer care costs for a leading financial services company. The Jupitermedia Corporation study suggests this kind of savings is in the ballpark of the typical opportunity: "Cost reductions are driving increases in outsourcing; Jupiter estimates that large contact centers handling 300,000 inbound customer contacts each month can save $2 million, or 15 percent annually, by outsourcing their support operations entirely; their trade-off is a lack of control over daily operations."[9]

Regarding lack of control, mostly there is legitimate concern about who is talking to the customer, and how well they will represent the company. Here is where the best outsourcers shine. Their agents are hired, trained, and compensated on the basis of efficient and superior service. Just a few anecdotes of bad customer experiences with an outsourcer can jeopardize a mutually beneficial relationship.

Having the right people saying the right things is critical. Marilyn Spittle and Humberto Trueba from the Human Resource Department at TeleTech state in a CommWeb article, "Implementing guidelines on hiring, training, retention and compensation of agents is a key element in outsourcing your customer service." The ultimate impact is made when "the customer who calls customer service and gets an able agent, believes completely that he is talking with your company. The best agents in the marketplace are the ones that are the most transparent and whose agents communicate passion, energy, accountability, and enthusiasm for the uniqueness of the client they represent. In fact, when those customer service reps are interviewed, they invariably say that they feel the customers they interact with really are their clients."[10]

Pay for Performance . . .

Customer care outsourcing companies typically get paid for handling calls (pay-per-call), or providing the staff to handle calls (per-minute fees or agent-hour fees). The contracts become quite complex with minimum monthly fees regardless of call volumes, and ways to increase rates if calls become more complex (therefore requiring more call time and more agent training). These fee structures do not always work in the best interests of your company.

The Jupitermedia Corporation report suggests one solution, "One way . . . to pay outsourcers [is] on a per-case or per-incident basis, which provides an incentive for outsourcers to improve their first-contact-resolution ratio by striving to satisfy customers' needs in one contact. Based on the industry average (i.e., first-contact resolution rates of 65 percent), businesses could save another 5 percent by structuring agreements on per-incident pricing."[11]

First-contact-resolution pricing and per-incident pricing schemes still have problems. Think about the cases where the majority of customer calls should not occur at all. Many calls occur because something went wrong (e.g., expectations were mismanaged, work was done improperly, products failed or were delivered late). The information that is gleaned from those calls and contacts is valuable, especially with regard to upstream process problems. Customers call when things have gone wrong. If things had not gone wrong the contact would not have occurred.

Now think about the customer care center being paid on the basis of call volume or agent hours—there's no incentive for them to help reduce calls altogether. Whether outsourced or not, the value proposition for a customer care center should encompass the ability to define the root cause of the calls and assist the organization in reducing call volumes, through fixing the upstream process failures. The value proposition should be in lowering total service costs per customer, whether that customer is actually served or not. In other words, one big value of customer care operations is in the capture and use of information to strive for flawless service delivery in the first place.

The next logical extension of promoting the value of service/support in this manner is to pay for services in this manner. This approach could work much like the way doctors are paid fixed capitation rates for prospective patients, whether they actually become patients or not. A customer care center (in-house or outsourced) could promote and price their services on the basis of cost per customer (whether they interact or not). This payment scheme encourages the customer care center to continuously help the overall corporation improve its operations and service delivery processes based on knowledge gained from customer contact. Also, since the customer care center will be paid on the basis of the entire customer base, there is great incentive to help the overall corporation drive acquisition, retention, and referrals—while driving down the number of service recovery contacts.

So while customer care firms such as TeleTech can provide great value because they are so good at what they do, there is one caution: Make sure they have a role and an incentive to help you eliminate the calls and contacts that should not happen at all. (See Chapter 11, "Strike 8: Link and Learn—Unclog the Flows of Knowledge.")

Fire the Intermediaries

On one hand I just described opportunities to improve process performance by hiring an intermediary; on the other hand, I will suggest just the opposite. While at first glance this appears contradictory, it isn't. There are situations where each approach is called for, even desirable—even simultaneously within one company. For instance, there are many companies whose products and services can be ordered directly over the Web. However, those same companies recognize some customers prefer phone or face-to-face contact. Therefore they provide the means for customers to exercise their preference, including hiring intermediaries to handle phone contacts while at the same time trying to eliminate intermediaries through the use of the Web.

Other companies have gotten very aggressive about eliminating intermediaries altogether, or at least no longer paying them as their agents. For example, the airlines have all but eliminated any compensation to travel agents for the booking of domestic flights. Since the agent is no longer valued by the airlines, it is now up to the passenger to decide what value, if any, a travel agent provides.

Here is what appears to be a classic surgical strike. The airlines just up-and-did-it: cut payments to travel agents. When it worked, they did it again and again, until the payments went to zero. However, the reason they were able do it is that the airlines have spent years getting their infrastructure ready to handle the order taking by themselves (their own call centers, their own Web sites, the industry Web site— Orbitz.com). So given a state of readiness, it was a surgical strike to cut the payments. But if you view the cost reduction effort as encompassing the preparation required, it was hardly a small, targeted action with a rapid and big result. It was a huge complicated undertaking over an extended period of time—with a big result.

In any case, the point is to consider the opportunity to eliminate the need for intermediaries (Figure 8.6). Consider the question: Are there opportunities in your organization to bypass the usual conduits to the customer?

Figure 8.6. Eliminate the Middleman

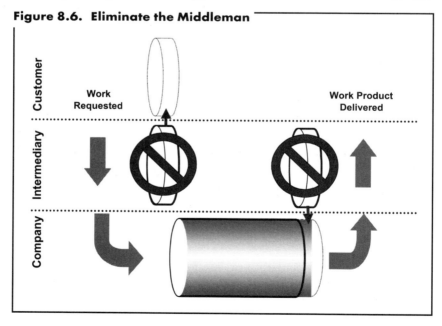

In your consideration of the question, you will wonder if it will work. What would it take to make it work? What are the risks? What are the benefits? In thinking about benefits, it goes beyond just compensation to agents and intermediaries. Intermediaries create the potential for miscommunication, process delays, even mischief.

Speaking of mischief, in the case of one insurance company with which we worked some years ago, some of their agents began issuing their own insurance-coverage cards (credit-card size to carry in a wallet) with their name and logo alongside the insurance company's logo. For the agents to issue coverage cards on behalf of the insurance company was not only a problem with the company, it was illegal. But rather than prosecute, the company looked at the rationale. In essence the customers were covered by the paperwork but did not feel comfortable without the card. Initially customers were told by the agents to wait for the company to provide the cards to the agent, and that they would in turn provide them to the customer. They put pressure on the agent for some kind of card they could put in their wallet. After badgering the insurance company to provide the cards faster, they gave up and did it themselves. So the root cause was really the slow, inefficient process by which the insurance company produced and delivered the cards. So here's a case where the insurance company's confused and slow process contributed to additional needless work on the part of an intermediary, and ultimately needless aggravation and confusion on the part of the customer. In this case, they fixed their card production process and began delivering rapidly—and directly to the customer—bypassing the intermediaries.

No Middleman, No Mess

So a surgical strike also may be found in redistributing the work from an intermediary or supplier back into your organization (a la "vertical integration"). It depends upon circumstances and your strategy.

In our Process Redesign Game, we start Round One with thirteen employees, one of which has the title "customer service manager." That person's job is to take the order *from* the customer and give it to the operations manager, and then deliver the completed order *to* the customer. They are an intermediary between the company and the customer—all work and information between these two parties flows through the customer service manager.

As mentioned before, in Round One the customer is annoyed with poor delivery (the orders are unfilled), poor quality (phones that are delivered are defective), and poor service (the process is in such a state of confusion the customer can't get the attention of their customer service manager). But as the game progresses through Round Two, quality and delivery improve dramatically and the service is responsive. There is even time for dialogue about forthcoming orders, constructive communication about the few remaining quality problems, and the potential for more work.

Typically by Round Three the customer service manager's distinct intermediary role is eliminated. Sometimes the participants in the game rearrange the tables so the final assembly table touches the customer's table. The order is taken and delivered without an intermediary, no manager, and no material handler. Perhaps more important, if there is a quality problem, there is direct and immediate communication from the customer to those who are completing the assembly. Problem phones are identified quickly, the root causes identified, and corrective actions taken before many more problem phones are created.

Removing the intermediary role ends up by improving all dimensions of performance in the game: quality, delivery, cycle time, and cost.

Strike 5: Redistribute the Work

Strike 5 actions typically encompass:

- Enabling customers to perform activities previously performed by the company
- Outsourcing non-strategic work to third party vendors
- Eliminating agents and other conduits to your customers
  —Remove agents from the business model entirely, or
  —Bypass the agent/intermediaries for a portion of the process, or for some key interfaces with the customer

Strike 5 starts with an understanding of the company's strategic intent and process flows, then a review of the work redistribution options, and selection of those changes with the greatest benefit (relative to implementation costs and day-to-day operating costs). The typical Strike 5 opportunity entails the following steps:

- Review your process profiles (e.g., core process definitions and process maps).

- Assess activities that you do that might be performed by customers.

- Assess and define what processes and activities are core to your business strategy.

- Consider as candidates for outsourcing those processes and activities that you do but are not core to your business mission.

- Consider as candidates for bringing in-house those processes and activities that others do, but that are core to your business mission.

- Prepare an impact assessment of the options (including risks of new hand-offs).

- Develop an action plan and execute!

Strike 5, Redistribute the Work, is about capitalizing on targets of opportunity to shift work, and the related processes, to or from other organizational entities—whether it be customers, suppliers, or intermediaries.

CHAPTER 9

Strike 6: Manage Fluctuations in Work Volume

The businessperson who resists chaos will find in time his business will only grow brittle and irrelevant.
—Mel Ziegler, founder, Banana Republic Company

Have you ever gone to get your hair cut, arriving on time, only to be told you will have to wait, since "We're running behind?" You were probably caught up in a peak work situation (or it's aftermath). Recently it happened to me. When told I would have to wait over an hour, I walked out and got my haircut elsewhere. I never returned—ever. So not only did they lose the revenue from that day's haircut, they lost my business forever.

Fluctuations in work volume are inevitable, but many times these fluctuations are overlooked and/or mismanaged, leading to poor productivity and/or service performance. Rather than clip the peaks and fill the valleys with work, companies do things to exacerbate the peaks and valleys of work. Staffing levels get out of sync with the workload. Either work doesn't get done (too much work, too few staff), or the staff is idle while waiting for work (too little work, too many staff). The surgical strike is to either manage staff levels to the ebb and flow of workload, or manage the ebb and flow of workload to the staff level (Figure 9.1).

Clip the Peaks and Fill the Valleys

There are a number ways to manage fluctuations in work volume such as:

1. Expand and contract the "pipe" (e.g., staff levels) that processes the work.

2. Keep the pipe full continuously—by encouraging work to be requested during off-peak times instead of peak times.

3. Shift some activities to off-peak times.

4. Merge groups of workers when their peaks are at different times.

Figure 9.1. Increases and Decreases in Workload

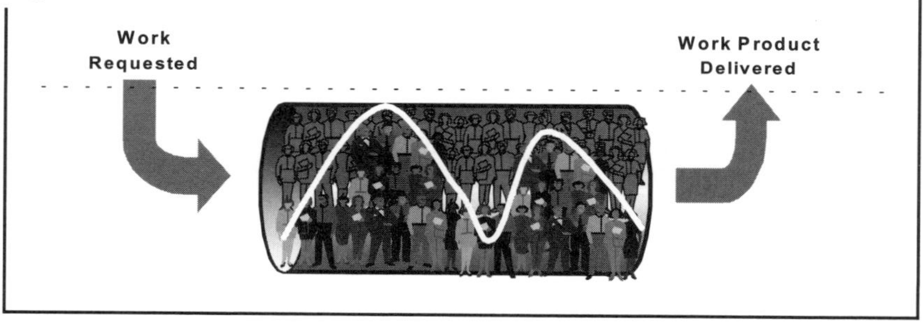

Sometimes the increases and decreases in workload are random and rapid. However, in many cases the ups and downs are cyclical and predictable. On a weekly basis, a call center may be busier on Mondays, especially if they are closed over the weekend. On a daily basis a call center may have a morning peak load, and a lesser peak in the afternoon. Other businesses have annual surges of work (H&R Block with taxes, Christmas for retailers). Many manufacturers have end-of-the-quarter spikes in shipping (typically self-induced). In any business there are times of peak workload and times where there are lulls in the action.

Many businesses use a combination of the approaches described above to best deal with surges in work volume. For instance, a well-run haircut salon staffs up for the after-work crowd (Point 1). One haircut salon has instituted 20 percent higher prices at peak, and 10 percent lower prices during off-peak times (Point 2). This pricing scheme encourages those who are more flexible to come during off-peak times. Finally, after buying a few more scissors, combs, and so forth, the cleaning of those items is now done entirely during off-peak times (Point 3), keeping the peak time focused on serving customers and cutting their hair. The intent is to handle more customers at peak time with peak pricing. The net impact was said to be a 10 percent profit increase, plus the customers were satisfied—having been served at the time promised.

Let's look at some examples of managing fluctuations in the corporate world, beginning with an example of "merging groups of workers when their peaks are at different times" (Point 4).

Twin Peaks

We worked with a leading metropolitan newspaper with a troubled classified advertising business. Nearly 10 percent of the ads had some kind of error, leading to complaints and, in many cases, reimbursed fees. The classified ad reps took the ads over the phone, and their performance at getting the advertisements right in the first place had not changed for years.

We began an investigation with a cross-functional task team from the classified ad department, the proofing group, credit, and customer service. This team analyzed the workload characteristics, and developed a profile of the current process.

The workload characteristics included a profile of volumes and types of ads, volumes and types of complaints, incidents of error, types of error, and so on. The profile also included a breakdown of the workload by day of the week.

To develop the process profile, a map of the current process was created. This map, combined with the other analyses, led to a discussion of possible reengineering actions. Figure 9.2 is a simplified reproduction of parts of the map for the current classified advertising workflow that was drawn during the task team meeting. The top horizontal band, above the shading, displays customer contact with the newspaper and its classified advertising department. Below the customer contact band, there are three horizontal bands to illustrate the hand-offs within the newspaper's offices. The zigzag cut out simply means there is a section of the map that is missing—the preparation, production, and distribution processes.

Figure 9.2.

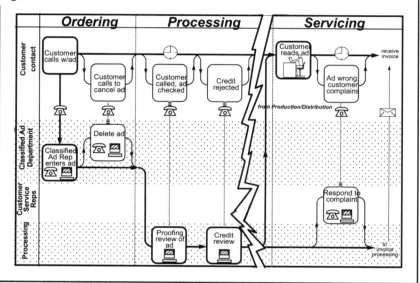

This map, the workload profile, and related discussion, brought out the shortcomings of the existing process. First, the team noticed that there was no effective feedback loop from complaints to the classified ad reps. Second, the ad reps could abdicate responsibility for the integrity of the information since they relied on the proofing group to catch and fix any errors. Third, as illustrated in Figure 9.3, the peak volume of work for the ad reps is on Thursday and the peak volume for complaints is on Monday.

So the typical scenario was that the classified ad reps would be swamped with calls on Thursday and Friday. They would rush through the calls, making more errors than they would earlier in the week. At the same time the customer service reps would be nearly idle, after spending the first half of the week swamped with complaints and problem solving for the ads placed over the previous weekend. In both cases customer service suffered at the peak times when there was more volume than the reps could handle.

Figure 9.3. Respective Work Volumes for Placing Ads and Calling with Complaints

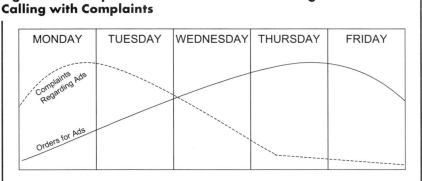

The surgical strike was to merge all the activities related to the entire life cycle of a classified ad. The new classified ad group would be responsible for proofing (and credit check), plus hear the complaints and be responsible for understanding and correcting the root causes of their problems. Also, such a merger would effectively balance the workload throughout the week.

In other words, not only would a merging of the functions lead to an improvement in ad accuracy and timeliness, but the workload could be handled by fewer people in total. The classified ad and customer service departments were staffed to nearly handle their peaks in volume with some significant idle time during the rest of the week. To make the example simple, lets just look at the ad rep and customer service functions. Assume there were ten people taking the ads and four people handling the complaints. The ten people taking the ads were not quite enough on Thursdays, but as much as four people too many for the workload on Monday through Wednesday. Likewise the four people handling the complaints were short handed on Mondays, but over-staffed for the rest of the week. By merging the groups only ten people would be needed, not the fourteen currently employed, to provide the same level of service. However, by initially having eleven or twelve people available, the Thursday peak load could be handled leading to fewer errors made in the first place, and providing time for root cause analysis and corrective actions to be taken.

Over time, the ability to get the ad copy right in the first place (with new tools and training), combined with attrition, would enable a reduction to eight people in the group, a $\cong 40$ percent reduction in staff with an 90 percent reduction in errors!

Why Exacerbate Peak Loads?

In other cases it makes sense to shift the work rather than shift the workers. In a leading telecommunications company, one call center operation was buried in calls every morning. To their credit, they were more interested in rewarding "call closure" than call time. However, in this case we found a sole emphasis on call closure may not be in the best interest of the company or the customer.

Let's look at the details as originally described in my *Quality Progress* magazine article.[1] A study by my colleague Chuck Malovrh showed the peak in incoming call volume was twice as high in the morning as it was in the late afternoon. As depicted in Figure 9.4, upon closer inspection it was found that the peak load occurred during the first two hours of the morning.

Line 1 at the bottom shows that work in process, in this case calls waiting, could be kept to a minimum. A combination of available specialists (Line 2) and associates (Line 3) shows a peak load (Line 4) in the opening minutes of the day.

Figure 9.4. Staff Required to Keep Up with Workload

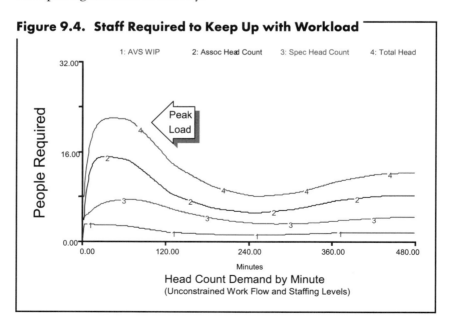

So to provide the same service levels throughout the day, more staff is needed in the early morning hours than during the rest of the day. Unfortunately, hiring good part-time help for two hours per day was not practical. The job required more skills than could be effectively learned in a mere two hours per day, even with advanced training.

The company found itself in a tough situation. It wanted to minimize its head count requirements and level the load of work. At the same time, it did not want to sacrifice service levels or dissatisfy its customers.

Again, a detailed analysis of calls was required. The calls were classified by customer, type of call, duration of call, and so on. It was found that for some customers, and some types of calls, a callback or fax with information later in the day was not only acceptable but desirable.

The dynamic simulation model was put together to test the new policy idea. The new policy said that, for certain calls during the first two hours of the morning, the procedure would be to accept the inquiry but provide the answer later. So while the number of calls would remain the same, time for calls would lessen during the peak hours of the day. The new policy enabled a flat staffing level (Figure 9.5).

However, there was a trade-off, as depicted in Figure 9.6. The number of pending calls could be expected to grow until the peak during the mid-morning. Fortunately, upon closer inspection of the model, very few calls would be left on hold longer than the desired service level.

The surgical strike was to change the first time call closure policy and allow some callbacks at an off-peak time (Point 3). The mantra, measure, and culture of "first time call closure" would need to change—at least for two hours per day. The net impact was a reduction in staffing level from twenty-three to fourteen people, a $\cong 40$ percent reduction!

Level the Workload

A simple profile of the workload along a timeline can be very powerful, not so much in providing the answers, but in providing the right questions. For example, look at the day-by-day changes in volume of work over the course of one month. Figure 9.7 shows that there is a clear pattern repeated each week.

Figure 9.5. Shows the Impact of This Policy on Staffing

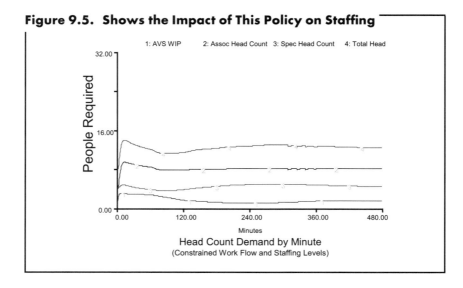

Head Count Demand by Minute
(Constrained Work Flow and Staffing Levels)

Figure 9.6. Peak Acceptable Work Queues

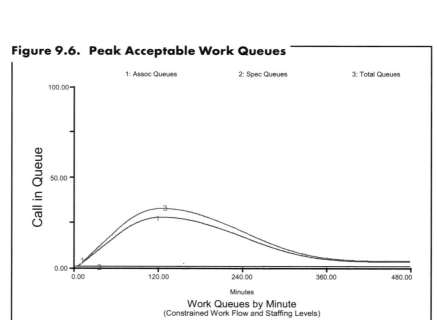

Work Queues by Minute
(Constrained Work Flow and Staffing Levels)

Figure 9.7. One-Month Profile of Work Volume by Day

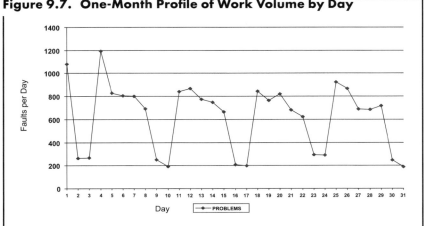

In this case we were working with the information technology department of a leading telecom company. A huge portion of the job for more than 800 people entailed installing changes to the software and hardware over the weekend, and then fixing the hundreds of "faults" that occurred during the week, most of which occurred early in the week. To make matters worse, the faults that occurred on Monday and Tuesday tended to be the most urgent and the most difficult. In other words, more labor hours were required per fault for those faults that occurred and were corrected on Mondays and Tuesdays.

So fault volumes and related labor requirements fluctuated significantly (and predictably) while available FTEs remained flat. The net impact was that on average 30 percent of the fault labor appeared to be unutilized (based on an average number of faults/day x time/fault). However, the 30 percent (or 247 FTEs) unutilized capacity is consumed during the peak load days. See Figure 9.8.

Again, a cross-functional team determined that a redesign of the business processes could free up as many as 247 FTEs through "level loading" of work and productive use of off-peak time.

The surgical strike was to level load the work (Point 2). Some changes could be done on Wednesday night, instead of over the weekend. Any faults that occurred would show up and be fixed during Thursday and Friday—previously underutilized days.

However, to start, the recommendation was to reschedule and rebalance the changes and related faults—but not reduce the staff by a

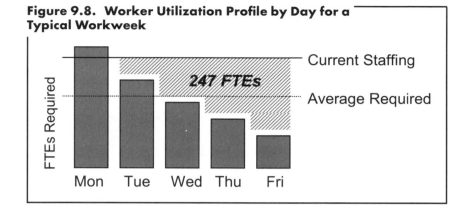

Figure 9.8. Worker Utilization Profile by Day for a Typical Workweek

corresponding percentage. Instead of cutting out all 247 (30 percent of the staff), the intent was to start with half that and use the additional capacity to eliminate the root cause of faults in the first place. An investment of 10–15 percent of the capacity in root cause analyses and fixes today, would lead to a 40–50 percent savings in the long run.

The Appearance of Flexibility, the Reality of Efficiency

In our Process Redesign Game, the customer issues one order every minute. The order quantity can vary from two phones to eleven phones—a huge fluctuation in work volume from minute to minute. To make matters worse, the fluctuation is random. There is no cyclical pattern.

In Round One, there are some groups who attempt to build-to-order. They take the order to Workstation 1 and attempt to push the order through the process. It doesn't work. Very few orders are delivered—and none on time.

By Round Two all the groups figure out the way to succeed is not to build-to-order. Rather they build to meet a longer-term commitment, and put a process in place to also meet the demanding fluctuations in volume. So first they understand that the customer commits to ordering sixty phone units over the course of ten minutes in quantities ranging from two to eleven per order. Then they design the process to steadily produce at least six phones per minute (plus they start each round of the game with five units of work-in-process).

Now as each order is received from the customer, the finished units are "picked and packed" from Workstation 5, the last step in the process. So the fluctuations in order volume now become irrelevant to the process. The workflow and volumes are level and steady throughout the ten-minute round for everyone in the process, except the one person who picks and packs the order for delivery to the customer.

So here is a case where product-oriented businesses have an option that many service businesses do not. They can level the workload, and maximize the utilization of labor, equipment, and space, and still meet the demands of fluctuating order volumes. However, as we all learned with the just-in-time movement, the trick is not to build-to-stock, but rather build-to-order—in this case to the overall customer commitment for the round, not the minute-by-minute demand.

Strike 6: Manage Fluctuations in Work Volume

Strike 6 is about recognizing the inevitable peaks and valleys in work volume, and doing something about it.

Strike 6 primarily starts with facts and data about the volumes and types of workload profiled over time. The time span could be a day, a week, a month, a quarter, or a year, or some combination; whichever time horizon is most significant to highlighting the swings in work volume.

Strike 6 actions typically encompass:

- Expanding and contracting the pipe (staff levels) that processes the work
- Keeping the pipe full continuously
  - —By encouraging work to be requested during off-peak times instead of peak times
  - —By building product at a steady pace to meet longer term demands (and hopefully commitments), rather than day-to-day demands
- Shifting some activities to off-peak times, or
- Merging groups of workers when their peaks are at different times

Strike 6 is about understanding the impact of peaks and valleys of work volume, and then pinpointing targets of opportunity within businesses to clip the peaks of work volume and fill the valleys with productive work.

CHAPTER 10

STRIKE 7: FOCUS THE FLOWS

To do two things at once is to do neither.
—PUBLILIUS SYRUS, FIRST CENTURY B.C.

I sn't it nice that supermarkets have a "10 items or less" line, so you don't get stuck behind someone with one hundred items or more? Isn't it nice when the Department of Motor Vehicles allows you to renew your car registration by mail, phone, or Internet, instead of in person? Here are cases where the simple transactions are put on a designated fast track, and the more difficult transactions are handled on a separate track.

Isn't it nice when you call your health coverage company and they know about the doctors in your area; they know about the local regulations and coverage plans? Sometimes these companies have teams dedicated to serving geographic regions of the country.

Wouldn't it be nice to call the information technology department in your company with an enhancement idea and not get the runaround? Instead of excuses, wouldn't it be nice to get a solutioncentric team that has all the resources (people and equipment) to spec out, develop, and deliver your desired solution rapidly?

In all of these cases, the flows of work are focused—focused on complete and rapid delivery of the desired service. The common theme is that work is segmented into a few key types of work, and distinct processes are put in place to excel at processing each type. Like hot and cold water, there are separate pipes to "focus the flows" (Figure 10.1).

Figure 10.1. Focus the Flows

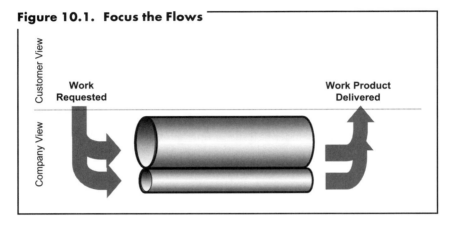

The surgical strike is to clearly distinguish a few key types of work, then develop, and establish clear distinct process flows for each type.

There are many ways to slice and dice the workload. But for the purpose of focusing the flows, the predominant distinctions seem to be made based upon the following:

- Degree of difficulty: Fast, easy-to-process work versus slow, difficult, customized work

- Geography: support and service requirements sometimes vary because of climate, laws/regulations, and/or population densities

- Segment: Focused processes can sometimes better serve distinct products and/or customer segments

Slow-Track Versus Fast-Track Work

Think about that supermarket checkout line. If you have only a few items, but get behind a person with over a hundred items, you will have to wait a long time. However, if you are in the "10 items or less" line with only a few people in front of you, your fast-to-process checkout is not slowed down by a long-to-process checkout. (You would have to be behind many people to equal the delay of being behind the one person with a hundred items.) The same is true in the corporate environment—segregating slow from fast work improves workflow efficiency, effectiveness, and, in many cases, the customer experience with both types of work.

Rapid Review and Response

In one case, we worked with a leading medical device manufacturer. Their delicate little devices are used in surgery. Since product failure in this industry can lead to serious injury or death, the FDA closely monitors medical device manufacturers, and all product inquiries, complaints, and product returns (even minor) are subject to stringent federal regulations. This company had grown to the point that it had a small department that received and handled over a thousand product inquiries, complaints, and returns per year. Although it sounds like a lot, as a percentage of units shipped these complaints are statistically insignificant (.0005 percent). However, because of their impact on human lives and potential penalties for noncompliance with FDA regulations, the product complaint process is essential to the company's long-term stability and growth objectives.

The company needed a product complaint process that would guarantee a response to each complaint within the federally mandated time frame (thirty days), and ideally full resolution within that same time. This task was made more difficult because of the range of complexity within the 1,200 complaints. Even so, labor times per complaint were relatively low (from two to twenty person-hours depending upon the type of complaint) while elapsed time to resolution for nearly all complaints exceeded ninety days.

Without getting into details, it was found that there were three types of complaints—with some *requiring* much more work than others, yet all were directed through nearly the same process anyway. For example, in many cases a returned product that did not need to be decontaminated and tested (e.g., still in original package) was decontaminated and tested anyway.

The elapsed time, from initial receipt until "case closed" (90+ days), to process simple complaints was taking as long as the difficult complaints. Simple complaints went in line with everything else and waited their turn for processing—basically a first-in first-out system.

An analysis of the workload and subsequent new process design created three distinct streamlined processes with a fast track, medium track, and slow track. A slow track was designed for returns requiring testing and extensive investigation, roughly 10 percent of the workload. A medium track was designed for returns and complaints requiring some tests to be performed, roughly 50 percent of the workload. And a fast track for 40 percent of the workload was put in place for inquiries and complaints for which no test or investigation was required.

The new design called for dramatically reduced average elapsed times from submission to resolution. The combination of focused flows, along with reduced steps and time, enabled a three-day turnaround on the fast track, a fifteen-day turnaround on the medium track, and a twenty-five-day turnaround on the slow track, all greatly improving upon the ninety-plus-day turnaround time on the old process.

Fast-Tracking Software Services

A number of years ago within a leading telephone company, the software service and support organization had to reengineer themselves to better meet the needs of their customers, the product managers. The product managers were responsible for new products/services such as the ability to charge reduced rates for special conditions (like MCI's Friends and Families program at the time).

The division manager believed the business improvement craze of the 1990s, process reengineering, could help turn around their software services group, where change requests took too long, cost was too much, and customer focus could only be categorized as blurred. "Rapid delivery of new products and services is very crucial to our company's competitive position," the division manager explained. "Our internal customers are Product Managers and our job is to support them by providing consultative and system enhancement services. When they identify a new product or service based on market interests, Software Services assesses the technical feasibility, cost, and implementation time of the idea. If the idea evolves into a product or service, Software Services is responsible for developing or changing code, testing it, and producing the methods and procedures from which people delivering the new service operate. If we can't make the necessary changes, or can't make them within the time frame our customer demands, both our ability to give customers what they want and our time to market suffers. This situation results in lost customers and a weakening of our competitive capabilities."

The division manager put a reengineering team together and asked them to clearly define a mission and project scope for redesigning software services, which employed nearly 1,200 people. She was confident the process needed to be redesigned for three basic reasons: (1) a software change took too long to implement; (2) the procedure for making changes was ambiguous, making changes difficult to process; and (3) the number of product/service ideas and related software changes desired by their customers exceeded capacity. Software services faced up to their internal problems, decided it was time to reevaluate the way they were thinking about customers, processes, and people, and actually did something about it.

In the analysis phase, the redesign project team looked closely at the software group's service delivery process, beginning to end, from product management's perspective. These customers, along with intermediaries, were interviewed to determine common characteristics and delivery requirements. The team found that some product managers needed changes completed in four months, while others required a two-month turnaround time.

The redesign team also went through the tedious process of manually analyzing a sample of the change forms product managers used. "This analysis was the only way to get detailed data on how customers and work simultaneously go through the process," said a company project team member, who was responsible for analyzing workload volumes and characteristics. "Instead of looking at single variables, such as a customer's time requirement for a simple change, we captured a variety of variables from this review: customer, location, systems the change went through, cycle time, etc., . . . which during analysis could be sorted in many ways. It seems basic, but this had never been done before and it provided valuable information. All code developments or enhancements went through the same steps, whether they needed to or not. The requests could be clearly segmented by type and complexity——how many systems would be affected by a change. A large group was considered "simple" and could be processed much more quickly if they didn't get bogged down with complex work. Likewise, the more extensive or complex changes were not getting the concentrated attention they required."

The reengineered process called for self-managed teams with fifteen to twenty people who are responsible for end-to-end support for specific product managers. The teams are further aligned by the complexity of changes: simple requests go through a fast track, leaving a separate path for complex change requests. The new design contained 100 steps, reducing the number of activities necessary to deliver software changes by 60 percent. For one type of change, the average cycle time declined from 14 months to 4.5 months, which meant the ability to reduce time-to-market by 9.5 months.

While just the design portion of the telephone company's project took months, the same types of redesign projects are now possible within a matter of weeks. A small e-commerce software firm in Seattle redesigned their software development process and organization over six weeks. Working with Joe Barrett, a founder and vice president, as their project manager we convened a team of eight people from various departments to redesign the process.

Ultimately, like the telephone company, the most significant surgical strike action was to focus the flows. The team design alternative workpaths depending upon the size and complexity of the software development effort. In addition, the new design called for the developers to be organized into teams focused on the primary customer of their development work. For this e-commerce firm, this meant a "merchantcentric development team," a "consumercentric development team," and an internal capability team, as well as a small group of project managers to manage any cross-team integration issues.

In the end, the design provided a process capable of reducing unplanned work, focusing work toward a team with a clear customer, and having distinct processes within the team on which to route fast-versus slow-track work. The net impact was a capability to reduce throughput time from months to weeks for most projects, practically eliminate the most severe defects, and, with focus, develop better quality software with half the effort.

Even Television Can Fast Track

Assume a station where their share was not eroding, but where it has long ago leveled off in a lagging position. Focus groups of viewers suggest that there is nothing to clearly distinguish the station from the others in its market. More detailed research showed that viewers in this market are looking for a newscast that "scoops the competition." They are saying "the station could differentiate itself by giving viewers a hard-hitting and dynamic newscast that is aggressive about being on-the-scene first and covering the news as it happens."

Unfortunately, the station was wrapped up in a conflicting strategy and a strategy that had effectively been usurped by one of its rivals. The station was attempting to be known as "the station of record," and, as such, was intent on giving viewers a serious, professional, and businesslike newscast that provides in-depth coverage and analysis of the news. The implication was profound, especially with regard to the basic processes of the business. In many respects the processes for selecting, gathering, producing, and delivering the news for a "station of record" were ineffective for a station that could routinely "scoop the competition."

The mapping and subsequent analysis conducted by the task team demonstrated the potential to reengineer the news process with a few breakthrough improvement actions required to become the station with the newscast that "scoops the competition."

The map graphically depicted how the development of a news story became dispersed and uncoordinated. The reporter did her thing in relative isolation from the photographer, who did his thing, and the editor, who did her thing. While it always came together in the end, the picture and the words did not always match. Nor did the story always live up to its original intent.

The team discussed the "unexpected," last minute, late-breaking stories. They described how they couldn't be planned. The team went on to mention that their best people worked days and were unavailable if late stories broke before the 11 P.M. news. Yet, the team insisted that while late-breaking stories were critical, quality could not suffer. So they are left with their "second-string" players to do a first-rate job in a fraction of the time.

They decided that the solution might be found in planning for a "late breaker" every night and using the best people to staff a "late-break team." The "best people" are typically quick, flexible, self-starters, and highly competent—exactly the skills needed for a "late-break team." A time slot would be left available every night to be filled by this team.

On the new business process map this team's activities would be depicted as a separate "fast track" process flow leading directly to the newscast. In effect, the "late-break team" of best professionals would develop and operate their own rapid-response process, unencumbered by the usual delays, approvals, and so on. Other work would traverse the less intense path.

The main difference on a redrawn map of the new process is not that all the activities disappear, but that the whole job is done by one group of people. On the new map there are fewer distinctive horizontal bands, and there is less movement between the remaining bands.

The team described how in the current environment, on a typical news day, every story was equal when it came to contention for the edit booths. With the new emphasis on "scooping the competition," the team discussed how all the resources could be made available to this "late-break team" for preparing their story in the hour or so before deadline. Any other story would have to be completed before (or after) "crunch time." For example, it was determined that many human interest stories and "puff pieces" can wait if necessary and use the edit booths during an off-peak time. Even if these types of stories had to air the next day, they are not particularly time-sensitive. When the edit booths are a bottleneck, especially just before airtime, the late-break team would always have priority.

So here is a great example of how strategy drives process, and in this case the need for a fast-track process and supporting organizational structure.

Geographic Orientation

Dramatic breakthrough improvements in process performance (quality, delivery, time, and effort) can be achieved by focusing the flows of work to serve geographic regions. For example, my partner at Corporate Renaissance, John Feather, worked with the individual medical underwriting unit at Time Insurance Company, where they focused the flows and realized a variety of improvements. His article in *Quality Progress* magazine described specific improvement results such the following:[1]

- 60 percent reduction in reissuances of policies

- 50 percent increase in measured customer satisfaction ratings

- 10 percent reduction in cost per policy issued

- 80 percent reduction in process cycle time for fast track applications

- Significant increases in revenue from higher customer retention

The redesigned process had quantitative results, but perhaps more importantly the improvements were perceptible to their customers (the insurance agents) and employees. Here are some comments about the newly designed underwriting process:

A general agent in Texas: "The Texas team is so responsive. They follow up and keep on top of everything." The Texas regional sales manager: "It's worked very well. The agents really like the fact that the team is working so hard and aggressively to get their business issued." An underwriting analyst noted: "We talked about the team concept when I was in business school. It's really exciting to see how it actually works."

How were such dramatic improvements achieved? First a little background.

At the time, the principal challenge for Time's individual medical insurance business was to increase the company's effectiveness in dealing with an increasingly uncertain and changing environment where local and regional differentiation requires rapid and flexible competitive actions. This meant that the organization had to become much more nimble in identifying and taking local marketplace initiatives, while simultaneously achieving substantial improvements in operating costs and service. A critical element involved the identification and redesign of Time's key business processes so as "to simultaneously minimize cycle time and waste while providing superb quality service to policyholders and agents."

Meanwhile, it was already apparent that the individual medical underwriting department was in trouble. Policy issuance for the past two years had remained flat, unit cost was increasing, and reissuing of policies had reached an alarming 10 percent. In addition, customer calls to the help desk for application-related problems were increasing by 50 percent each year. The second vice president decided that incremental improvement would not help her operations and that radical change was needed.

A project team was formed with nine members from Time and two members from our consulting firm. This project team was charged with the tasks of developing a new process design and testing it in a pilot operation.

As part of the analysis, the project team developed a customer-segmentation analysis (needs assessment by customer type); a work-load profile (volume and mix of work); activity-value analysis (steps in the process that add value to the customer); developed design specifications (specific customer demands such as twenty-four hour turn-around) and design options (range of options used to customize the design); and then constructed a business process map, which detailed the flow of work to the customer.

Both the workload analyses and process-mapping efforts were found to be more difficult than anticipated. Each of the fifty states has different regulations. In addition, the company had a variety of contractual differences with agents, leading to differences in what needed to be delivered when.

In other words, the analyses clearly showed that the physical materials, the processes, and process timings had to be tailored to meet geographic differences. The means by which an application goes through the process—gets quoted, sold, processed, delivered, and serviced—varies, depending primarily upon geographic location.

It became obvious that no one individual or centralized department could excel at servicing all fifty states. But, small $\cong 8$-person teams, with processes designed and tailored for their constituency within a few states, would work. Team members could get to know the legal and contractual requirements of the area they serve, understand the materials required, the timing requirements, and the process to follow to meet the specific needs of their constituency.

Segment Focus

Sometimes there are clearly distinct customer segments each with their own service requirements that are currently being served by one department and one messy process. In other cases there are distinct product/service segments that have traditionally been lumped together and delivered by one group of people, also using a messy or unclear process. In either case the solution may be to divide and conquer—set up dedicated processes (and sometimes dedicated organizations) to best deliver each product or best serve each customer segment. In one case we found the product segmentation and the customer segmentation amounted to the same thing.

At a technology-driven Fortune 500 corporation, with thousands of employees, the logistics of providing voice (phones) and video (video conferences) services was enormous. To further complicate matters, the rapid and continuous advances in the technology were enabling new modes of operation—and of course, in a technology-driven company, everyone wanted to be up to date with the latest and greatest. The telecom department, a ≅700 person organization, was responsible for meeting the entire corporation's ≅300,000 employees' needs for such services, but was having trouble keeping up:

- New installations and service changes took too long.
- Too many installations and changes were done incorrectly.
- The work was costly (a simple order brought in $325, but cost over $450).

The catalyst for action was further driven by a couple of factors:

1. External competition required the business units to react faster and cut costs (pressure to reduce the $325 transfer price)

2. The corporation's policy changed to allow competition for the internal telecom services group, so the business units could now do it themselves or use outside services

Internally, the telecom service department had spent time and energy trying to improve, yet with little success. Most of the effort had gone into managing and improving isolated process silos, such as those depicted in Figure 10.2.

A redesign team was convened to figure out where the biggest opportunities lay and answer the key question: Where would the surgical strikes be found? This question led the redesign team to more questions and ideas for redesign as shown in Figure 10.3.

Figure 10.2. Isolated Process Silos in a Telecom Company

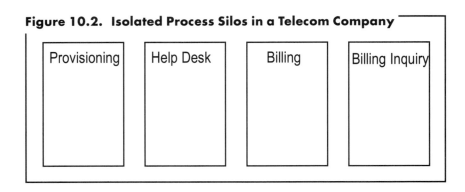

Figure 10.3. Questions and Ideas for Redesign

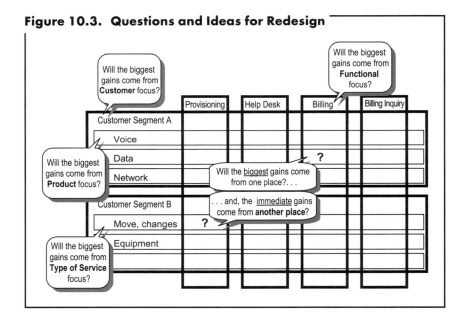

In the end, it was determined that there were three kinds of orders:

1. Development projects within the information technology group, of which Telecom was part

2. Complex solutions/installations (set-up buildings, entire call centers, video conference rooms)

3. Simple orders (e.g., install, move, change phones and phone service, plus video reservations)

These three kinds of orders were delivered to three segments of customers:

1. The Information Technology group, and its development project managers

2. Other business units and their telecom coordinators and project managers

3. End users

As it turned out, the product segments matched the key customer segments (Figure 10.4). The simple orders (install, move, change phones and phone service) were done for end users. The more complex development orders were delivered primarily to technicians, while complex installation orders were delivered to coordinators and project managers throughout the organization—but not the end users directly.

Figure 10.4. Process, Product, and Customer Segments

Process Segment/Team	**1** New Product Introduction	**2** Business Unit Solutions/Projects	**3** End User Transaction Services
Team Purpose	Manage service process for new products	Handles complex provisioning, from beginning to end for large projects/solutions affecting multiple users	Provides complete servicing of simple orders for specific locations
Customers: External		Coordinators & Project Managers	End Users
Internal	IT Project Managers		
Product/Service Focus	New products/ services	SDN, Broadcast video, Mega 800, Advanced 800, video installations, ISDN, packaged solutions, T1/T4s, Centrex	Install, Move, Change 5 phones or less; translations, video reservations, service assurance, service recovery, billing inquiries

With focused processes and focused delivery organizations, combined with error reduction and streamlining, the benefits were huge. The "End User Transaction Services" group could now focus on excelling with the delivery of small transactions with end users. In particular it was the simple things that made the greatest difference. The new simplified dedicated process would cut the overall labor required by 50 percent; yet at the same time essentially ensure that the installations and changes would be done correctly. With nearly perfect up-front quality and delivery performance, the help calls and billing inquiries would diminish dramatically. The net result from this surgical strike, as illustrated in Figure 10.5—a nearly 50 percent reduction in overall process cost!

Figure 10.5. Focused Flows Impact Assessment

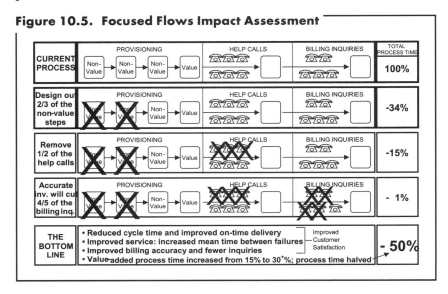

Focus the Flows on Performance to the Customer

In our Process Redesign Game, there is one customer and one product and one small process. To "focus the flows" in a single flow environment is impossible. However, the game represents an environment where the flow has already been focused. It is precisely that focus that readily enables the game's participants to easily see the process flaws and the customer's expectations.

The games' participants are not distracted and confused by an intertwined array of products, services, processes, and customers. To oversimplify—Strike 7, Focus the Flows, is about getting a business process to the point where it resembles the game—one process, one product, one customer segment. In the game this focus and visibility to process performance allow for rapid process improvement. As described earlier—this clarity and focus leads to improvements being made almost by intuition. As many participants suggest during our post-game debrief: "It's a no-brainer."

> By focusing the flows in your operation, such dramatic perform-
> ance improvements can also become a no-brainer.

Strike 7: Focus the Flows

Strike 7 is about clearly distinguishing a few key types of work, then developing, and establishing clear, distinct process flows for each type.

Strike 7 primarily starts with facts and data about the types of workload and customer segments being served. In this case, the intent is not to identify and eliminate workload or segments based on profitability or value-added. Here, the intent is to distinguish clear types of work, based upon similar processing characteristics. For the purpose of focusing the flows, the predominant distinctions tend to be made, based upon the following:

- Degree of difficulty: Fast, easy-to-process work versus slow, difficult, customized work

- Geography: Support and service requirements sometimes vary due to climate, laws/regulations, and/or population densities

- Segment: Focused processes can sometimes better serve distinct product and/or customer segments

Strike 7 actions typically encompass:

- Designing dedicated process flows to best deliver a type of work or to best serve a particular customer segment

- Restructuring the organization to best operate the new process (more on this in Chapter 13)

Strike 8: Link and Learn—Unclog the Flows of Knowledge

Don't be afraid to make a mistake. But make sure you don't make the same mistake twice.
            —Akio Morita, chief executive officer, Sony,
                              to his young managers

E arlier strikes talked about unclogging the workplace and unclogging the flows of work. This surgical strike is about unclogging the flows of knowledge. However, unlike the amorphous concepts of "knowledge management," this strike is about tangible and immediate results. The results come from defining and using specific feedback and "feed-forward" of information regarding the business and process performance to immediately take actions and make improvements.

By feed-forward I mean the transmittal of information from an upstream process to a downstream process. A downstream process should know of a decision, or action, or condition that is or will be relevant to its future performance. For example, customer service should be informed by the product designers about a potential product defect prior to receiving complaints from customers. Likewise, marketing needs to provide customer service with information regarding promotions prior to customers calling with questions.

Feedback is more obvious, as in the billing inquiries example. If billing inquiries result from hard-to-understand bills, then those who design the bills and/or manage customer expectations need routine feedback from those who handle the inquiries. With effective feedback the bill's design and/or the management of expectations can change immediately—for the next billing cycle, not months later. Typically, such instant-action links are lost in large organizations and nothing improves, or if improvements are made, they are done as a one-shot project over a long period of time. So even if a one-shot project results in a "Strike 2: Eliminate Work"-type success, the gains will then likely plateau or regress.

Strike 8 is about putting in place the structure so the processes and people who create the pain feel the pain, yet they also create the gains and feel the gains—therefore, no plateau, no regression in process performance. As an executive overseeing a troubled process, it is good to know there is a surgical strike action that will quickly lead to additional strikes and related performance gains. So even if an executive cannot pinpoint the source of the gains, the strike is to enable others with the easy and rapid movement of critical information from where it is created to where it is needed.

You could argue that Strike 8 is not, in and of itself, a strike with direct results—it is a means to an end. By unclogging the flows of knowledge the people close to the work will see and act on the now obvious targets of opportunity. So, although indirect, Strike 8 actions can get huge results rather quickly. So what are these actions? Let's first set the context.

There are two vantage points from which to view the need to unclog the flows of knowledge:

1. The first is to view the need to close the feedback loops from *within* a core process, as shown in Figure 11.1.

    Unclogging the flows of knowledge within a core process is likely to be relatively simple. Typically there are fewer organizational enti-

Figure 11.1. Feedback Within a Core Process

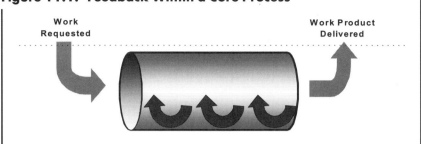

ties and executives with whom to contend. And there is likely to be one kind of work product (new products for the new product introduction process, maintained and repaired products for the after-sales service process)

2. The second is to view the need to move information *among* core processes (Figure 11.2):

Figure 11.2. Feed-Forward and Feedback Among Core Processes

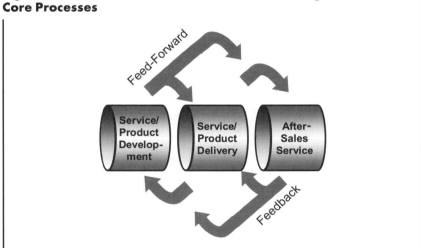

Among core processes such a strike is more difficult. Typically each core process is under the charge of a separate top executive, with dedicated people focused on their process, each core process using a language of it's own. For instance, the new product introduction people think in terms of a few products per year, each developed over many months, if not years. While at the same time the service-recovery people are processing thousands of customers, transactions, and phone calls per day. However, perhaps because of this difficulty in communication, it is *among* the core processes in which there is the most to gain from Strike 8, Link and Learn— Unclog the Flows of Knowledge.

Therefore the bulk of this chapter will be spent on unclogging the flows of knowledge *among* core processes. However, I will begin by briefly discussing the application of Strike 8 *within* a core process.

Close the Feedback Loops from *Within* a Core Process

In our Process Redesign Game, the game represents a microcosm of a relatively simple core process within a business. As mentioned before, there is one customer and one product and one small process. In Round One the tables are spread around the room and no one knows what the other does to assemble the toy phone. Communication consists of loud, blaming, disparaging comments directed at no one in particular, as in: "Who made this mess?"—referring to a faultily built subassembly.

By Round Three, the tables have been pulled together so that they are touching. The assemblers are right next to one another. Communication is immediate, quiet, and constructive. For example: "The antennae was placed one notch too far from the top." The antennae assembler immediately understands the fix and now places the antennae correctly.

In the game there is no sophisticated information system, no grandiose knowledge-management project. Simply locating people next to each other and encouraging problem solving and productive discussion was a surgical strike action that led to great results.

There are a number of examples of how getting people together to unclog the flows of knowledge has enabled a number of improvement actions:

■ At the classified ad department of a newspaper, the merger of the ad-takers and the complaint-takers enabled dramatic improvements in performance. The people who create the pain (by taking incorrect ad info) would feel the pain (by taking the complaint call). The combination of personal pain (having to take the complaint calls) and peer pressure ("I took a call on an ad you messed up!") worked. Rather rapidly, the correct ads went from ≅90 to ≅99 percent.

■ Likewise, at a health insurer—the people who paid or rejected a claim did not take the calls themselves or even hear about the subsequent problem and complaint calls. While in this case the answer was not found in merging the responsibilities so each individual performed both tasks, the answer was found in locating the claims-payers among the call-takers. The claims payers then focused on getting more claims done correctly and on time, and then saw call volume drop by 25 percent.

■ In a circuit board assembly operation, a U-shaped floor layout was created. The test and repair stations were located next to the initial assembly steps. Again, if something was found to be incorrect, the feedback was informal, yet fast and effective. The combination of one-at-a-time processing and instant feedback cut defects by nearly 90 percent.

The main lesson in all of these cases was that proximity counts. Proximity counts when it comes to root cause identification and corrective action. But more importantly, proximity counts toward the speed with which actions happen and results are realized, and the simplicity by which information is communicated. Unclogging the knowledge flows can be simple.

The next chapter will focus further on the importance of visibility to the results of one's work, and how such visibility is a key strike for improving process performance.

Move Information and Knowledge Among Core Processes

The movement of information among core processes is not so simple. In some cases, with the way things are structured, the flows of knowledge are obstructed and distorted, leading to a real disintegration of an organization's effectiveness. First I will describe a situation and provide examples of such disintegration at a leading consumer phone manufacturer. Then, using the HMO as an example, I will describe the means to systematically evaluate an organization's opportunities to link and learn among its core processes.

Dis-Integration by Design

Your company can achieve breakthrough improvements in performance by aggressively moving toward the re-integration of product design, process design, and day-to-day production (and repair). The organization has the core skills and technical ability to succeed dramatically with such an effort . . . and initially it doesn't have to be a huge undertaking. However, if the current dis-integration continues, the company is likely to become increasingly uncompetitive on quality, delivery, and price.

This was the lead-in to my report on the effectiveness (or lack thereof) of a leading manufacturer of simple consumer-oriented wired and wireless phones. I observed and conducted interviews within their U.S. headquarters and seven manufacturing plants in the Far East (some company owned, and some outsourced to OEMs, or original equipment manufacturers).

Essentially, I observed that they had embarked on a strategy of disintegration by design. While the intent may have been to isolate components of the business into bite-sized manageable entities, the effect was a dis-integration according to every definition:

Dis-in-te-gra-tion

1. Reduce to particles, fragments, or parts; break up or destroy the cohesion of.

2. Separate into its component parts; break up.

3. Decay.

All of these definitions applied to the way their workflows, organizations, and related knowledge flows had been designed and structured. So what were some of their specific problems and opportunities?

Feedback and Feed-Forward for Manufacturability

This dis-integration showed itself in the broken link between product design and product manufacturing. There were numerous examples in the production lines where the assembly effort appeared excessive due to the product design such as: excessive jumper wire connections and reworking boards where tight component locations created missed insertions. Had there been a tighter link among product designers and product assemblers, these inefficiencies could have been avoided.

They needed to select any product (existing or new) and challenge one or two product designers and one or two manufacturing engineers to work together to design the product for manufacturability. With clear aggressive objectives around process impact, final product quality (e.g., Six Sigma) and time to market a few small product design changes could make a significant difference in process performance.

In the longer term, distinction between product and process engineers needed to be blurred by having them both housed in the same facility and participating in each other's projects. To achieve this level of integration between manufacturing and the best product engineers would require that a plant or at least some production capability be located in close proximity to the product engine. In addition, we suggested they initiate a program to swap engineers with the best OEMs for a year or so at a time.

Feedback and Feed-Forward for Effective Procurement

Each manufacturing plant was responsible to source their own components and parts. There were huge problems with quality and delivery (one plant rejected 10 percent of their incoming material). Every facility appeared to have problems with their ability to provide 100 percent of the components required for completion of a circuit board assembly. So they produced partially completed boards and finished them when the components arrived. One of the high-leverage opportunities is in reducing the incoming quality problems and part shortages experienced by all the OEMs.

This phone manufacturer needed to use its immense clout with vendors in the procurement of components, especially to support the OEMs. The effort could begin by establishing a small (six to eight people) core group of purchasing and technical (product/process engineering, or quality assurance) representatives from each of the product lines (corded, cordless, and answering systems). Their assignment would be to:

1. Define/analyze the purchased components and sources across the three product lines.

2. Select the key components and evaluate the performance improvement potential.

3. Define selection criteria; evaluate and select key vendors.

4. Define the major obstacles to establishing a value-managed purchasing arrangement.

5. Meet with key vendors; establish a pilot program.

6. Define a roll out plan and a measurement/monitoring system.

Feedback for Reliability and Serviceability

The factories had minimal participation in, or knowledge of, field failures, returns, and repairs. Particularly disturbing was the repair operation that was run as a distinct operating entity. The objective of the repair organization was almost exclusively centered on receiving the returned goods, refurbishing those goods, and shipping them back to the marketplace. Little attention was paid to the identification of failures and root cause analysis. There was not even any real effort to identify the returns by factory. Obviously, knowledge of failures and participation in their resolution on the part of the factories was impossible if the basic information was not available.

No amount of reports, studies, or data can achieve the same level of understanding and problem solving as having the production function (workers, managers, and engineers) physically conducting the repairs to the products they produced. A significant production plant in close proximity to the returns-and-repair facility would help establish a tight linkage between repair-and-production operations. Furthermore, a close proximity of manufacturing/repair to the marketing/sales organization may help close another important performance gap related to the high return rate.

Again, such an initiative could start small. The effort, to demonstrate the benefits of integrating repair with production, could begin by establishing a production line for a relatively low-volume product in a repair center. All repairs for that low-volume product would also be directed to that repair center. Ideally, the center would also be in reasonable proximity to the other functions of the business, such as finance and marketing.

Feedback for Marketing and Sales

It may be that the product is performing to specification, but not to expectation. For example, if inexpensive cordless phones are returned because they don't sound as clear as corded phones, who managed the customers' expectations? Who is responsible to manage those expectations? The company is, of course. In this company's case, marketing/sales (or the retail salespersons) may not be properly managing expectations regarding the product's performance.

How to Link and Learn

While this phone manufacturer provides a great exposé of dysfunction and dis-integration, along with some sense of what can be done about it, it lacks a cohesive analytical framework. Having encountered numerous organizations with similar difficulties, a framework has evolved. A combination of "core process definition," a "knowledge flow grid," and process mapping, can provide the tools to define and design the most appropriate surgical strike and unclog the knowledge flows. The intent must be to "link and learn"—link information flows and enable learning from one process to another throughout the organization.

"We have eliminated our functional silos, and created process silos," states a cynical vice president at a leading telecommunications company. While she acknowledges the inroads that process-improvement programs have made, she is concerned about the linkages among the various processes.

She is not alone. Many are concerned that while process-improvement programs (TQM, reengineering, and the like) have made great strides in unclogging the flows of work, they have not unclogged and channeled the flows of information and knowledge. Yet for many business problems, resolution depends upon knowledge transfer among various business processes. For instance, the data from the order fulfillment process may be used to define a customer segment as unprofitable. Based upon that information, the business planning process may produce a declaration that the customer segment is undesirable. Then it is the customer acquisition process that will utilize the information to avoid that customer segment, or to re-price the product or service for that segment.

Like it or not, core processes are intertwined and interdependent. It is these undercurrents of knowledge flow that enables processes to do the right things well rather than the wrong things well. So how do we channel these undercurrents?

The CFO, like others, is intrigued by the emerging field of knowledge management, but expresses his highly cynical outlook: "It's a consultant's dream . . . big ideas, big picture, and big money . . . and little definition." To a degree he's right. It's an emerging field with lots of activity, including numerous definitions being floated, with no one definition receiving a consensus. Here are some possibilites:

Some Definitions of Knowledge Management

Policies, procedures, and technologies employed for operating a continuously updated linked pair of networked databases (Anthes, 1991).

Bringing tacit knowledge to the surface, consolidating it in forms by which it is more widely accessible, and promoting its continuing creation (Birkett, 1995).

Ensuring a complete development and implementation environment designed for use in a specific function requiring expert systems support (Chorafas, 1987).

Processes of capturing, distributing, and effectively using knowledge (Davenport, 1994).

Creation, acquisition, and transfer of knowledge and modification of organizational behavior to reflect new knowledge and insights (Garvin, 1994).

Identification of categories of knowledge needed to support the overall business strategy, assessment of current state of the firm's knowledge, and transformation of the current knowledge base into a new and more powerful knowledge base by filling knowledge gaps (Gopal and Gagnon, 1995).

Finding out how and why information users think, what they know about the things they know, the knowledge and attitudes they possess, and the decisions they make when interacting with others (Hannabuss, 1987).

Mapping knowledge and information resources both on-line and off-line; training, guiding, and equipping users with knowledge access tools; monitoring outside news and information (Maglitta, 1995).

Understanding the relationships of data; identifying and documenting rules for managing data; and assuring that data are accurate and maintain integrity (Strapko, 1990).

Facilitation of autonomous coordinatability of decentralized subsystems that can state and adapt their own objectives (Zeleny, 1987).

However, the CFO suggests that rather than worry about the semantics of "knowledge management," let's look at the basics. Data needs to be gathered, information produced and delivered and then used at various points in the business processes. The trick is in defining the collection points, the dissemination points, and the "big picture" priorities for managing these flows of knowledge. So where do we begin?

Begin with the Business Processes

I laid out the following clear connection between process management and knowledge management in *Knowledge Management* magazine a few years ago.[1] Basically the process work done by most corporations over the last decade provides the foundation for managing knowledge flows. Core processes have been defined and detailed process flows have been documented.

Broad strategic efforts, around core process definitions have enabled organizations to see the big picture of how their companies work. In the grand scheme of things, product development comes before customer acquisition that comes before service delivery or after sales service. Some call this view "life cycle management." For some organizations, the "life cycle" refers to the product, for others it refers to the customer experience. In either case the intent is to view the entire business as a complete process. With this "big picture" view, companies can be sure they focus on improving and managing complete processes from the customers' perspective (new product introduction: from product idea to product available for sale; or order fulfillment: the day-to-day order through delivery of the product or service).

From the HMO example, here is the core process view from Chapter 2. Figure 11.3 portrays seven core processes, supported by various enabling processes.

For this HMO, the "big picture" core *process* flow is clear, especially if we think of what it takes to start a business from scratch. It begins with a business plan, then development of the product/service. Next, the infrastructure is prepared to deliver the service, and then customers are acquired. Data must then be entered and maintained, in order to effectively deliver member wellness programs and to provide patient health care. As time goes on, this flow continuously repeats itself, as new plans are developed, services introduced, and so on. Experience begets knowledge and renewal. It is the knowledge transfer among the core processes, vaguely depicted by the lines and arrows above the seven blocks, which enables that renewal.

Focus on Knowledge Flows

The first step of many companies has been to unclog the linkages and to enable access to information and knowledge. The various incarnations of technology-based "knowledge management" solutions (e.g., data warehousing, data mining, intranets, and Lotus Notes) has enabled the availability of more and more critical information throughout the business.

Unfortunately, while these technologies have been liberating, in many cases they have become a catalyst for information chaos and overload. The unclogged and freeform flows of knowledge now need to be channeled. As suggested by the top lines and arrows on the HMO's core process diagram, the all-encompassing flows (where everything is related to everything) are not particularly helpful.

It is in the individual point-to-point flows where the value of knowledge can be examined. For example, what specific information is created in the Business Planning Process that would be of great benefit

Figure 11.3. Core Processes for a Health Maintenance Organization

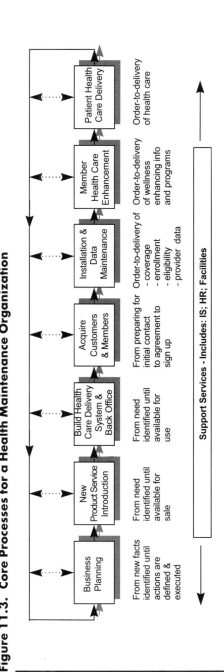

well downstream in the Service Delivery Process and vise-versa? This one example suggests there are two flows, a feed-forward and a feed-back, for every pairing of core processes. So how can we sort through all the possible point-to-point flows for all the core processes?

The Knowledge Flow Grid

The core process framework (see the example in Figure 11.3) provides the means to evaluate the point-to-point knowledge flows at a high level. It is at this high level where the major benefits of channeling knowledge flows will emerge. Much like the process-management work of the past decade has broken down the functional silos, a focus on knowledge flow can break down the process silos.

At the core process level, each interconnection deserves a look. At first it sounds unwieldy to list each core process and determine how knowledge might flow to and from each. However, the Knowledge Flow Grid (shown in Figure 11.4) provides the means to perform such an evaluation.

In this grid, the HMO's core processes are depicted in order from left to right. Much like a mileage table on a map, the grid is intended to show how one place relates to another. However, in this case we look at two distinct connections: (1) the "Feed Forward" of informa-tion downstream, and (2) the "Feedback" of information upstream. Hence, the blocks on the top represent the feed-forward relationships, while the lower blocks reflect the feedback linkages.

In this HMO example, where there are seven core processes, the number of interfaces requiring evaluation is 42; 21 for all the possible feed-forward relationships, and 21 for all the possible feedback rela-tionships.

While the intent should be to evaluate every single box on the grid, only three examples are displayed in the HMO grid (Figure 11.4):

1. **Business Planning → Acquire Customers & Members:** It is the plan-ning process that defines and selects specific customer segments as targets. Once defined—and as these targets are continuously re-fined—the information needs to be "fed forward" to the acquisition process. The acquisition process can then build in specific points where selected customer segments are whisked through the process,

Figure 11.4. The Knowledge Flow Grid

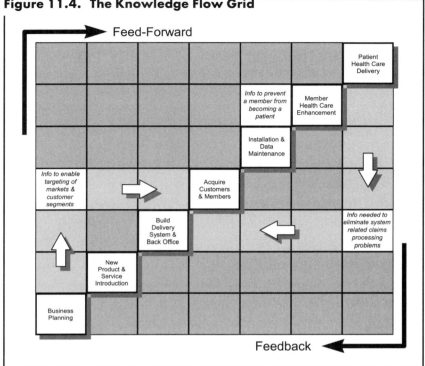

while the nontarget customer segments are encouraged to go else-where.

2. **Installation & Data Maintenance → Member Health Care:** The intent of the member health care process is to prevent a member from becoming a patient. Therefore, it is imperative that member specific health information that enables preventive health care be "fed forward" to drive specific points of preventive care actions in the member health care process. For instance, a member with heart disease might require—and the HMO should desire—more frequent and specialized physical examinations.

3. **Patient Health Care → Build Delivery System and Back Office:** As claims are processed, it is not unusual to have a significant portion "suspend" for one reason or another. These suspended claims then require labor-intensive intervention to process. To reduce the delays and extra labor, information regarding the portion of suspended

claims which are due to inherent system deficiencies needs to be fed back to the systems development operation. The information is vital to determining priorities relative to other problems, and to designing and implementing the fix. Again, the key is in defining where the information is most vital and where it truly becomes valuable at a specific point-of-use in the process.

The intent of the knowledge flow grid is to force an evaluation of each one-to-one link among the core processes. This evaluation means first defining the key information needs and content (whether available today or not) for every intersection on the grid. Next, an evaluation of priorities among the blocks can help narrow and focus any knowledge-flow development work. Then the concept of a knowledge flow needs to be converted into a pragmatic design for implementation and day-to-day use.

From Concept to Reality

Each of the three examples mentioned specific points where information is needed. But we also need to be concerned with specific points where information can be collected. A point-to-point knowledge flow requires a clear starting point, a clear ending point, and a clear articulation of how the information will be used at the ending point.

Again we go back to our process management foundation. This time, the detailed business process maps provide the means to design and document the specific point-to-point knowledge flows. These detailed process maps depict how the work gets done on a day-to-day basis, usually for an entire core process.

In places where information is collected in one place but used in another, the use of symbols in the information band can portray these linkages. The example map contains symbols for computer terminals as examples. Assume this symbol represents a particular computer system. The computer terminal on the left is depicted as collecting data early in the process, while the terminal on the right suggests where the data is used. The same situation occurs if the symbol were a hard copy book, where information was gathered and prepared as a book (product specs book or company phone directory) and used later in the same, or another, process. See Figure 11.5.

Figure 11.5. Business Process Map for Information Collected One Place and Used in Another

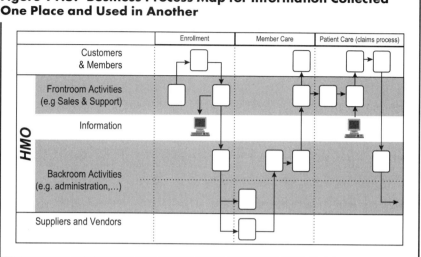

While the discussion has centered on the use of technology, documentation, and the like, there are many occasions in which simple face-to-face communication is more effective. For instance, at the end of a project or at the end of making a deal with a customer, there is a lot to be learned from the experience. However, building in reporting requirements, data-collection points, measurement points, and other vestiges of bureaucracy may not be the best way. Perhaps a couple of simple debriefing sessions, one with the customer and one without, will unearth the key findings. If this is the case, the process map can depict the specific step at the end of the process where such a session will take place and (with more steps, lines, and arrows) delineate how and where the information from the session will be packaged and disseminated.

Channeling the Undercurrents of Knowledge Flow → Knowledge Management

The undercurrents of knowledge flow enable business processes to do the right things well, rather than the wrong things well. Channeling these powerful undercurrents is the essence of effective knowledge management. In other words, knowledge management is about flow: "the processes of capturing, distributing, and effectively using knowledge." (Davenport 1994).

The key question is: "How can we channel these undercurrents?"

■ First, define the core processes of the business:
  To ensure that, in the big scheme of things, the important process silos are permeated by the flows of information and knowledge.

■ Second, identify the information and knowledge content that needs to flow between each core process link (feed-forward and feedback):
  To evaluate all the possibilities and then select the priorities for designing and managing the flows that matter.

■ Use detailed process maps:
  To design and establish explicit links within day-to-day work processes for capturing, distributing, and effectively using knowledge.

The undercurrents of knowledge flow can resemble either a strong tailwind or a vicious crosswind affecting your organization. The former will get you to your intended destination with great speed and efficiency; the latter will tear at your people and resources, pushing them off course in unexpected and potentially dangerous directions. The trick is finding and channeling the right flows of knowledge, whether in the front lines, the back office, or in the boardroom.

Feed-Forward and Build Revenues, Not Just Fix Problems and Cut Costs

Not only is it advantageous to unclog the flows of knowledge across processes, but also across companies. Think about the potential cross-sell opportunities for huge conglomerates such as General Electric. GE is sitting on a gold mine and has all the elements in place. GE has multiple businesses with mutual interests. GE is a process-driven company (having excelled in its execution of Six Sigma). GE believes in change, and GE believes in boundaryless behavior regarding the movement of information among its organizational entities. So while there are great opportunities within the businesses, GE can establish very profitable links among the businesses.

GE can become even more boundaryless, without disrupting the focus each business unit must have on their own success. Those ideas revolve around two essential foundations: (1) defined process flows, or in this case *knowledge flows*, among the businesses, and (2) *knowledge brokers*—an organizational entity, perhaps a business unit, whose mission is to build and manage the knowledge flows (for a cut of the additional profits).

1. *Knowledge Flows:* Information from one business can be mined and creatively applied to create a new business or assist another business. For instance, as illustrated in Figure 11.6, big project financing might identify a subsequent need for modular space or technology assistance, or the need for mortgage services to new hires and relocated employees. Subsequently, data that is mined from the mortgage businesses might provide opportunities for both the credit card businesses and GE's appliance businesses.

2. *Knowledge Brokers:* I suspect no one in a business unit has the inclination to set up intra-business knowledge flows—especially if the benefits will be seen downstream in other business units. However, if a business unit were to receive compensation (as well as the accolades from corporate management) for providing information, and the effort were not too great (the knowledge flows were built and managed by others), their cooperation would be more than forthcoming.

Figure 11.6. Linking GE's Businesses—To Convert Knowledge to Dollars

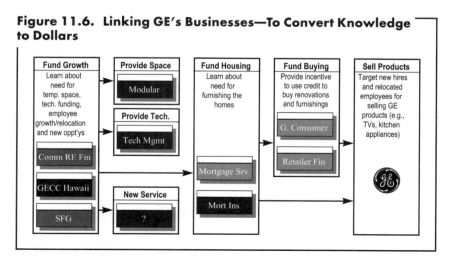

A distinct organizational entity (perhaps a business unit) may be required to make this work. I can see the potential of having a group of knowledge brokers totally dedicated to making money on brokering the knowledge flows among GE's businesses. This group would have the mandate and incentives to build and maintain these knowledge flows, and receive compensation based on brokering an arrangement among the information supplier, themselves, and the information receiver. In other words, the knowledge flow will have to appear profitable or it won't get built, and will have to be profitable or it won't be maintained.

Again GE has the opportunity to lead. If GE were to design and build its knowledge flow brokerage service, such a project would play to GE's strengths in engineering new services, processes, and management techniques where the focus is on value creation, not cost reduction.

Likewise, the whole idea of "supply chain management" and boundaryless behavior across companies and even industries is a huge opportunity, although not a quick hit on a grand scale. However, the use of analyses and tools such as process mapping, the knowledge flow grid, and the like, on an entire supply chain will likely uncover some specific and actionable quick-hit surgical strike actions.

Strike 8: Unclog the Flows of Knowledge

Strike 8 is about defining and using specific feedback or feed-forward of information regarding the business and process performance to immediately take actions and improve.

Strike 8 primarily starts with the fear that things are messed up and not getting better. The feeling picks up steam with facts and data about the lost opportunities when something that should have been known and should have been acted upon is not. Then the missing links are identified and connected.

Strike 8 actions typically encompass:

- Providing the means to rapidly move the right information to the right place at the right time
- Locating people within close proximity to each other, and/or
- Providing clear and specific points in the day-to-day processes in which data is captured and in which the data is used

CHAPTER 12

STRIKE 9: SHOW THE RESULTS

Men who experience a great deal of accountability make accurate decisions.
—KARLENE ROBERTS, INDUSTRIAL PSYCHOLOGIST

When the outcomes of change are seen and felt (for better or worse) the impact is quite powerful. When the outcomes are invisible, intangible, or somehow obscured in a morass of data, the impact is nonexistent. Simply making the results of day-to-day work visible and rewarded can drive huge gains in process performance.

Like Strike 8, Strike 9, Show the Results, is a means to an end, not an end in itself. Showing the results indirectly enhances process performance. Supported by executive attention, clear indicators of performance will instigate behavior and drive actions that result in performance gains.

"Clear indicators" are not necessarily confined to performance scorecards and measures. For example, the simple visibility of work piling up can drive corrective actions and performance improvements. However, I will begin with the surgical strike of instituting performance scorecards and measures.

Establish Down-to-Earth Balanced Measures of Performance

In the Process Redesign Game: The four-quadrant scorecard we use (see Figure 12.1) provides clear focus for everyone as to the criteria and expectations for process performance. The scorecard balances external measures of quality and delivery to the customer, with internal measures of cycle time and waste (or cost as an indicator of waste reduction).

Figure 12.1. Process Performance Scorecard

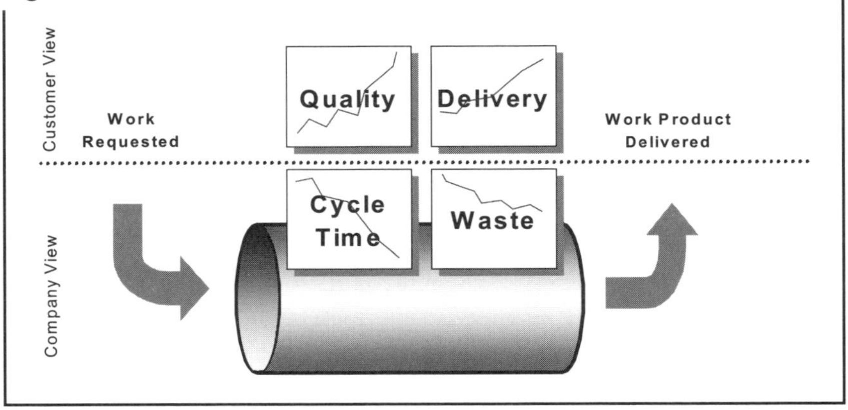

During the post-game debrief, we always ask about the role of the measures. We hear from the participants that, as results improve, they become more motivated. They say that the visible results drive visible improvement, which drive visible results, and so forth.

So we ask if measures are so beneficial, should we have a scorecard at each of the five assembly tables in Round One? Everyone says no. A scorecard at each table would drive individual attempts to improve in isolation. Perhaps the tables would never be pulled together. In addition, the collection of data and maintenance of so many scorecards would take too many people away from real work—assembling phones.

The lesson from the game is that it takes a group to deliver value to the customer. A simple scorecard that focuses attention on overall value to the real customer drives the right behavior. People get together for the good of the overall scorecard.

The role of measures cannot be overemphasized in the game or in the workplace: They must be balanced, tangible, visible, and actionable. Then they will motivate behavior leading to dramatic improvements in all aspects of performance, or help sustain the improvements that have been made.

Scorecard in Action

So one form of surgical Strike 9—Show the Results—is to put a scorecard in place. We suggest a balanced scorecard like the one depicted. There are measures of process performance to the customer: quality and delivery. There are measures of concern to the insiders: cycle time and waste.

"Quality" refers to meeting customer expectations through the delivery of defect-free product or service. Quality has to do with features, performance, durability, reliability, aesthetics, perceived quality, and so on. It measures the quality of product or service output to the customer, user, and/or next department; as defined by those who receive that output.

"Delivery" refers to timeliness and quantity. Good delivery is when the desired quantity of goods and services is received by the "customer" of the process on time (not too late or too early).

"Cycle Time" refers to the internal capability of the process—the speed with which it can produce the product or service regardless of the delivery promise. For instance, a process may be capable of doing the work in a few minutes, but the delivery promise may be for a one- or two-day turnaround.

"Waste" refers to the non-value-added activities, resources, and ultimately costs, incurred in meeting the requirements of the customer. These problems are internal in that they are money and effort spent to get the product right before it is passed on to the customer (or downstream department). In our game, and in many companies, a measure of cost per unit is used to provide an indication that waste is being ferreted out.

Since developing this four-quadrant scorecard over a decade ago and describing the approach in detail in our book *Measure Up!*,[1] the uses have proven unlimited. We have applied it in product development organizations, software development, customer service functions, and administrative workflows, in a whole host of industries and companies, including the television station.

With the TV late break news team (and elsewhere), we found that a reengineered process makes it easier to define and implement effective measures of performance. For example, with no reengineering it might make sense to measure separately the quality and delivery of reporters' work and photographers' work. In the reengineered process, the reporter/ photographer/editor partnership on the late break team could be measured on the quality and delivery of their combined effort.

In the new workflow, there are only two key customers for the late break team: one external and one internal. The external customer is the viewer. The internal customer is the control room. These two key constituencies rely upon the quality and delivery performance of the late break team. Therefore, any reporting of performance for the late break team must contain measures of quality and delivery to these two constituencies.

Internally, the late break team will need to measure their performance regarding the reduction of cycle time and waste. Cycle time is the time from receiving a story idea until it is handed off to the control room. Waste is some indication of the activities (time and effort) expended above and beyond what is essential to meeting the quality and delivery requirements of both constituencies.

An example of what the performance report card for the late break team contains is shown in Figure 12.2.

For the TV station their new redesigned process map provided the means to develop the critical measures. The map provided the sequence of events and a clear delineation of the most critical hand-offs. It is these critical hand-offs where the performance scorecard can be used to measure results and motivate behavior that will lead to improvements.

The Right Measure and Real Value

If measures drive actions and results, then you better measure the right thing. Measuring the wrong thing can easily sub-optimize performance. To make matters worse, the whole idea of pay-for-performance even further complicates the search for the right measure(s). So there are some circumstances where defining and using the right measure is the surgical strike.

Let's revisit our customer contact center operation. Typically an in-house operation gets measured and rewarded on the basis of calls han-

Figure 12.2. Process Performance Scorecard for the Late Break Team at a TV Station

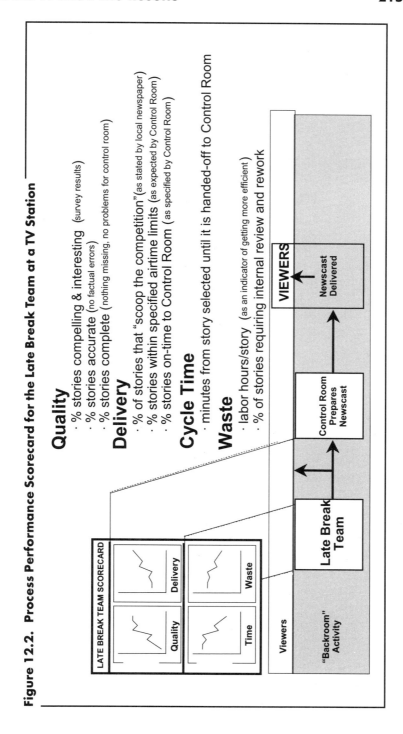

Quality
· % stories compelling & interesting (survey results)
· % stories accurate (no factual errors)
· % stories complete (nothing missing, no problems for control room)

Delivery
· % of stories that "scoop the competition" (as stated by local newspaper)
· % stories within specified airtime limits (as expeced by Control Room)
· % stories on-time to Control Room (as specified by Control Room)

Cycle Time
· minutes from story selected until it is handed-off to Control Room

Waste
· labor hours/story (as an indicator of getting more efficient)
· % of stories requiring internal review and rework

LATE BREAK TEAM SCORECARD

Quality Delivery
Time Waste

Late Break
Team

Control Room
Prepares
Newscast

VIEWERS

Newscast
Delivered

Viewers

"Backroom"
Activity

dled efficiently (reduced call times), but no real incentive or measure to encourage reducing calls altogether. Likewise for the outsourcer, getting paid on the basis of calls and call time, and/or agent time, provides no incentive to understand root causes of phone calls. There is no incentive to suggest ways in which calls might be eliminated.

The implication is that, for the customer interaction center as a whole, a broader overall measure is required. For instance, call centers and help desks might measure "customers per employee or per seat" (total customers/total interaction center employees or seats). In other words, the center gets credit for serving customers, whether they call or not. This measure encourages the center to provide the rest of the organization with useful feedback on the calls, with the intent of eliminating a large portion of the calls altogether. It also enables the center to juggle the relative priorities of the micro-measures ("call resolution," or "talk time") in a way that best enhances the overall measure of customers/employee or customers/seat.

For example, in the health care case the majority of customer calls should not occur at all. Calls occur when customers' and doctors' expectations are mismanaged, or claims are submitted improperly, or claims are paid slowly. The value proposition should revolve around the interaction center's ability to define the root cause of the calls and assist the organization in reducing call volumes, through fixing the upstream process failures. The value proposition is in lowering service cost per customer, whether the customer is served by the call center or not.

The next logical extension of promoting the value of service/support in this manner is to price services in this manner. This could work much like the way doctors are paid fixed capitation rates for prospective patients, whether they actually become a patient or not. A customer interaction center (in-house or outsourced) could promote and price their services on the basis of cost per customer (whether they interact or not). This payment scheme encourages the interaction center to continuously help the overall corporation improve their operations and service delivery processes based on knowledge gained from customer contact. Plus, since the interaction center will be paid on the basis of the entire customer base, there is great incentive to help the overall corporation drive acquisition, retention, and referrals, while driving down the number of service recovery contacts.

Therefore, the real value of a service and support operation is in designing and providing the most customer-centric and profitable solution to customer care. In other words, the value is in the capture and use of information to strive for flawless service delivery.

It is service cost per customer, not the cost per seat for service recovery, that counts. For example, let's assume an interaction center management team eliminates calls and call time amounting to 40 percent of the call handling effort and takes on a 500-seat center and turns it into a 300-seat center. Assume that in either case the center supports an installed base of 1 million customers. The 500 seats supported 2,000 customers/seat, while the 300 seats support 3,333 customers per seat—a dramatic improvement in productivity, and better service (the customers do not call when the product or service works right in the first place).

Assume the center was paid on the basis of a capitation rate at .015 dollars per hour per customer. This equates to $15,000 per hour to handle the customer base, whether it takes 500 seats or 300 seats.

Perhaps, the center and the rest of the organization could split the savings. Even when traditional "per agent, per hour costs" are used, the benefits are clear. A 300-seat center at $40 per agent per hour is a lot cheaper than the 500-seat center at $30 ($12,000 per hour versus $15,000 per hour—a 20 percent savings). The value in the higher agent-hour price is for the expertise in the root cause analyses, feedback, and assisting in the fix (which will eliminate contacts), not just the day-to-day management of calls and contacts. When viewed in a broader context, the interaction center is not high priced—even at $40 per hour per agent.

Make Clear Priorities Visible

On occasion there are too many measures and unclear priorities. A simple declaration of priority can be a surgical strike that leads to gains where they count. But unless expressly defined and reiterated, priorities can be lost or assumed—and sometimes the assumptions are not correct.

In the Process Redesign Game we use the four-quadrant scorecard. We never say which quadrant is most important. One day we ran three games simultaneously for a *Fortune* 100 corporation. The company's managers wanted to give a little prize to the "winner."

At the end of the game and debrief, the three teams posted their final scorecards:

	DELIVERY	QUALITY	CYCLE TIME	COST
TEAM 1:	90%	100%	.9 min	$52
TEAM 2:	95%	92%	.5 min	$29
TEAM 3:	100%	95%	.6 min	$35

So who won? Without much thought they said Team 2 was the winner, because they achieved the lowest cost.

But what if the phones were for the military and espionage behind enemy lines? From which team would you choose to buy your phones? Team 1. Even though they were late on one order and phones cost more, quality is most important.

Interestingly enough, even though it is not shown on this table, Team 3 would be declared the winner from the view of an investor or venture capitalist. They started Round One with a cost of $1,200 per phone and brought it down to $35. The other teams had it under $900 right-off-the-bat in Round One. So the greatest turnaround and productivity gain, and probably the greatest return on an investment risk, would have occurred with Team 3.

Declaring priorities for performance does not always have to be done through pronouncements about which measure is critical. Sometimes a very simply visual cue can provide the required guidance.

Dress Up the Workers

We once worked with a soap manufacturer. They produced everything from cheap airplane soap to elegant bath rope soaps. The workers would get confusing mixed messages about performance priorities. From day to day, sometimes within a day, priorities changed—and for good reason. When making inexpensive bars of soap for the airlines, margins were thin and cost was paramount. As a utilitarian product for an airplane's bathroom a few speckles in the soap did not matter. When making designer-name rope soap, the emphasis was on perfection. The soap itself had to be clear and spotless, the rope had to be just right, and the labeling and packaging were to be crisp and properly centered.

A colleague of mine at the time, Doug Howell, had a great idea.

When the workers were producing inexpensive soap for the airlines, let them continue to wear their jeans and tee shirts. However, to send a clear message about the need for quality and perfection, have the workers wear white lab coats for high-grade soap production. This way the production lines could remain flexible to produce what was needed when it was needed. But the worker would change their appearance to signal the performance priority.

Dress Up the Work

Once we worked with an order processing operation that had just automated. The new system resulted in eliminating tons of paperwork, but the process performance suffered. Orders that used to take days, now took weeks. The work-in-process exploded, but it was nowhere to be seen. "Work Pending" was simply a number on the computer screen.

The new system made things worse by hiding the best visual cues— stacks of work waiting to be processed. When the stacks got too big in any one area everyone jumped in to help out and relieve the bottleneck. Over the years a more sophisticated scheme using color-coded folders enabled work to be tracked by type and by day—ensuring attention was paid to the most pressing priorities.

They eventually had to replicate the old visual cues within the new system. A combination of work-in-process information on every desktop computer screen and large-screen monitors in the office area enabled their old visual cues to be restored. They finally got the payback originally promised by the new system.

Build Camaraderie and Teamwork

Perhaps more in the category of "reward the work," "build camaraderie and teamwork" is not so much a surgical strike, as it is a rather nice platitude. However, there are specific actions that can be taken to help build camaraderie and teamwork.

For a great example, look at Barry and Eliot Tatelman, the former owners and current leaders of Jordan's Furniture in the Boston area (now owned by Warren Buffet, who knows a good thing when he sees it). They took all of their employees to the beach. And not just any beach on a summer day in Boston. They took the nearly 1,300 employees of Jordan's Furniture, to Bermuda for the day—on a cold spring day in Boston. As reported by the *Boston Globe*, they went "on this most civil of resort islands for exactly one afternoon, all expenses paid, courtesy of Barry and Eliot."

This was no small feat. All the stores were closed and four jets were chartered for this exotic day-trip. The *Globe* tried to characterize the trip, but ultimately let it be characterized by Barry, Eliot, and their employees.

Barry and Eliot believe success and excellence are built on a two-way street. Although you could be cynical, the *Globe* article shows they are onto something:[2]

> **An elaborate, expensive publicity stunt? Perhaps. Another exercise in self-aggrandizing? Maybe. A generous and successful way to run a family business? Absolutely. In a corporate age when the haves take more and the have-nots are given less, Barry and Eliot Tatelman cut against the proverbial grain, believing that work should be fun, that good business goes beyond the bottom line, that happy employees are crucial to economic success.**
>
> **"If you do normal things, you only get normal things back," Eliot explains as he stands on this perfect beach, now crowded by so many furniture saleswomen and men, deliverers, and designers. "If you do something special, you get something special back."**

Furthermore, the article lends credibility to their view by publishing the employees' perspective:

> **The J-Team members [all employees] swoon in their presence. They crowd the stage when brothers Barry, 48, and Eliot, 52, briefly welcome the group to the island. They shout their affection when the pair drive by in a golf cart.**

> **"I've never seen anyone give a damn about their employees like these guys,"** says Larry Barocas, a salesman in the Natick store, in a sentiment echoed by colleagues. **"With these guys, what you see is what you get."**

So what's the upshot? Do such antics count as a surgical strike? You decide. Such antics, along with similarly outrageous advertising, good prices, and a fun store environment have contributed to great success—Jordan's Furniture is perhaps the most successful furniture retailer in the country. It takes a lot to get Warren Buffet's attention—let alone his money!

Strike 9: Show the Results

Strike 9 primarily starts with an objective to influence people in two areas:

1. To do the right things in their day-to-day work
2. To focus on a few key areas requiring improvements

Strike 9 actions typically encompass:

- Defining, prioritizing, and articulating/communicating the right things
- Providing clear direction on priorities for improvement
- Making the results of day-to-day work visible
  —Through measures
  —Through visibility to work queues and the like

Strike 9 is about making visible and tangible the priorities and outcomes (good or bad) from one's work.

CHAPTER 13

STRIKE 10: IMPLEMENT CUSTOMERCENTRIC TEAMS

The reason I am enthusiastic about self-directed teams is simple: They really do work.

—DAVID HANNA,
MANAGER OF ORGANIZATIONAL DEVELOPMENT,
PROCTER & GAMBLE

So is there any way to get all the surgical strikes and related benefits in one big coordinated multistrike hit? The answer is yes.

And it can be done quickly. When we first started helping companies conduct major reengineering projects, they tended to take six to nine months from analysis, through design, until piloting the new process. And after all that work, regardless of industry, the designs came out nearly the same—streamlined processes enabled by customercentric teams. So now, with this experience, our fundamental redesigns have taken as little as six weeks to accomplish the same thing.

In some cases, in true quick-hit surgical-strike fashion, customercentric teams are pulled together practically overnight, especially in times of crisis. In these cases the project team is the work team—and the processing of work begins immediately, not unlike our game.

In our Process Redesign Game the participants are both the workers and the process designers. They work to produce the phones during the rounds and work to redesign the process between the rounds. There is not time for a major redesign, just time to come with a concept and try it. Plus, they have to live with what they design— probably a sound principle for the real world.

As a working/design team, the participants always come to the same conclusion and take the same actions—through instinct and common sense (no need for extraneous or cumbersome methodology). After ten minutes of experience with the workflow in Round One, the biggest immediate action is to pull the isolated assembly tables together and create a team environment for Round Two. Starting in Round Two, performance improves, the internal dissension wanes, and the team members then work together to meet the needs of the customer.

The whole approach to management changes dramatically. In Round One of the game, the designated operations manager frantically tries to figure out what's going on. He or she yells and screams for the workers to produce good phones, but to no avail. No amount of management declaration and edict can overcome the defective process. The whole situation is frustrating for the manager and the workers. By Round Three, when everyone is working together as a cohesive team, the manager's role is essentially gone. The manager either produces phones, or acts as the liaison with the customer (eliminating the customer service rep job), or sometimes acts as a coach. The wild-eyed, ineffective dictator from Round One is gone.

The same is true with real redesign initiatives. Workers who participate in a redesign project, after looking at the current state (the Discover Stage) and the opportunities (the Inspire Stage), will design-in a self-managed small-team-based work flow and work environment that focus on results for their customer.

So teams are the answer—when workers and managers are given a chance to rethink and redesign the way a process operates and the way it is organized—but is it the answer for everyone? I have facilitated major process redesign initiatives in a variety of industries (e.g., a steel factory, electronics products, a "yellow pages" business, software development organizations, technology solutions providers, insurance, banks, and other financial services). I have facilitated process redesigns in all core processes such as new product development, customer acquisition, order fulfillment, service delivery, and service recovery. We reached, in each case, the same conclusion. The small self-managed customercentric team structure is a common solution. And rather than taking months to design and implement such a structure (as was the case during the glory days of reengineering), such teams are now designed and implemented (at least piloted) in a matter of weeks.

So how do companies reach this conclusion? And what are the key characteristics of small self-managed customercentric teams? I will start with the first question.

Group Think—How Did I Get Here?

Companies reach the conclusion to move to small self-managed customercentric teams when three things happen. First, a team is put together to redesign the process—made up of people from within and throughout that process. The team is made up of some of the company's top talent—signaling the seriousness of the challenge. Second, before starting their design work, the team is grounded in the facts about the customer, the work, and the process—including where performance suffers and how much it needs to improve—and why it needs to improve. Third, the design team is given a clear directive from the senior management, along with dedicated uninterrupted time (at least a week) to develop a redesigned process. In this context, we have repeatedly seen these redesigns spell out radically streamlined processes, enabled by self-managed customercentric teams.

Let's look at the case of a Yellow Pages business. In every region of the country the local Yellow Pages business was a division of the local phone company. It was part of the entrenched phone company's bureaucratic morass. However, with deregulation and a lucrative profit margin, significant competition appeared. The phone companies recognized that their Yellow Pages business would be assaulted by competitive service offerings from other directories, plus newspapers, cable companies, on-line services, CD ROMs, and probably others to be invented. To complicate the issue, these companies served a wide geographical area encompassing rural and urban locations, where the nature and basis of competition varied from place to place. All dimensions of performance—productivity, flexibility, and customer satisfaction—were coming under pressure. The incumbent leaders had to change their ways. Simply getting the Yellow Pages out every year would not be enough.

Let's look inside one of these incumbent phone companies and their Yellow Pages business. The business processes needed to become flexible and responsive, yet efficient, at meeting the expectations of a variety of different customers in a variety of different markets. Unfortunately, the company's processes and supporting structures were not suited to the emerging reality.

They recognized the need for a complete redesign. Each department was focused on its own specialty knowledge, skill, and internal efficiency to the detriment of serving the other departments and the paying customers. To oversimplify the case, let's assume four departments each had five employees. Selling the ads, preparing the ads, managing the billing, and handling after-sales service and complaints—each function was the focus of its own separate department. These disconnected functional silos had virtually all of the problems mentioned in earlier chapters. Each had its own entrenched bureaucracy with extraneous people, nonsense work, extraneous nonvalue process steps, and so on. Furthermore, the customer would get the runaround when trying to deal with the company.

So what did they do? An off-site meeting was convened over a period of two weeks to review and redesign the entire process by which the Yellow Pages were put together. In attendance were representatives from the direct flows of work (sales, artists, billing, and service), plus the critical support departments (human resources and information technology).

In the interest of a quick-hit surgical-strike approach, the initial analysis and Discover Stage was cut to a bare minimum—a week or so of work by three subteams. The subteams were pulled together to prepare overviews of the facts, not based on new investigation and analyses, but by simply summarizing all the work that had been done to date. One subteam reviewed the customer experience—current problems and future requirements. Another subteam developed a quick yet detailed process map (based on existing flow charts) and provided and overview of the process—number of steps, the percent value-added, number of hand-offs, and various key processing and cycle times. A third subteam reviewed the current workload—volumes, types of work, extent of service recovery work, refunds, and so forth. At the start of the off-site session each subteam was given an hour or two to ground everyone else in the facts of current business, along with desired performance changes.

After hearing the facts, the group worked to boil down the findings to its essence—a mission statement for the design team. The mission statement defined what was to be done by when. In this case, the conceptual design was to be done and documented in a couple of weeks, with the detailed design effort to follow. The design itself was intended to achieve a number of improvements in performance, based on the findings. There were quantitative goals expressed as design specifications for four key constituencies: (1) sellers (people who sell services in the Yellow Pages); (2) buyers (people who use the Yellow Pages to buy services); (3) management (specifications regarding efficiencies and the like); and (4) employees (regarding job satisfaction levels). Constraints and limits were also clarified and made part of the specifications (e.g., we will use these software and hardware systems).

We gathered ideas, big and small, that might be incorporated into the new design. As a catalyst for a brainstorming session we put the design team members through our process redesign game. With the game experience and a clear mission, the design team then spent a few days or so brainstorming design options. Hundreds of ideas were boiled down and summarized into forty big ideas that might (or might not) be incorporated into the redesigned process.

The rest of week was spent on the redesign. First, we focused on the work flow design—the activities and their sequence. Then the redesign effort continued by determining what key supporting structures would enable the process flow to work. In the end, the team placed great importance and emphasis on the deployment of small self-managed customercentric teams as the key component and characteristic of the new design (Strike 10).

Broken Silos

In the Yellow Pages business there were numerous departments each with their functional specialties spread over multiple states. The headcount for the entire business totaled over a thousand. Originally the redesign task seemed overwhelming. It really wasn't. By first focusing on the process—and what needed to be done for whom—the redesign became simple. And conceptually it is a simple process. The customer, a "seller," agrees to have an ad placed in the Yellow Pages, agrees to the look and content of the ad itself, and then pays for it—and sometimes calls for service if the ad or the bill is wrong. So what's so hard about that?

For the sake of simplicity, let's assume that in the current process the work traverses through four distinct departments, each with five employees. When the work comes in, such as a sales order, it is given to one of the five employees for processing. The work order then moves on to one of the five employees in the art department for creation of the ad, and so forth. In the end, the work could be processed by any one of the twenty people. Now think of thousands of work orders and a thousand employees in eight to ten departments, each with subdepartments! Random allocations of pieces of work among multiple employees in multiple departments typically create a convoluted network of unmanageable flows. In the specialty-department structure it is not unusual to have large batches of work, buffers of work, and significant WIP (work-in-process).

In addition, sophisticated control and tracking systems are attempted, usually with questionable results. In the end no one "owns" work or the customer experience. So what can be done about it?

Typically these customercentric work teams are made up of a person or two from each of a few previously isolated functional departments. Each work team, using a Strike 7-style focused flow, is then dedicated to serving a segment of customers.

If we revisit our greatly simplified example, we can see in Figure 13.1 that customercentric teams can be extricated from the silos.

In this case, "Customer Satisfaction Team 1" is made up of one employee with skill "A," one with skill "B," one with skill "C," and one with skill "D." So rather than a spider web of possible flows, the flow is straightforward. Plus there is clear accountability as to who "owns" the work and the customer experience—the customercentric work team does.

Of course there's a trade-off. Small work teams do not function well if everyone sticks with their specialty skills. These teams require generalists, not specialists. For example, in this case if a customer calls to complain about the artwork, it might be the former billing specialist

Figure 13.1. Customercentric Teams Cut Across the Organization's Silos

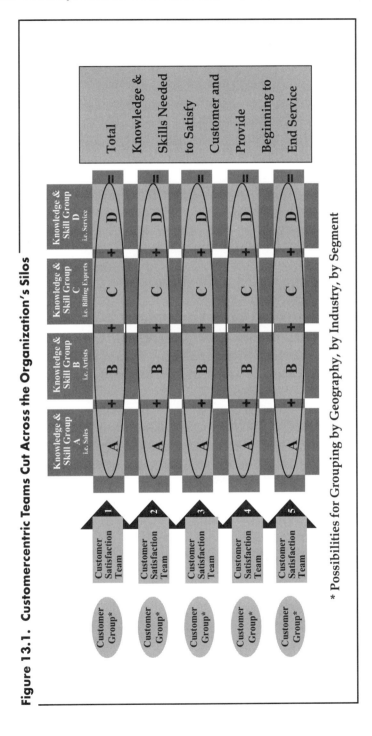

* Possibilities for Grouping by Geography, by Industry, by Segment

that takes the call and handles the complaint. The majority of artwork complaints are relatively simple—and while working together, the artist has transferred some skills to the billing specialist, so now only the difficult ones need be routed to the artist.

A customercentric team contains all the knowledge and skills needed to satisfy the customer and provide beginning-to-end service. As a group and as individuals, there becomes a more tangible relationship between their work, their product, and its impact on the company.

These teams are customercentric in that they are organized to support all customers in a specific geographical area, or a specific industry, or other definition of customer segment. These options were described in some detail in Chapter 10 when I covered Strike 7, Focus the Flows.

Fast Team—Fast Results

Implementing a cross-functional customercentric team does not have to take weeks, in true surgical-strike fashion it can be done this afternoon. Just look at what happens naturally in times of corporate crises. I was talking about this with Greg Maguire, vice president of claims at a leading health care insurer. He told me a story of what typically happens.

He remembers the last crisis when the claims department was accumulating a serious claims backlog. They were in danger of violating the required turnaround times for thousands of claims—and the backlog was growing. It turned out that numerous claims were caught in a corporate "do loop." These claims could not be automatically adjudicated, and were kicked out of the system for review by a claims processor. The claims processor would see that many problem claims required another specialist's review (e.g., the eligibility group, the provider group, or legal group), and the claims were forwarded. The next department might see these problem claims as partially their issue to resolve but also requiring another specialist's review and/or a management sign-off. The bottom line was that no one department and no one individual felt they could make the decision on these problem claims, so these claims meandered and accumulated until finally exploding into view as a massive pileup and crisis.

So what was done? A "SWAT team" was pulled together and located in a "War Room" to resolve the crisis. Any claim that had to have a multi-discipline review was routed to this group. Essentially this working/design team started processing problem claims. The 80/20 rule came into view right away. For the few issues that created the most problems corrective action was taken—usually in the form of a quick process redesign—to prevent the next similar problem claim from coming to the group. The remaining problem claims were dispatched with increasing speed as the team worked together and got to know some degree of each other's expertise. The pile was whittled down in a matter of a few weeks and "success" was declared.

Then the SWAT team disbanded. Each functional department wanted their person back.

It is interesting to note that such cross-functional customercentric teams are routinely put in during times of crisis, and then abandoned after the crisis has been abated. Why, if putting cross-functional teams together to rectify a crisis is common sense, is it not common sense to organize that way? Basically because there is a long history of these functional departments, not just in the company, but for the industry as a whole. No one in power gives serious thought to any alternative. In addition, department heads worked hard through their entire careers to get where they are, and have every incentive to maintain and grow their empires. Finally, they argue, one team can work for a short time, but using multi-teams for the everyday processing of work could not be supported. I beg to differ: companies can provide the structure to support a multi-team-based organization.

Multi-Teams and the Supporting Environment

Let's look at how a multi-team environment can work. The basic concept explained here has been applied in both high volume and low volume workflows in a variety of industries, and the issues are the same. However, for the sake of variety, I will use an example from a small company conducting a few transactions per month.

Not all companies, or departments within companies, process thousands of units of work per day for thousands of customers. So let's look at how a $\cong$200-person technology solutions company deployed permanent customercentric work teams in their launch process.

First a little background. We came to this solutions company at a critical stage in its evolution. The entrepreneurial zeal and individual heroics that worked so well were no longer sufficient. The need for more structure, and a repeatable scalable process, had become especially apparent in the new client launch process. They defined their launch process as encompassing all the activities from the time a customer approved the contract until the technology solution was configured, installed, and operational.

The existing launch process was ill defined and performed poorly. Basically to meet and succeed with the growth plans, the company needed a launch process that would perform exceptionally well in all dimensions of performance such as:

- Quality—would work as promised and as expected by the client (instead of never)

- Delivery—on-time: commitment date for delivery met (instead of never)

- Cycle Time—capability to implement within four weeks (instead of six to eight weeks)

- Cost—$\cong 300$ person-hours per implementation (instead of $\cong 1,000$ person-hours)

This design effort was made even more difficult since the sales were rolling in, and the company could not stop to get this done. In effect the design team needed to "change the engines on a moving jet" with resources stretched to do it. But there was no other option (the jet would crash if they didn't change the engines!).

A design team was assigned to the project and, at best, devoted half their time to the project for six weeks. The Discover and Inspire Stages were completed within two weeks, with the high level design done during week three. The remaining three weeks were used to produce detailed designs and related documentation (detailed process maps and procedure sheets for each step), and to prepare for piloting the new process.

Anyway, not unlike the Yellow Pages project, their design called for semiautonomous launch teams made up of expertise from the various functions: essentially a couple of software developers, a project manager, an HTML specialist, quality assurance, and someone from production. However, not every team looked the same.

They established two types of teams. One would handle the "fast track" projects. These projects did not entail lots of new specialized code. They simply required the company's off-the-shelf software solution to be configured to order and integrated with the customer's systems. The fast-track launch team would be the primary contact with the company for 80 percent of the customer deals. This five-to-six-person team contained the capability to initiate and complete the launch/installation in the majority of cases.

The second type of professional services team was established to handle "custom track" work. Here the customer required consulting help and new specialized code and/or customized code to integrate the solution with its systems. The customer required more people, and typically would have them for a longer period at the customer site.

The design team prepared the slide in Figure 13.2 to depict how they envisioned the organization working.

The Resource Pool

As this organization took form, there was one big problem, one big cultural hurdle to overcome. From the company's founding, the software developers had few constraints and participated in both new product development and client launch. The developers even liked being the heroes when pulled in to bail out troubled launch efforts. However, the company had now grown to the point where some focus was in order. Product development suffered as developers were continually pulled off development work, and the launch process suffered while waiting for the bailout.

As hard as it was, the company had to dedicate some resources to each core process: development and launch, with just a few top developers capable to help either side. Along with the segregation they had to think through the career path. It made sense to start entry-level developers in the fast-track configuration team, then migrate them to the "custom track." Later, the big promotion would be to product development, followed by assignment of the best and brightest to a "resource pool." The intent of the resource pool was to have a core group of talent that could bail anyone out of any problem—in essence, a SWAT team.

Figure 13.2. Team-Based Organization

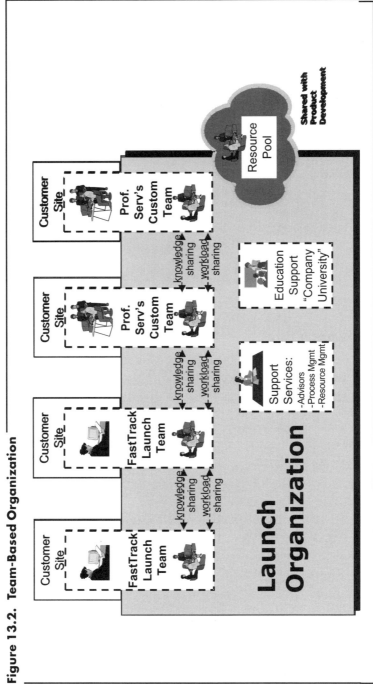

In addition to the resource pool, the work teams would need to be supported by training and education support. In this case, the education group had three roles. They provided a broad array of learning tools and services to: (1) customers regarding the company's technology, portal use, custom track implementations; and (2) employees regarding technology proficiencies, technological advances, quality improvement and problem solving techniques, human resources and teamwork skills, project management, and the like, as well as (3) collecting and disseminating knowledge and learning among the teams and support services.

Sharing Work and Knowledge

Knowledge sharing is built into the process. A mechanism based on Web technology and facilitation by the education group was designed to allow easy sharing of ideas and solutions that have worked (or have not worked). The intent was to share such knowledge among all the teams and support services.

The design team also recognized that workload imbalances among the teams were not only likely, but also inevitable. Workload sharing among the teams would be needed. An underloaded team would seek to assign one or more members to assist an overloaded team. A combination of measures, incentives, and resource-management techniques were needed to make this work.

At the end of the six-week design project, a pilot of the new process, for one fast-track team, demonstrated the design worked. By every measure the design was a success: the installation was on-time, it worked as promised, it was done within four weeks, and just under 300 person-hours. This one team alone represented a quick hit surgical strike for 20 percent of the company's launch workload.

Dedicated Support

For other companies, and other processes, a team-based design is likely to contain the concept of dedicated support. This comes out of working the capacity planning numbers when calculating the required staffing levels for the teams. Sometimes every team requires half a person. In such circumstances the designs have called for a person to be assigned and dedicated to serving two teams—essentially every team gets their half a person.

Common Themes

The ideas contained in these designs are common outcomes in nearly every team-based operations design. The idea of a resource pool has been included in many designs where the top talent with a particular expertise needs to be shared. The idea of support services and especially the need to share knowledge and share workload come out of nearly every team-based operations design. "Dedicated support" shows up routinely.

The Dominoes of Change[1]

In our 1994 book *Corporate Renaissance: The Art of Reengineering*, we used an illustration to make the point that an effective new process design encompasses more than process. If you knock over the process domino, you will hit "organization design," "job design," "physical layout," "measures," "compensation," and so on. See Figure 13.3.

As part of our surgical-strike initiatives we use the dominoes as a checklist. The intent is to spend a little time thinking through the implications of a new process design on each of the dominoes, and ask some key questions such as:

- Does the organization structure support or hinder the new process design?
- Do job titles, boundaries, descriptions support or hinder the new process design?
- Is the facility and workspace set up to reinforce and enable the success of the new work design?
- Are the day-to-day measures of performance aligned with the performance objectives for the new design?
- Is the way in which employees are reviewed and compensated consistent with the process design's intent and the supporting measures?

Figure 13.3. Dominoes of Corporate Change

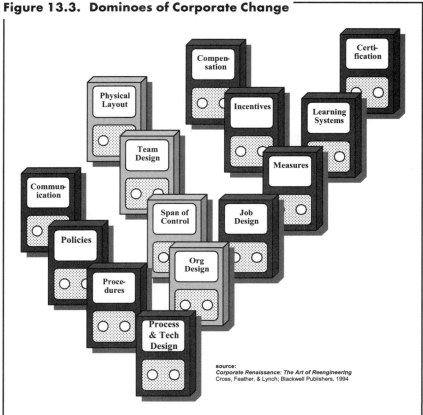

source:
Corporate Renaissance: The Art of Reengineering
Cross, Feather, & Lynch; Blackwell Publishers, 1994

The point is to ask such questions and think these things through before rolling out the new design across the organization. You can either plan and design how these dominoes will fall, or just wait and see what happens. At the very least you need an answer when questions are raised. The answer may be: "We recognize the need to also redesign how this or that will work, and in a general sense we see it working like this, but we want to try the process first in a pilot mode. The pilot will help determine the best course of action for this or that domino."

There are a couple of key dominoes that appear to be particularly critical to the success of these customercentric teams. The first is proximity and the physical layout, and the second is the use of measures to drive *team* performance.

Proximity

A recurring theme in this book and a key feature of these customercentric team designs is proximity. As much as possible these designs call for each work team to have its members located right next to each other. Sometimes this is the most tangible, and threatening, feature of the design. People can nod their heads in mindless agreement to the concept of teams, but they can't ignore their desk being moved. I remember one case in which we asked for the workspace to be reorganized for the first pilot of a new work team. First we were told there was no budget—it couldn't be done (after they invested well over a few hundred thousand dollars on the project to that date). A meeting was convened to discuss the re-layout where there were more people at the meeting than were needed to move the furniture. In the end the corporate bureaucrats had to be overruled by the executives in charge of the redesign. In that case we had capitulation and compliance, but not commitment (more about building commitment in Chapter 14). Although we got off to a rocky start the re-layout was essential and enabled the pilot to succeed.

Measures

In the traditional work environment individual performance is a primary driver. For instance, in our technology solutions company the "lines of code per developer" was an indicator. In our game the "subassemblies produced per assembler" seems important. However, it does no good for one link in the chain to be twice as strong as the others. The stronger link has to help strengthen the others. Teams require a new way of thinking—it is the team's overall performance that counts. Individual performance will be visible to the other team members without a lot of detailed measurement. Teamwork (and some peer pressure) will go a long way toward encouraging improvement in individual performance for the good of the team. In many respects the performance of the team will be seen and measured much like individuals used to be measured.

For example, in our technology solutions company the key performance expectations were expressed for the team as a whole, where they said: "A six-person 'launch pod' will be expected to: launch 32 deals per year, manage 3.3 active deals at any one time, and deliver .7 deals per week."

In addition, they established measures for the four-quadrant score-card to capture and make visible the team's performance for every launch project (Figure 13.4).

Figure 13.4. Launch Team's Process Performance Scorecard

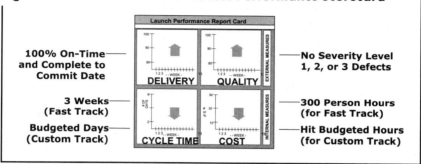

At our tech firm any observation or measure of individual perform-ance was left to the team.

Culture Clash?

Team-based work is a major cultural shift for some companies. At companies where individual performance has been recognized and re-warded for years to the exclusion of team performance, a Strike 10 solution should probably not be tried. For instance, in the extreme case, there are companies where piecework-based pay schemes have been the norm for years. Some people thrive in that environment and do not want day-to-day contact with other people. To move such an organization into a team-based environment would likely require the hiring of a new workforce.

In other companies the cultural clash is less obvious, but real none-theless. In such cases it may be helpful to conduct a workforce readi-ness assessment. While such assessments may appear mushy, they can provide critical guidance with regard to the specific areas where the workers have concerns. Only by understanding their concerns can a combination of adjustments to the new process design, a communica-tions plan, and a transition plan alleviate what would have been some significant implementation obstacles.

However, for the majority of companies that can find a way to implement customercentric teams, the benefits can be enormous and fast.

Strike 10: Implement Customercentric Teams

Strike 10 primarily results when a cross-functional team of workers is given support and some dedicated time to redesign their own workflows.

Strike 10 actions typically encompass:

- Creating a team of six to ten workers, with expertise from all functions engaged in processing the work from beginning to end of a core business process
- Locating the workers next to each other as much as possible
- Measuring and rewarding team performance

Strike 10 is about getting a few workers together with all the skills required to serve a set of customers. It succeeds when there is a belief that the work teams themselves can best manage and improve their own performance—given the right environment.

CHAPTER 14

CONDUCT THE STRIKE(S)

Nothing succeeds like success.

—ALEXANDRE DUMAS THE ELDER

In a business climate requiring quick hit operating improvements, using the ten key surgical-strike solutions to obtain those quick hits is the way to go. Our collective experiences with TQM, Six Sigma, reengineering, and the like, have provided clear guidance as to the solutions that work. Why reinvent the wheel?

Simply conduct a brief, but intelligent, analysis of your current process(es). Cut to the chase and find the facts; without conducting a "science project," but enough to be directionally correct. Use the facts to identify and focus on a few key areas of greatest opportunity.

You can then obtain quick hits by pulling in the surgical-strike solutions already proven to work in the real world. These solutions were built upon the tried and true principles of all types of process-improvement methods. They represent a fast, yet balanced and moderate approach, between incremental improvement and radical redesign.

Typically these surgical-strike actions represent projects with low costs, low risks, and high benefits. They are small-scale projects with broad organizational scope and impact where the emphasis is on a big bang for the buck.

Obtain the Gains, Sustain the Gains

"You can win the war, but lose the peace." This saying applies to corporate change initiatives as well. Without engaging people throughout the change process, there is a strong likelihood of significant implementation problems, and an increased risk that long-term sustained success may be compromised.

So what can be done to ensure a successful and sustainable surgical strike?

- Communicate, communicate, communicate.
- Pilot the strike.
- Strike again.

Communicate, Communicate, Communicate

As soon as an executive thinks of conducting a surgical strike the word gets out. The rumor mill takes over and expands, distorting and contorting the thought into an unrecognizable horror story. So the best remedy is to get out in front and "manage the press." There are plenty of good texts on change management and communications[1], so I won't delve into the topic in too much detail. Rather I will hit some of the highlights that I have seen work well with surgical-strike initiatives.

I have been using a one-page "communications guideline chart" as depicted in Figure 14.1. The intent of the chart is to assist me and design teams to evaluate and select the most appropriate vehicle(s) for communicating various pieces of information as they arise.

The intent has been to achieve a better alignment between the information that is to be communicated and the means of communicating. It is not that companies don't use a wide variety of media, it's that more thought should go into classifying information and then selecting the best means of communication. For example, while there are no hard and fast rules, some information is best conveyed in face-to-face encounters, while other information can be communicated via a routine newsletter.

The factors that dictate the appropriate mode of communication

Figure 14.1.

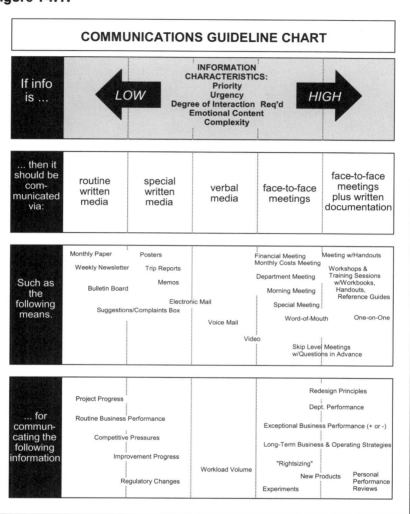

are the information's priority, urgency, and the degrees of interaction, emotional content, and complexity. If any one of these factors can be rated as "high," the mode of communication needs to become more personal, perhaps backed up by less personal means of communication. If most of these factors can be rated as "low," it may be possible to use more impersonal modes of communication such as memos and newsletters only.

What follows is a brief description of the factors:

- *Priority:* There are a number of issues that come up and are critical for everyone or a selected group of people to know about. You can't count on the people that absolutely need to know to see and read a memo, bulletin board, or newsletter. Issues that will significantly alter people's day-to-day activities, or change their perception of either long- or short-term objectives, are examples of the kinds of information that can fall into the "high priority" category.

- *Urgency:* Other issues and information can't wait. An obvious good example would be the announcement of an acquisition. No employee likes to hear what the company is doing from the general media. They like to hear it first from their management. Other urgent issues might include a change in production schedule, management/organizational changes, or immediate safety issues.

- *Interaction:* There are some issues that can't be (or shouldn't be) addressed with a one-way mode of communication. There are issues where discussion, questions and answers, or additional information must come from those to whom an issue must be communicated. Also, interaction is required when the issue is of high emotional content (see next item).

- *Emotional Issues:* Issues related to job security, reporting and working relationships, major changes in management style, new assignments, and anything that affects pay or benefits can be emotionally charged. These issues require great care in how they are presented in order to ensure a positive response. Emotional topics require factual information conveyed with understanding and sensitivity for the audience (and how the information could be perceived).

- *Complexity:* The more complex the information is, the more likely that every nuance and interpretation won't be anticipated. Therefore, the written word (or voicemail, or video) may not be appropriate by itself as the means to convey complex information. It should likely be used to make the initial explanation followed by face-to-face communications where questions can be answered and specific concerns of each segment of the audience can be addressed.

The chart suggests the range of media options to be employed depending on the assessment of the factors described above. At the bottom of the chart are some specific topic examples, according to the factors above. However, these topics are rather general and subject to interpretation, and are only meant to elicit some thinking and further discussion.

The point is to be conscious of what information you wish to communicate and select the most appropriate media. The "most appropriate" is the media that gets the job done and is most cost effective. For example, it may be useful to review the list of topics covered in a typical morning meeting and see which topics require face-to-face communication and which topics could be done via other media (memo or voice mail). It is not that face-to-face communication is ineffective for those topics that could be conveyed via written media; it is that other topics requiring face-to-face communication are crowded out. However, there is one caution. Sometimes it is simpler and more cost-efficient to provide one or two sentences or paragraphs at a meeting than it is to issue a formal memo. Again, awareness of the issue and conscious selection of the means to convey the message will go a long way toward effective employee communications.

Position the Project

First and foremost in any surgical strike is the need to build the case—the compelling need for change. This typically has to come from the top. The case needs to be made to the masses, who see a few of their colleagues called out for a few weeks to participate in a surgical-strikes project team.

Plus the case has to be made even more clearly and directly to the project team. It is the project team that feels out on a limb. They need to be sure their role is strongly sanctioned and supported from the top, and know that their peers and immediate superiors can see that as well.

Again here is where the results of an organizational readiness assessment can provide input as to the relative priorities of what needs to be communicated. Usually there is good news and bad news from such assessments. The good news—more often than not, the organization was "change ready," meaning that most employees recognized the need for and welcomed change. Sad to say, but in more cases than we like to admit there was a general lack of trust that management would really make any of the changes that the employees would recommend. In these cases the employees were right to be skeptical. The company's history of fanfare followed by inaction spoke for itself. The widespread perception of "all talk, no action" cannot be refuted with more talk— all the more reason to conduct an effective surgical strike as fast as possible.

Report Progress

Simply making the case at the onset is not enough. Even though the skeptics don't believe anything will happen, they still want to know what is going on. For example, at Time Insurance, "a communication mechanism was established in the form of a bi-weekly divisional meeting that was intended to inform and include the entire organization in the project. Monthly communication forums were also established as well as day-to-day participative mechanisms for employee involvement. The day-to-day mechanisms were in the form of a newsletter, an e-mail mailbox set-up for ideas and inquiries, a suggestion box, and a 'living list' that included all of the ideas that employees felt should get incorporated into the design."[2]

Engage Others in Discovery

That last point about capturing the ideas of all employees, not just those in the project team, is great. There are many ways to get their input.

One project team at a leading software company used their 141-step map of the current process to get ideas. The map was blown up (3′ high by 21′ long) and posted on a wall in the main hallway. They posted instructions on the wall, provided markers, and asked for comments on sticky notes. They provided three colors of sticky notes for three categories of ideas. The instructions said:

- Use yellow sticky notes where a new process, procedure, or policy may be helpful (e.g., we should eliminate this intermediary hand-off and send it directly to . . .).

- Use blue sticky notes where the interaction among people needs to improve (e.g., editors should be involved in selecting/hiring writers).
- Use pink sticky notes where a technological solution will help (e.g., we need a new system to . . .).

They were a relatively small group, yet they received fifty-one comments over a couple of days. Thirty-one out of the fifty-one comments were on yellow sticky notes and were process related. This was good news for a surgical strike—in that they weren't all technology related. A technology-dependent change will tend not to be surgical strike, but rather a long meandering road that goes halfway to where you want to go.

Engage Others in Inspiration

Other project teams have engaged their peers in brainstorming sessions. The technology solutions company made up a phony business magazine cover. It consumed the front page of a one-page handout. The headline read, "Solutions Company of the Year—Outstanding Launch Process Explained." The back page contained the following instructions for their "Design Options & Ideas Exercise:"

LAUNCH PROCESS DESIGN
Design Options & Ideas Exercise: January 17

In the April issue of this leading business magazine, there is a feature article highlighting the stellar performance of our efficient and effective launch process. The article opens with a description of outstanding performance:

- Customer Satisfaction—from 3–4 to 4+ satisfaction rating
- Employee Satisfaction—4+ satisfaction rating
- Quality—No severity Level 1, 2, or 3 defects
- Delivery—100% on-time & complete to commit date
- Cycle Time—from 8+ weeks to 3 weeks
- Labor—from 1,000 person hours, to 300 person hours

Within the article there are several headlines and sections outlining specifically how we accomplish this performance. What are the highlights of the article? Suggest specific characteristics of the new process that would have to happen to make such performance a reality.

Service Experience (from the client's perspective): This refers to the perception the client has regarding their overall experience and specific day-to-day service encounters with us *during the launch process.* Expressed as quotes from our clients, what did they say? *Example:* "Your company provided us with . . ."

Management Style: This refers to the way that people are organized, trained, managed, and rewarded. *Example:* "The Company has instituted client-focused two-person implementation teams."

Process Techniques: These can be specific ideas relating to changing company operations or generic ideas that may relate to the application of the basic principles of good workflow. *Example:* "Launch process is streamlined by . . . eliminating [what activities] . . . and adding [what activities] . . . changing [what activities]."

Technology Enablers: These are the tools that will enable the launch process to achieve the outstanding performance.

Write the highlights/headers that would be found within the business magazine's article. The sky is the limit; however you want it to be concrete enough that it can stand alone as a separate thought. A good indicator is if you can return to the highlight a week later and still understand the underlying concept.

The exercise worked. Well over one hundred ideas were generated with contributions from throughout the company.

A week or so later, the project team had a surgical strike defined and a design of how things would look after the strike was made. The project team went back to the workforce, showed their design, and made sure everyone knew the degree to which the ideas submitted were incorporated into the design.

Manage the Water Cooler

Most formal communications are treated with a degree of skepticism. Most people seem to trust the insight they gain through informal conversation—over the lunch table, at the water cooler, or over a few beers after work. These are the situations where the project team itself can do the most good—or the most damage—to the project.

The rank-and-file employees need to hear the same thing from the members of the project team. If one team member says one thing and another team member says another, then confidence in the team's work may be eroded. However, if people compare notes and the story is consistent, the team will appear to have its act together.

At the end of each day, the project team can use a flip chart to write down and agree upon the talking points for the day. One team even used the talking points to get constructive feedback on ideas. For instance, the talking point was: "Today we had some disagreements around whether to . . . , what do you think?" As long as everyone on the team was aware that the issue would be mentioned publicly, it could work in the team's favor. The team would appear to be open and not hiding anything, plus the project team would get some constructive feedback.

Project teams need to be reminded that half their job is to develop the most appropriate surgical-strike actions. The other half of their job is to communicate and promote their work.

A critical time for communication is when the project team is ready to make the strike, even if it is done on a small scale as a pilot. Before conducting a pilot, the project team members may conduct a communications "road show." Their mission: to inform all employees involved about the surgical-strike plan, explain how it was derived and how they might play a role in it.

As seen in a software services organization, it was most important to address the impact on headcount. "It was critical to tell people that although a reduction in man-hours could be attained, it was our intention to use these resources in revenue-producing functions such as completing more change requests," said the software services director.

"After everyone understood the pilot concept, we asked for volunteers for the first self-managed team who would implement and test the new process design on a small scale for three months. They were trained for two weeks, using the process maps and procedure-level documentation of each new activity, which had been completed during the design phase."

Pilot the Strike

Sometimes a surgical strike can be a no-brainer. Strikes 1 through 6 are particularly suited to "just do it." But even so, surprises crop up. Anytime there is change, there are likely to be unintended consequences. Also, don't expect to get the full benefits right out of the starting gate.

First, a word about unintended consequences. On one occasion we piloted a much better way of handling customer service calls for a bank. The customers were so pleased with the way in which they were handled that they continued to call back for everything (account balances, and transaction information), even though the information was readily available on the Internet and easily accessible on the automated phone system. We found if we made the service encounter too good, the calls and call time went up. The bank had two choices: degrade the service slightly or find a way to offer the premium service for a price. The bank ended up with a premium line for its best customers.

> **In the Process Resign Game** the three rounds make a great case for the importance of a pilot. After Round One, the game's participants get to figure out how to fix the process and implement as many surgical-strike improvements as they desire. The process is redesigned; tables are reconfigured; job roles are changed; and Round Two begins.
>
> In most cases Round Two shows great improvement, but not nearly to the degree required. For example, the unit cost is too high, while quality and delivery are also inadequate. Remember this chart from Chapter1? Figure 14.2 shows the average performance levels during each round:

Figure 14.2. Performance Takes Practice

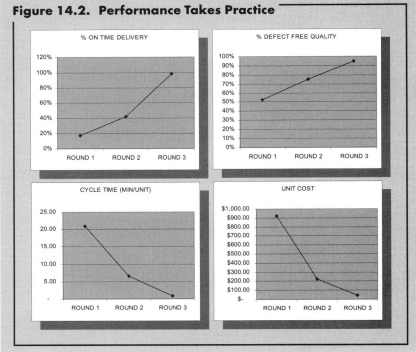

After Round Two, the results are usually disappointing to the participants—they thought they had it figured out. It takes the mid-course corrections between Rounds Two and Three to nail it.

Round Two can be viewed as a pilot of the surgical-strikes improvement. Additional process flaws are identified and corrected, and then the participants succeed in winning the game.

The same situation occurs with real surgical-strike improvements. Unfortunately, there are occasions where there is no opportunity for Round Three. We have seen cases where the management team does not have the patience to learn from a pilot experience and try again. The plug was pulled on the project, just when some great lessons were learned and success was imminent. Again, great communications and setting expectations for pilot performance and learning can go a long way toward alleviating this problem.

During the debrief after a successful and major surgical strike, the project manager stated that "during the pilot, we expected that problems or new ideas would arise, requiring modifications in order to smooth out the process. In fact, this is one reason why the pilot was so important and a wise choice over immediate company-wide implementation, especially when you are dealing with organizations the size of ours. Also, a pilot of the new process proved the concept worked with action and facts rather than words."

Strike Again

There are many cases when you can jump to these ten proven surgical-strike solutions, and skip the rigor, delay, and cost of drawn-out process improvement methodologies.

Strike 1: Unclog the workplace

Strike 2: Eliminate work

Strike 3: Streamline the workflow

Strike 4: Reclaim lost time—Utilize capacity and expand capability

Strike 5: Redistribute the work

Strike 6: Manage fluctuations in work volume

Strike 7: Focus the flows

Strike 8: Link and learn—unclog the flows of knowledge

Strike 9: Show the results

Strike 10: Implement customercentric teams

With simple good intelligence that is directionally correct about current process performance and operating characteristics, the most appropriate surgical strikes can be applied.

If the solution is legitimately obvious, then "just do it." The intent of the ten surgical strikes described in this book is to make some tried-and-true solutions legitimately obvious.

THE TEN
SURGICAL STRIKES

Strike 1: Unclog the Workplace

Strike 1 is essentially a significant and rapid downsizing, that may be warranted in cases where:

- Employee growth has significantly exceeded revenue growth, and/or
- Revenue per employee greatly lags that of your competitors

If warranted, Strike 1 typically needs to focus on:

- Specific areas (functions, departments, or processes) in the company where headcount growth has far exceeded revenue growth and the growth for other areas; and
- The areas of extraordinary growth that are not justified to that degree by today's strategic objectives

Strike 1 is a beginning, not an end. The elimination of excessive bloat and related confusion is what allows the organization's participants to see their work and how it flows. With such visibility, more precise and more significant surgical strikes can be identified and carried out.

Strike 2: Eliminate Work

If appropriate, Strike 2 typically needs to:

- Eliminate some customers: Uncover and stop doing business with undesirable and unprofitable customers; and/or

- Eliminate some products and services: Uncover and stop doing or offering undesirable and unprofitable products and services; and/or

- Eliminate non-value-added nonsense work: Uncover and stop doing work with no value
  —Eliminate failures and failure-related recovery.
  —Eliminate inspections.
  —Eliminate set-up, movement, and storage.

Strike 2 is about eliminating the need to have a process. If there is no work to do, there is no need for a process. The next strikes are about pinpointing targets of opportunity within processes.

Strike 3: Streamline the Workflow

Strike 3 starts with facts and data about the process. There are typically four steps to getting the facts:

- Define the workload.
- Map the process.
- Quantify the process.
- Identify the key priority areas for action.

Strike 3 actions typically encompass:

- A focus on the few process steps that consume the most time (labor time and cycle time)

- The elimination of non-value-added nonsense process steps:
  —Eliminate failures and failure-related recovery activities.
  —Eliminate inspection steps.
  —Eliminate set-up, movement, and storage steps.

- The reduction in labor time and cycle time to perform the value-added steps:
  —Through proficiency
  —Through orienting the work
  —Through sequencing the work
  —Through automation

Strike 3 is about pinpointing targets of opportunity within processes.

Strike 4: Reclaim Lost Time—Utilize Capacity and Expand Capability

Strike 4 starts with facts and data about where time is spent. There are typically a few categories of lost time:

- Wait time
- Unavailable time
- Utilized time
- Unutilized time

Strike 4 actions typically encompass:

- Reclaiming lost time by eliminating the wait for work:
  —Relieve the bottleneck.
  —Use generalists rather than specialists.
  —Get people together.
  —Schedule work.
  —Schedule workers.
- Putting unutilized time to work
- Expanding capabilities
  —Enhance the process.
  —Enhance the customer experience.
  —Enhance sales and expand the customer base.

Strike 4 is about opportunities to improve utilization of people's time by finding and eliminating time that is wasted, and by ideally putting that freed-up time to good use.

Strike 5: Redistribute the Work

Strike 5 actions typically encompass:

- Enabling customers to perform activities previously performed by the company
- Outsourcing nonstrategic work to third party vendors
- Eliminating agents and other conduits to your customers
  —Remove agents from the business model entirely, or
  —Bypass the agent/intermediaries for a portion of the process, or for some key interfaces with the customer.

Strike 5 starts with an understanding of the company's strategic intent and process flows, then a review of the work redistribution options, and selection of those changes with the greatest benefit (relative to implementation costs and day-to-day operating costs). The typical Strike 5 opportunity entails the following steps:

- Review your process profiles (e.g., core process definitions and process maps).
- Assess activities that you do that might be performed by customers.
- Assess and define what processes and activities are core to your business strategy.
- Consider processes and activities that you do, but are not core, as candidates for outsourcing.
- Consider processes and activities that others do, but that are core, as candidates for bringing in-house.
- Prepare an impact assessment of the options (including risks of new hand-offs).
- Develop an action plan and execute!

Strike 5: Redistribute the Work, is about capitalizing on targets of opportunity to shift work, and the related processes, to or from other organizational entities—whether it be customers, suppliers, or intermediaries.

Strike 6: Manage Fluctuations in Work Volume

Strike 6 primarily starts with facts and data about the volumes and types of workload profiled over time. The time span could be a day, a week, a month, a quarter, or a year, or some combination—whichever time horizon is most significant to highlighting the swings in work volume.

Strike 6 actions typically encompass:

- Expanding and contracting the "pipe" (e.g., staff levels) that processes the work
- Keeping the pipe full continuously
  —By encouraging work to be requested during off-peak times instead of peak times
  —By building product at a steady pace to meet longer-term demands (and hopefully commitments), rather than day-to-day demands
- Shifting some activities to off-peak times
- Merging groups of workers when their peaks are at different times

Strike 6 is about understanding the impact of peaks and valleys of work volume and then pinpointing targets of opportunity within businesses to clip the peaks of work volume and fill the valleys with productive work.

Strike 7: Focus the Flows

Strike 7 is about clearly distinguishing a few key types of work, then developing and establishing clear, distinct process flows for each type.

Strike 7 primarily starts with facts and data about the types of workload and customer segments being served. There are many ways to slice and dice the workload and segments. But for the purpose of focusing the flows, the predominant distinctions seem to be made based upon the following:

- Degree of difficulty: Fast easy-to-process work versus slow, difficult, customized work

- Geography: support and service requirements sometimes vary because of climate, laws/regulations, and/or population densities

- Segment: Focused processes can sometimes better serve distinct product and/or customer segments

Strike 7 actions typically encompass:

- Designing dedicated process flows, to best deliver a type of work or to best serve a particular customer segment

- Restructuring the organization to best operate the new process

Strike 8: Link and Learn—Unclog the Flows of Knowledge

Strike 8 is about defining and using specific feedback or feed-forward of information regarding the business and process performance to immediately take actions and improve.

Strike 8 primarily starts with a fear that things are messed up and not getting better. It picks up steam with facts and data about the opportunities lost when something that should have been known and should have been acted upon is not. Then the missing links are identified and connected.

Strike 8 actions typically encompass:

- Providing the means to rapidly move the right information to the right place at the right time

- Locating people within close proximity to each other

- Providing clear and specific points in the day-to-day processes in which data are captured and in which the data are used

Strike 9: Show the Results

Strike 9 primarily starts with an objective to influence people in two areas:

1. To do the right things in their day-to-day work

2. To focus on a few key areas requiring improvements

Strike 9 actions typically encompass:

▪ Defining, prioritizing, and articulating/communicating the "right things"

▪ Providing clear direction on priorities for improvement

▪ Making the results of day-to-day work visible
—Through measures
—Through visibility to work queues and the like

Strike 9 is about making visible and tangible the priorities and outcomes (good or bad) from one's work.

Strike 10: Implement Customercentric Teams

Strike 10 primarily results when a cross-functional team of workers is given support and some dedicated time to redesign their own workflows.

Strike 10 actions typically encompass:

▪ Creating a team of six to ten workers with expertise from all functions engaged in processing the work from beginning to end of a core business process

▪ Locating the workers next to each other as much as possible

▪ Measuring and rewarding team performance

Strike 10 is about getting a few workers together with all the skills required to serve a set of customers. It succeeds when there is a belief that the work teams themselves can best manage and improve their own performance, given the right environment.

NOTES

Chapter 1

1. *"Bureaucracies Love Kaizen,"* The CEO Refresher, *www.refresher .com,* Refresher Publications Inc., 1998.
2. Hal Clifford, "Six Sigma," *Continental Magazine,* November 1997.
3. Gary Hamel, *Leading the Revolution* (Cambridge, Mass: Harvard Business School Press, 2000).

Chapter 2

1. Kelvin Cross, "Wang Scores 'EPIC' Success With Circuit Board Redesign," *Industrial Engineering,* January 1988.
2. The Associated Press, "First Union Staffs Up as Customers Demand Tellers," July 19, 1999.
3. Peter S. Pande, Robert P. Neuman, and Roland R. Cavanagh, *The Six Sigma Way* (New York: McGraw-Hill, 2000), p. 158.
4. Richard Lynch and Kelvin Cross, *Measure Up! Yardsticks for Continuous Improvement* (Malden, MA: Blackwell Publishers, 1991), p. 46.
5. Britt Beemer, "The New AT&T: Now for the Hard Part," *Upside,* September 1999.

Chapter 3

1. Richard L. Lynch and Kelvin Cross, *Measure Up! Yardsticks for Continuous Improvement* (Malden, MA: Blackwell Publishers, 1991), pp. 57–58; and Kelvin Cross, Richard L. Lynch, and John

Feather, *Corporate Renaissance: The Art of Reengineering* (Malden, Mass.: Blackwell Publishers, 1994), pp. 71–72.

2. Reprinted from "The New Industrial Engineering: Information Technology and Business Process Redesign" by Thomas H. Davenport & James E. Short, MIT Sloan Management Review, Summer 1990 by permission of publisher. Copyright © 1990 by Massachusetts Institute of Technology. All rights reserved. (Thomas H. Davenport and James E. Short, "The New Industrial Engineering: Information Technology and Business Process Redesign," *MIT Sloan Management Review,* Summer 1990.)

Chapter 4

1. Excerpts from *Parkinson's Law*, Copyright © 1957, 1960, 1962, 1970, 1979 by C. Northcote Parkinson. Reprinted with permission of Houghton Mifflin Company. All rights reserved.
2. Ibid.
3. Project on Government Oversight (POGO), March 1998.
4. Fred Vogelstein, Paul Sloan, and Bill Holstein, "Corporate Dowagers Go for a Makeover," *U.S. News & World Report,* November 6, 2000.
5. Carol J. Loomis, "How AT&T Managed to Have Excess Managers," *Fortune,* December 25, 1995.

Chapter 5

1. Rick Brooks, "Unequal Treatment," *The Wall Street Journal,* January 7, 1999.
2. Ibid.
3. Ibid.
4. Kelvin Cross, "Call Resolution: The Wrong Focus for Service Quality," *Quality Progress,* February 2000, pp. 64–66.
5. Kelvin Cross, John Feather, and Richard L. Lynch, *Corporate Renaissance: The Art of Reengineering* (Oxford, England: Blackwell, 1994), p. 85.

Chapter 6

1. Richard L. Lynch and Kelvin Cross, *Measure Up! How to Measure Corporate Performance,* 2nd ed. (Oxford, England: Black-

well, 1995); and Kelvin Cross, John Feather, and Richard L. Lynch, *Corporate Renaissance: The Art of Reengineering,* (Oxford, England: Blackwell, 1994).

Chapter 7

1. Eliyahu M. Goldratt and Jeff Cox, *The Goal* (Croton on Hudson, NY: North River Press, 1984).
2. Richard L. Lynch and Kelvin Cross, *Measure Up! How to Measure Corporate Performance*, 2d ed., (Oxford, England: Blackwell, 1994), p. 211; Kelvin Cross, John Feather, and Richard L. Lynch, *Corporate Renaissance: The Art of Reengineering* (Oxford, England: Blackwell, 1994), pp. 135–137.
3. Kelvin F. Cross, "Making Manufacturing More Effective Through Reduced Throughput Time," *National Productivity Review,* Winter 1986–1987, pp. 43–45.
4. Peter Katel, "Bordering on Chaos," *Wired 5.07* (July 1997).
5. Frederick F. Reichheld, *The Loyalty Effect* (Boston: Harvard Business School Press, 1996), p. 13.
6. "Pushing the Customer Service Envelope," *Inc.* (July 1993), p. 24.
7. John J. Feather, "The Upside of Process Improvement," *IIE Solutions,* December 1998, pp. 42–45.

Chapter 8

1. James L. Heskett, W. Earl Sasser, Jr., and Leonard A. Schlesinger, *The Service Profit Chain* (New York: The Free Press, 1997), p. 13.
2. From their 10K Filing to the Securities & Exchange Commission, March 2002.
3. Daniel McGinn, "I'll Help Myself," *Newsweek,* April 29, 2002, p. 52.
4. "The Era of Efficiency," *Business Week,* June 18, 2001.
5. Scott Thurm, "Selectron Becomes a Force in Stealth Manufacturing," *The Wall Street Journal,* August 18, 1998.
6. From Fiserv's Web site (*www.fiserv.com*).
7. IDC Report #24532, "Opportunities Abound: A Look Into the Demand for Outsourced e-Customer Care," by Brian Bingham, Manager, CRM & Customer Care Research, IDC, 2001.

8. David Daniels, David Schatsky, and Mike Herzlinger, "A Call for Outsourcing: Building Customer Service Cost Efficiencies While Ensuring Quality," Jupitermedia Corporation, July 10, 2001, p. 1.
9. Ibid.
10. Marilyn Spittle and Humberto Trueba, "To Outsource or Not to Outsource, That Is the Question," Commweb.com, July 17, 2001.
11. Daniels et al, p. 2.

Chapter 9

1. Kelvin Cross, "Call Resolution: The Wrong Focus for Service Quality," *Quality Progress,* February 2000, pp. 66–67.

Chapter 10

1. John Feather, "A Time for Quality," *Quality Progress,* April 1997, pp. 113–115.

Chapter 11

1. Kelvin Cross, "Knowledge Flows: The Undercurrents of Process Flow, " *Knowledge Management,* January 1999, pp. 88–92.

Chapter 12

1. Richard L. Lynch and Kelvin Cross, *Measure Up! How to Measure Corporate Performance,* 2d ed., (Oxford, England: Blackwell, 1994).
2. "Barry, Eliot Go Against Tide," *Boston Globe*, May 11, 1999.

Chapter 13

1. Kelvin Cross, Richard L. Lynch, and John Feather, *Corporate Renaissance: The Art of Reengineering*, (Oxford, England: Blackwell, 1994), p. 150.

Chapter 14

1. Arnold Judson, *Changing Behavior in Organizations* (Oxford, England: Blackwell, 1991).
2. John Feather, "A Time for Quality," *Quality Progress,* April 1997, pp. 113–115.

INDEX

abandonment rates, 77
activity-based costing (ABC), 75
airline industry, 157–158
Americas Research Group Inc., 32
AT&T, 59–60
automation, 100–101, 111

backroom processing, 152–153, 154
Bankhead, Tallulah, 87
banking industry, 23–24, 73–74, 80,
    89–91, 101–103, 140, 153, 154
Barrett, Joe, 180
batch processing, 104–106
Beemer, Britt, 32
benchmarks, for SG&A (Sales, General,
    and Administration), 64
Bingham, Brian, 155
"blank canvas" approach, 4
Boston Chicken, 27
bottlenecks
    eliminating, 115–117, 219
    utilization and, 125
boundaryless behavior, 208–210
British Navy, 58
Buffet, Warren, 219, 221
bureaucracy, 53–60
    British Navy and, 58
    in the business world, 59–60
    kaizen and, 3
    nature of, 53–57
    teamwork versus, 225–228
    U.S. Project on Government Over-
      sight (POGO) and, 59–60
business planning, 25–27, 204–205
business process maps, 36–40, 90–91,
    92, 180–182, 199

call centers
    call closure focus, 77, 168–169
    call-handling efficiency in, 124–125
    managing work volume in, 164
    occupancy factors in, 122–124
    performance measures in, 214–217
    service cost per customer, 216–217
    unnecessary calls to, 77–78
    unnecessary movement of work in,
      83–84
    workload profiles in, 89–91
capability expansion, 130–138
    through expanding customer base,
      133–137
    through improving customer experi-
      ence, 131–133
    through process enhancement, 131
    through sales enhancement, 133–137
Cemex, 127–130
change process
    dominoes of change, 236–237
    gains in, 242
Christie, Agatha, 139
circuit board assembly, 195
Citibank, 140
clear indicators of performance, 211
Coburn, Steve, 1
Cohn, Lawrence, 24
communication, 242–249
    communications guideline chart,
      242, 243
    complexity of, 243, 244
    among core processes, 193–199
    degree of interaction in, 243, 244
    emotional content of, 243, 244

communication (*continued*)
  engaging others in discovery,
    246–247
  engaging others in inspiration,
    247–248
  informal communication, 248–249
  organizational readiness assessment
    and, 245–246
  priority in, 243, 244
  progress reports, 246
  urgency in, 243, 244
communications guideline chart, 242,
  243
complaint processes, 177–178
complexity, of communications, 243,
  244
computer-based spreadsheets, in process quantification process, 92–93,
  94
continuous improvement, 3
contract manufacturing, outsourcing
  of, 150–151
core customers, 20
  core processes and, 25–28
  customer segments, 22–23, 176,
    184–188
  naïve, 20–23, 73
  profitable, 72–75
  savvy, 20–23, 73
  as strike zones of opportunity, 32–33
core processes, 20
  advantages of using, 29–31
  closing feedback loops from within,
    192–193, 194–195
  components of, 31
  defining, 29, 31, 199, 201–202
  intent of, 35–36
  moving information among,
    193–194
  moving information and knowledge
    among, 195–199
  omission of, 28–29, 29
  process map framework for, 36–40,
    90–91, 92, 180–182, 199
  redesign of, 4, 6
  as strike zones of opportunity, 32–33
  types of, 25–28
  unclogging knowledge flows in,
    192–193

costs and costing
  activity-based costing (ABC), 75
  cost per customer, 156–157,
    216–217
  customer-valued, 66
  in process performance scorecard,
    232
cross-functional teams. *see* teamwork
cross-selling, 133–137, 208–209
culture clash, 239–240
customercentric teams. *see* teamwork
customer contact centers. *see* call centers
customers
  acquiring, 27, 133–137
  complaint processes, 177–178
  customer-discrimination strategies,
    73–74
  customer segmentation, 22–23, 176,
    184–188
  eliminating bad, 72–75
  enhancing experience of, 131–133
  as excuse for poor utilization,
    126–130
  self-service approach and, 140–149
  see also core customers; teamwork
customer service
  eliminating pesky customer contacts,
    76–77
  outsourcing customer care opera-
    tions, 153–156
  root-cause analysis, 77–80
  unnecessary calls, 77–78
Customer Value-Needs Profile, 22–23,
  66, 73
cycle time, 96, 103–109
  one-at-a-time processing and,
    104–107
  parallel processing and, 107–109
  in process performance scorecard,
    213, 214, 232, 250
  proficiency and, 109–111
  work schedules and, 119–120

Davenport, Thomas H., 46
dedicated support, 235–236
delivery, in process performance scorecard, 213, 232, 250

De Mar Plumbing, 132
Deming, W. Edwards, 19
deployment options, 46
design specifications/options, 184
Design Stage, 41, 47
direct labor
    full-time equivalent employees
        (FTE), 63–64, 93, 96–103,
        171–172
    time loss and, 113–114, 122
Discovery Stage, 41–44, 232, 246–247
dis-integration, 196–199
Disney World, 143
DMAIC framework (Define, Measure,
    Analyze, Improve, and Control), 8
documentation, 91
dominoes of change, 236–237
Donnenfeld, Judy, 141, 147
downsizing
    reengineering versus, 51–52, 63
    see also workplace unclogging
Dumas, Alexandre, the Elder, 241
Dunlop, Albert, 62–63

e-business revolution, 4, 7, 21–22
efficiency, call-handling, 124–125
elapsed time. see cycle time
emotional content, of communications,
    243, 244
engaging others
    in discovery, 246–247
    in inspiration, 247–248
excess capacity, 117
external failure, 80, 81

failures and failure-related recovery,
    76–80, 81
fault volumes, 171
Feather, John, 133–137, 182–184
FedEx, 100
feedback
    closing feedback loops, 192–193,
        194–195
    defined, 192
    for effective procurement, 197–198
    for manufacturability, 197
    for marketing, 199
    for reliability, 198–199

for sales, 199
for serviceability, 198–199
for workload, 166
feed-forward
    for building revenues, 208–210
    defined, 191–192
    for effective procurement, 197–198
    for manufacturability, 197
first-contact-resolution pricing, 156
first-time call resolution and closure, 77
First Union Corp., 23–24, 32, 73–74
Fiserv Custom Outsourcing Solution,
    152–153
flip charts, 249
focus groups, 180–181
full-time equivalent employees (FTE),
    63–64, 93, 96–103, 171–172

General Electric (GE), 12–13, 61,
    208–210
generalists, specialists versus, 117–118,
    228–230
geographic orientation, 176, 182–184
Goal, The (Goldratt), 116
Goldratt, Eli, 116
government bureaucracy, 58–60
growth rates, for SG&A (Sales, Gen-
    eral, and Administration), 64–66
Gulf War, 24

Hamel, Gary, 17
Hanna, David, 223
Harmon, Larry, 132
health maintenance organization
    (HMO), 30, 77–79, 196, 202–206
Howell, Doug, 218–219
H&R Block, 164

IDC, 154
in-chair occupancy, 123
industry benchmarks, 64
informal communications, 248–249
infrastructure development, 27
inspection/control, eliminating unnec-
    essary, 81–83
Inspiration Stage, 41, 44–46, 232,
    247–248
installation, 27, 205

insurance industry, 81–83, 133–137, 159, 182–184, 195, 230–231, 246
interaction, in communications, 243, 244
intermediaries, 157–160
internal failure, 80, 81

Jennings, James, 143
Jordan's Furniture, 219–221
Jupitermedia Corporation, 154–155, 156

kaizen, 3
knowledge brokers, 209, 210
knowledge flow grids, 199, 204–206
knowledge flows, 192–193, 202–209
knowledge flow unclogging, 16, 191–210, 258
  core process definitions and, 201–202
  feedback in, 192–193, 194–195, 197–199
  feed-forward in, 191–192, 197–198, 208–210
  knowledge flows in, 202–209
  knowledge management and, 191, 200–209
  linking and learning in, 199–210
  moving from concept to reality in, 206–207
  moving information among core processes, 193–194, 195–199
knowledge management, 191
  defining, 200–201
  knowledge flows and, 202–209
knowledge sharing, 235

labor time, 119–120
launch team performance measures, 234, 239
Leading the Revolution (Hamel), 17
life cycle management, 201–202
Loyalty Effect, The (Reichheld), 131–132

magazine subscription service, 84–85
Maguire, Greg, 230
Malovrh, Chuck, 168

manufacturability, feedback and feed-forward for, 197
marketing, feedback for, 199
McGee, Ken, 60
McGowen, William G., 51
middlemen, 157–160
Miller, J. Irwin, 69
Miller, Rick, 62
Morita, Akio, 191
movement/storage, eliminating unnecessary, 81, 83–85
multi-team environment, 231–236

naïve customers, 20–23, 73
new economy, 64
newspaper industry, 165–168, 194–195
non-value added work, 80–85
  analyzing loss of value, 95–96, 97
  external failure and, 80, 81
  inspection/control, 81–83
  internal failure and, 80, 81
  movement/storage, 81, 83–85
  reducing value-added time, 109–111

occupancy factors, 122–124
  in-chair occupancy, 123
  telephone occupancy, 123–124
officer inflation, 58, 59
one-at-a-time processing, 104–107
Orbitz.com, 158
organizational readiness assessment, 245–246
organizational silos, 227–230
outsourcing, 149–157
  of backroom processing, 152–153, 154
  of contract manufacturing, 150–151, 196
  of customer care, 153–156
  pay for performance in, 156–157
overhead rate, 75

parallel processing, 107–109
Pareto process, 42–44, 76
Parkinson, C. Northcote, 53–57
Parkinson's Law or the Rising Pyramid (Parkinson), 53–57

pay for performance, 156–157
performance measures, 16, 211–221,
    258–259
  in call centers, 214–217
  clear indicators of performance, 211
  clear priorities in, 217–218
  establishing down-to-earth, 212–213
  examples of, 213, 232
  individual, 238–239
  launch team, 234, 239
  process performance scorecard, 212,
    213–214, 215, 232, 234, 239, 250
  teamwork and, 232
per-incident pricing, 156
personal identification numbers (PINs),
    100
Peters, Tom, 1
PNC Financial Services Group, Inc.,
    152–153
pricing
  first-contact, 156
  per-incident, 156
  work volume and, 164–165
priorities
  bottlenecks and, 115–117, 125, 219
  in communications, 243, 244
  in performance measures, 217–218
  in workflow streamlining, 95–98
process analysis and design
  skills in, 12–13
  teamwork and, 225–228
  workload analysis and, 42, 89, 165–
    172, 184
  see also Process Redesign Game
process improvement, 1, 131
  larger context for, 20
  trends in, 5–7
process map framework, 36–40, 90–
    91, 92, 180–182, 199
process performance scorecard, 212,
    213–214, 232, 250
  costs in, 232
  for launch team, 234, 239
  for television programming, 215
process profile, 165–168
Process Redesign Game, 9–11, 39–40,
    48–49, 61, 63, 70–71, 87–88,
    109, 110, 119, 137–138, 159–160,

172–173, 188–189, 194, 212–213,
    217–218, 224, 250
process segmentation, 187
procurement, feedback and feed-for-
    ward for effective, 197–198
productivity
  busy-ness versus, 52–53
  improving, 132
products/services
  development of, 27
  eliminating bad, 75
  failures and failure-related recovery,
    76–80
  product returns, 104
  product segmentation, 187
  slow-track/fast-track work in,
    176–182
proficiency, 109–111
profitable customers, 72–75
progress reports, 246
Project on Government Oversight
    (POGO), 59–60
proximity, 118–119, 151, 238
Publilius Syrus, 175

quality
  dressing up workers for, 218–219
  dressing up work for, 219
  in process performance scorecard,
    213, 232, 250
  in TQM movement, 3–4, 7, 8, 71,
    131, 199, 241
Quick Hits Game, 9–11, 39–40, 48–
    49, 61, 63, 70–71, 87–88, 109,
    110, 119, 137–138, 159–160,
    172–173, 188–189, 194, 212–213,
    217–218, 224, 250

Rayburn, Sam, 35
Realization Stage, 41, 47–48
Reed, John, 140
reengineering, 1, 4–5, 7, 41, 71, 243
  downsizing versus, 51–52, 63
  example of, 179–180
  process improvement through, 131
Reichheld, Frederick, 131–132
reliability, feedback for, 198–199
resource pool, 233–235

returns, product, 104
rework, 76–80
Roberts, Karlene, 211
root-cause analysis, 77–80

sales
    cross-selling, 133–137, 208–210
    enhancement of, 133–137
    feedback for, 199
savvy customers, 20–23, 73
scheduling
    utilization and, 125
    work, 119–120, 168–172
    worker, 121, 165–168, 170
Scott Paper, 62–63
segmentation
    customer, 22–23, 176, 184–188
    process, 187
    product, 187
Selectron, 150–151
self-service approach, 140–149
    benefits of, 146–147
    gathering facts and, 141–143
    implementing, 145–146
    simulation model for, 143–145
    technology-enabled self-service,
        147–149
sequencing work steps, 111
sequential processing, 107–109
serviceability, feedback for, 198–199
service delivery, 27
Service Profit Chain, The (Reed), 140
service recovery, 28
SG&A (Sales, General, and Administra-
    tion), 64–66
    customer-valued costs and, 66
    industry benchmarks for, 64
    relative growth by function, 64–66
Short, James E., 46
Six Sigma movement, 3, 7, 8, 13, 29,
    71, 131, 197, 208, 241
slow-track/fast-track work, 176–182
    in medical device customer com-
        plaints, 177–178
    in software services, 178–180
    in television programming, 180–182
software services, 178–180, 231–236,
    246–247, 249

specialists, generalists versus, 117–118,
    228–230
Spittle, Marilyn, 155
Starbucks, 27
sticky-note communications, 246–247
Strike 1: Unclog the Workplace, 14, 51–
    67, 253
Strike 2: Eliminate Work, 14–15, 69–
    86, 254
Strike 3: Streamline the Workflow, 15,
    87–112, 254–255
Strike 4: Reclaim Lost Time, 15, 113–
    138, 255
Strike 5: Redistribute the Work, 15,
    139–161, 256
Strike 6: Manage Fluctuations in Work
    Volume, 15–16, 163–173, 257
Strike 7: Focus the Flows, 16, 175–189,
    257–258
Strike 8: Unclog Flows of Knowledge,
    16, 191–210, 258
Strike 9: Show the Results, 16, 211–
    221, 258–259
Strike 10: Implement Customercentric
    Teams, 17, 223–240, 259
strike zones of opportunity, 32–33
supply chain management, 210
Surgical Strike approach, 1–17
    communication in, 242–249
    Design Stage in, 41, 47
    development of, 2–5
    Discovery Stage in, 41–44, 232,
        246–247
    expertise needed in, 12–13
    game plan for, 40–41
    great results from, 11–13
    illumination of, 5–7
    Inspiration Stage in, 41, 44–46, 232,
        247–248
    intelligence and, 8
    list of surgical strikes for, 13–17,
        253–259
    as natural approach, 9–11
    nature of, 2, 5–7, 8–9
    piloting the strike in, 249–251
    Realization Stage in, 41, 47–48
    renovation versus obliteration in,
        7–8

Strike 1: Unclog the Workplace, 14, 51–67, 253

Strike 2: Eliminate Work, 14–15, 69–86, 254

Strike 3: Streamline the Workflow, 15, 87–112, 254–255

Strike 4: Reclaim Lost Time, 15, 113–138, 255

Strike 5: Redistribute the Work, 15, 139–161, 256

Strike 6: Manage Fluctuations in Work Volume, 15–16, 163–173, 257

Strike 7: Focus the Flows, 16, 175–189, 257–258

Strike 8: Unclog Flows of Knowledge, 16, 191–210, 258

Strike 9: Show the Results, 16, 211–221, 258–259

Strike 10: Implement Customercentric Teams, 17, 223–240, 259

striking again, 251–252

targets for, 19–33

trend toward, 1–2

SWAT teams, 230–231, 233–234

targets of surgical strikes, 19–33

core customers, 20–22, 25–28

core processes, 20, 25–31

missing the mark, 23–24

strike zones of opportunity, 32–33

Tatelman, Barry, 219–221

Tatelman, Eliot, 219–221

teamwork, 12, 17, 223–240, 259

broken silos and, 227–230

building, 219–221

bureaucracy versus, 225–228

culture clash and, 239–240

for custom track projects, 233

dominoes of change and, 236–237

for fast track projects, 233

individual performance and, 238–239

in insurance business, 230–231

multi-teams and, 231–236

for process redesign, 225–227, 230–231

proximity and, 238

resource pools, 233–235

sharing in, 235

in software development, 231–236, 238–239

SWAT teams, 230–231, 233–234

timing of communications and, 249

in Yellow Pages business, 225–228

technology enablers, 45–46

telephone occupancy, 123–124

TeleTech, 121, 122–125, 155–157

television programming, 180–182, 213–214, 215

Terayon, 151

Theory of Constraints (Goldratt), 116

throughput time, 116, 119–120

Time Insurance, 246

time loss, 15, 113–138, 255

capability expansion and, 130–138

customer chaos as excuse for, 126–130

from unavailable time, 113–114, 122–125

in waiting for work, 113–114, 115–121, 125, 165–168, 170

time per call, 79

time to answer, 77

timing of communications, 249

TQM movement, 3–4, 7, 8, 71, 131, 199, 241

Trueba, Humberto, 155

turnaround specialists, 62

turnaround time. *see* cycle time

unavailable time, 113–114, 122–125

efficiency and, 124–125

occupancy factors in, 122–124

utilization and, 126

urgency, in communications, 243, 244

utilization factors, 125–130

customer chaos, 126–130

unavailable time, 126

utilized time, 125

waiting time, 125

utilization measurement, 121

value-added time, 109–111, 135–136

Value-Needs Profile, 22–23, 66, 73

waiting for work, 113–114, 115–121
  bottleneck elimination, 115–117, 219
  generalists versus specialists and, 117–118, 228–230
  proximity and, 118–119
  scheduling work, 119–120, 168–172
  scheduling workers, 121, 165–168, 170
  utilization and, 125
Wang Laboratories, 20, 62
waste, in process performance score-card, 213
Weight Watchers International, 141–147
work
  dressing up, for quality, 219
  scheduling, 119–120, 168–172
  unnecessary movement of, 83–84
work cell design, 118–119
work elimination, 14–15, 69–86, 254
  bad customers and, 72–76
  failures and failure-related recovery, 76–80
  non-value-added nonsense work, 80–85
workers
  dressing up, for quality, 218–219
  scheduling, 121, 165–168, 170
workflow focus, 16, 175–189, 257–258
  customer segments in, 22–23, 176, 184–188
  geographic orientation in, 176, 182–184
  slow-track versus fast-track work, 176–182

workflow streamlining, 15, 87–112, 254–255
  assessing impact of, 98–103
  bottleneck elimination, 115–117
  cycle time in, 96, 103–109
  initial ideas for, 93, 95
  prioritizing opportunities in, 95–98
  process quantification, 92–93, 94
  value-added time in, 109–111, 135–136
  workload profile in, 89–91, 166
workload analysis, 42, 89, 165–172, 184
workload profiles, 89–91, 166
Work-Out (General Electric), 12–13
workplace unclogging, 14, 51–67, 253
  bureaucracy and, 53–60
  productivity improvement, 52–53
  radical cleanup and, 62–67
  routine maintenance and, 61–62
work process improvement, skills in, 12–13
work redistribution, 15, 139–161, 256
  customer self-service in, 140–149
  eliminating middlemen in, 157–160
  outsourcing in, 149–157
work volume, 15–16, 163–173, 257
  efficiency and, 172–173
  methods of managing, 164–165
  shifting workers for, 121, 165–168, 170
  shifting work for, 168–172

Yellow Pages business, 225–228

Ziegler, Mel, 163

About the Author

Kelvin F. Cross is a founding partner of Corporate Renaissance, Inc. (www.corpren.com), a business process design firm. He has worked to analyze, design, and dramatically improve process performance for a wide variety of processes in many industries. He previously co-authored *Corporate Renaissance: The Art of Reengineering* and *Measure Up! How to Measure Corporate Performance*. He is the author of *Manufacturing Planning: Key to Improving Industrial Productivity* and has published over fifty articles and papers.